To Maggie,
with thanks for all the love, light and laughter
you gave to Camas.

To Megan Alis Mhairi
– with thanks for your curiosity and delight.
May you and all future generations always be surrounded
by Love and nurtured by nature.

DOWN THE TRACK

A Camas anthology

Rachel McCann (Ed)

wild goose
publications

www.**ionabooks**.com

Contents of book © individual contributors
Compilation © 2022 Rachel McCann

First published 2022 by
Wild Goose Publications
Suite 9, Fairfield, 1048 Govan Road, Glasgow G51 4XS, Scotland
the publishing division of the Iona Community.
Scottish Charity No. SC003794. Limited Company Reg. No. SC096243.

ISBN 978-1-84952-807-8

Cover image © Rachel Daniels

The publishers gratefully acknowledge the support of the Drummond Trust,
3 Pitt Terrace, Stirling FK8 2EY in producing this book.

Overseas distribution
Australia: Willow Connection Pty Ltd, 1/13 Kell Mather Drive, Lennox Head, NSW 2478
New Zealand: Pleroma, Higginson Street, Otane 4170, Central Hawkes Bay

Printed by Bell & Bain, Thornliebank, Glasgow

Contents

Foreword

Every time I walk down the track to Camas, the same thing happens. Just as I reach the crest of the last hill and the sea comes into view, and then the roof of the building, I feel a weight lift from my shoulders (even if I'm carrying a rucksack). It doesn't matter what mood I'm in, or whether I'm worried about something, or nothing, or even whether I know who'll be there. Every time, my breathing relaxes and my heart sings. I feel that I am coming back to my senses.

The first time I tried to visit Camas, decades ago, with another volunteer from Iona, we got lost on the track, and then we lost each other. This is a little inexplicable, because it was a warm, sunny, summer's day, but I ended up at Kintra and she ended up in Bunessan. The tin of ice cream I was carrying for Camas from the Abbey kitchen (because Camas didn't have a fridge back then) gradually melted in the heat. We never got there, nor did the ice cream. It's a mystery how both of us ended up having quite responsible working lives thereafter!

But I got there the next time, and many times thereafter. Like the thousands who have walked down the track over the seventy-nine years of the Iona Community's association with Camas Tuath, I have found it a place of beauty and wonder, of hospitality and kindness, of listening and noise and silence, of peace and adventure. I have seen it change people's ideas about themselves, their abilities, their relationships, their lives. Mostly young people, but middle-aged ones and folk well into their seventies too have found community here, have learned to be attentive to rocks and sea and seals, to trees and stars and midges, have made lasting friendships and learned to believe in others and in themselves.

It is a great sign of hope for me that Camas exists as a place where people can discover what's really important, can learn to differentiate between wants and needs, and find a way of living that gives value to living gently on the earth – and that it is not grim or life-denying at all, but full of shared struggle and joy. I think this is summed up well by one of the contributors:

'Reflecting together on our time at Camas, one of the volunteers told us that such an experience of community spirit and relationship with nature

that we had at Camas is not an exceptional episode to keep as a memory, but an approach to life.' (Poppy Kohner)

The thing that strikes me most about reading the varied and creative contributions to this anthology is that it's actually a great outpouring of love! Thank you so much to all the contributors, and to Rachel, for whom this has indeed been a labour of love. And to all the people who have made Camas a place so full of love over so many years.

Kathy Galloway

INTRODUCTION

My first visit to Camas was on a dreich day almost twenty-five years ago, and the idea of a book about Camas floated briefly into my mind a few years later. In 2014 I was invited to be on the Camas Committee, and as a book hadn't been created in the meantime – I thought it was about time to get on with it!

To use a Camas metaphor, I cast the net far and wide to gather the writing: through research in *Coracle*, the magazine of the Iona Community, and other publications; through discussions and interviews; through the Camas blog; and by tapping into the informal Camas networks. I sought to include and represent as many Camas people as possible. The writing is by former Camas staff and volunteers, Iona Community members and associates, local Mull and Iona people, and adult guests and visitors; there are also a number of quotes from young people and youth group leaders throughout the book and it was important that these were included. There are over a hundred contributors – people involved in Camas from the 1940s and '50s and every decade through to the present day. Whilst they are often personal and anecdotal accounts, they convey the history, ethos and vision of Camas. It's clear that whilst Camas has evolved and developed over the years, its purpose and passion remain the same.

Whilst some of the writing has been published elsewhere, other con-tributions have been written specifically for the book. I have written a few short pieces in order to clarify a significant part of the Camas story, or to give voice to those who played a role but who are no longer with us. The chapters are made up of essays, short quotes, poems and reflections that explore each theme. The themes evolved organically from the research and writing and reflect the key aspects of life at Camas.

My hope is simply that the book will celebrate Camas and tell the story of those who have been involved. It matters that those voices are recorded, and it has been a privilege for me to gather them together. I would sincerely like to thank all the contributors for trusting me with their words and for being so supportive of this project. I also want to acknowledge people who are not named in these pages, both those from years gone by and those who will be involved in the future, because even as I write new people, experiences, ideas and stories will be developing at Camas. I hope they will feel honoured in the spirit of the book. Camas doesn't belong to any one person or group, but it certainly has a large network and an extended 'Camas family'!

I would like to note some personal thanks to friends and colleagues – to Sandra Kramer and Neil Paynter for their insight, support and work on this project. Thanks also to Kathy Galloway for friendship and for her consistent championing of Camas over many years. Thank you to Sandy Brunton for freely and graciously sharing his family's story. Thanks too to Simon, for his kindness.

I would also like to express gratitude to George MacLeod – though I never had the privilege of meeting him – for following the call of the Spirit to create a safe place of community amidst the wildness of Mull, however improbable it may have seemed. His mystical understanding of the cosmos – *'turn but a stone and an angel moves'* – was rooted in social justice and the down-to-earth reality that *'matter matters'*. Whilst Camas' spirituality has evolved, his vision and words remain not only relevant to life there, but also to our modern ecological crisis, where action grounded in a sense of the sacredness of all life is vital.

It has been a joy to create this book. I hope that it will be a joy to read.

All royalties from *Down the Track* will go to support the work with young people at Camas.

Thank you.

Rachel McCann, Biggar, Scotland, 2021

The Camas pioneers

1. The Story Starts with Stones

Camas Tuath is Gaelic for North Bay, and the landscape of the area reveals something of the history and culture of the Ross of Mull. The first people arrived on Mull at around 6500 BC. Standing stones, crannogs and ruins of crofts are all reminders of early inhabitants, and the legacy of the Highland Clearances can be seen on both the human and natural ecology of the island.

The history of Camas and those who lived and worked there is rich and varied, and Jan Sutch Pickard has researched this with the help of the Ross of Mull Historical Society and Mull residents.

A history of Camas

A flint tool

In the last year of the last millennium, a member of that year's Camas team, Peter Cinquini, from Tasmania, was working in the Camas garden – and found a shaped piece of flint. Peter, who, as it happened, had a degree in archaeology, knew that flint does not occur naturally on Mull. The tiny artefact – a Mesolithic scraper – was passed from hand to hand, admired, reported to colleagues on Iona – and put in a safe place. It is probably still there, somewhere in Camas, the place to which it was brought in prehistoric times and used in the daily lives of folk to whom this place was home. We know little about their lives, though we can imagine them fishing, hunting deer and seals and skinning them, foraging, and maybe planting seeds – just as that Camas volunteer was doing.

A pile of stones

For many centuries after that, Camas Tuath, sheltered from the prevailing south-westerly winds, will have been known by local people as a good place for fishing – even when it was not home. Attie MacKechnie, who grew up on the Ross of Mull, and became a member of the Iona Community who worked on the rebuilding of the Abbey, also fished at Camas. I remember him pointing out a pile of stones just back from the shore, toward the saltings – all that was left of a salmon fishers' bothy. Brambles have now taken over space where oars and nets were stored, a place where fishermen from the long coast of the Ross could shelter and sleep when too weary to walk back home by starlight, up the steep path to join the track used by cattle-drovers from Market Bay.

For centuries, Camas was used as a base for the summer salmon fishing – when the fish were migrating. The men slept down there to get up early. 'It was important to have the nets set when the salmon were running,' said Attie, whose father and uncle were fishermen. By then, they had a choice of places to sleep.

Rock to build lighthouses

No one else was living in the barracks ranged along the west side of the bay – those buildings that are so distinctive and have been so well used. The grey-pink granite of the Ross, from which they are built, is a key part of the Camas story. At the beginning of the 19th century, scores of ship-wrecks in the busy sea-lanes near Tiree prompted plans for a lighthouse on the Skerryvore reef. Alan Stevenson was commissioned to oversee the work. The Duke of Argyll, landowner on Tiree, Iona and the Ross of Mull, offered the Northern Lighthouse Board all the stone that would be needed. Stevenson, surveyor and civil engineer, decided that, rather than the gneiss of Tiree, the perfect material was Mull granite. He decided to open up a quarry at Camas, where the deep-water inlet would also allow barges to be loaded with stone.

In April 1839, work began. Over 4,300 blocks were blasted from the cliff. 50,000 tonnes of rough-cut rock were transported to Hynish on Tiree, where they were precision-cut by skilled masons, to build a tower out on the reef, held together not by mortar but by the power of the waves driving the stones into place.

Back at Camas, the quarry work had been begun by more-experienced workers from Aberdeenshire and the Black Isle. They were far from home, 'migrant labourers', like the Irishmen who joined them. They lived in bar-racks, built out of big blocks from the quarry opposite. These two-storey buildings, with flights of steps at each end, dormitories above and rooms with proper fireplaces, were very different from the traditional black-houses of the Ross. In conversation, Attie said that 'The quarrymen's quarters were salubrious compared to the small houses on the Ross of Mull – solidly built – a sign of Stevenson's meticulous care for his workers.' Instead of local reed thatch, the buildings were roofed with slates, probably brought by barge from Luing, another quarrying community in the Slate Islands of Argyll. Indoors, the stone walls would have been finished with lath and plaster.

The quarry – with the first railway on Mull, to transport the stone down to sea level – was one of several opened up by the Stevensons and other enterprising Victorians. They created work, and local men learned from the east coast incomers. Attie's great grandfather was a hammer-man at the quarry on Erraid – extracting stone for another lighthouse, Dhu Heartach, south of Iona. Quite a lot of local people were employed as hammer-men; two hammer-men would work with one borer, using tools called jumpers to begin to split the rock. The ruins of the smiddy can still be seen at the foot of the quarry.

Having acquired marketable skills, masons would walk miles from one quarry to another for work, carrying just apron and mallet. In the 20th century, those skills were welcome when the Abbey Church in Iona was restored, and then the Iona Community came into being, as the cloister buildings of the Abbey were rebuilt and brought into use. But a century before, as workers on the move settled down, families began to come to Camas. Their presence is marked in the 1851 census.

The Northern Lighthouse Board worked the quarry for ten years, providing stone for Skerryvore and Ardnamurchan Point lighthouses. Then a builder from Aberdeen took over the lease for another ten years and the quarry was source of stone for piers and polished memorials. Then, in the late 1850s, the work stopped.

Bread – or a stone?

Fish was, of course, a staple food, and there was plenty of it. But in 1847 many of the quarry-workers fell ill. The Stevensons (again showing care for their workers) brought a doctor from Glasgow, who diagnosed scurvy. The men had been living on a diet of salt fish, with no fruit or vegetables. This may have been when the lazy beds came into use – though there's no danger of scurvy in Camas today!

Failure of another staple crop – potatoes – caused great hardship in the middle of the 19th century. 1846 was *'the year the potato went away'*. The blight meant that many families went hungry, and their problems were made worse by the tough approach of the Duke of Argyll's Factor, John Campbell of Islay – 'Factor Mor' – who lived just over the hill from Camas, in the big house at Ardfenaig. In the spring of 1847 he wrote to his employer: *'Nothing but harshness and dread, I find will do. I have put a stop to their grinding of any of their grain and give them meal in exchange. I am making lists of emigrants. It is of utmost importance to have as many off this year as possible.'*

This is part of Mull's experience of the Highland Clearances when the population of the island went from around 10,000 to 3,000. It was in the interests of the landlords to move families who had farmed the land for generations, with their few cattle and goats, from the scattered 'townships' on the uplands down to the rocky coasts, to free up land for large flocks of sheep. Local people, seen as uneconomic compared to the landlords' sheep, were exploited with higher rents, or evicted outright. The suffering caused by the potato famine became another lever, and Factor Mor added to this the confiscation of the hand-querns, with which the people ground their homegrown oats and barley – so that they had to pay to use the Duke's mill in Bunessan. The Factor writes *'I give them meal in exchange'* – this was not a generous donation, but part of a food-for-work scheme. Roadbuilding and digging drainage ditches were two of the ways the population was pressed into service.

And, running alongside the track down to Camas, is another eloquent example: the wall. Such walls can still be seen in many places on the Ross, and on first sight are very beautiful, with their skilful use of the rounded granite boulders. The traditional field boundaries (of which traces remain too) were quite different – low turf dykes, overgrown with mosses, ferns and brambles. They would not stop a straying flock, but they defined the way the land was shared within communities.

But these new walls, built in the time of Factor Mor, stop wanderers in their tracks. They cannot easily be passed – they claim the land they contain. These, like the wall down the Camas track, are 'Galloway dykes', so called because the people who knew how to build them were the lowland shepherds who brought the flocks to graze land that had been 'cleared' of people. The men of the Ross were taught how to build the walls that divided up their land. And because their families were hungry, they had no choice.

Factor Mor himself died (and many rejoiced). The injustices of the Clearances on Mull were investigated by the Napier Commission. Many of the families who had been forced or made the hard choice to emigrate, and had survived dangerous journeys to Canada or Australia, sent back positive news. On Mull, crofts were established, as a new way of sharing the land.

Down at Camas, the sounds of quarrying had fallen silent. After the quarrymen left, fishermen were able to move into the accommodation used by the quarry-workers. The place had reverted to a fishing station, with nets drying on the tall poles on the grass, outside abandoned buildings, only occasionally used.

Like the stepping stones to the little island in Camas Bay, this piece has picked its way through the centuries: from that prehistoric flint scraper, to the salmon fishers' bothy, to the quarry face and the barracks, to the Galloway dykes.

Then, in the 1940s, new life and a new purpose came to Camas … But that's another story!

Jan Sutch Pickard

A map of the history of this place

A map of the history of this place
would colour whole continents in red,
discovered and colonised in blood;
contain tracts of swampland soaked in sweat,
salt marshes drowned in tears;
be surrounded by hills deep in purple mourning,
unable to recall the cataclysmic orogenies
that marked their birth,
and showing only hard, unyielding faces.

A map of the history of this place
would show a few meadows
where short-lived flowers of joy could bloom and die.

Highways and roads, paths and winding tracks
to aid communication: many disused,
divided by falls of earth,
washed away by streams or flooded rivers;
sometimes rebuilt or bridged
but often left untended.

A map of the history of this place
is dotted white with sheep grazing the ruins
of lives and dreams and hopes;
though, here and there, a new beginning,
a croft rebuilt, a hope, perhaps, reborn.

A map of the history of this place
would show it on the shoreline,
a place between, a place of jumping off,
an edge marked 'danger – do not stray too close',
a place of going from, a place to leave behind.

A map of the history of this place
would be old and tattered,
faded, smudges, parts indecipherable
and others merely blank
inscribed *Terra Incognita*
or 'Here be dragons':
redrawn and torn and incomplete,
reworked and reinterpreted.

But still strangely familiar
to those who follow after.[1]

Alix Brown

Work in progress

Slate calls to granite
across the moving waters –
a few sea miles, but
a giant step in geology.

Granite calls to slate,
with schist and shale
and sheer basalt cliffs
falling in between.

Slate calls to granite
where the land has been gouged out,
where the sea licks its wounds.

Granite calls to slate
where red rock bares its breast,
where lighthouses were born.

At Camas Tuath on Mull
the quarrymen's homes,
built of the stone they hewed out,
are roofed with big slates –
sea-grey, set with gold
from Cullipool on Luing.

Granite calls to slate,
telling stories of hard graft
and human community.

Slate calls to granite,
across the moving waters
granite calls to slate.[2]

Jan Sutch Pickard

Quarry, query

Why
did the work just stop
just then? Just here?
The hillside sliced clean
to a ledge with one ruined hut.
But the rocks that were blasted
baring land to the bone
are still stacked there,
or tumble into the bay
like a child's building blocks –
material for bridges that have not been built,
for homes un-hearthed,
for churches unhallowed.
Red rock:
barren aftermath
raw material
unused –
why?

Only these cottages
built as firm as a fortress
facing the quarry across the bay;
where generations have lived
and laboured and died,
working the hill for the red rock,
working the waves for the salmon;
where string nets catch air and light
and fish are gutted on the stone,
meals made, fires kindled,
words and silences shared.

Sit on the doorstep,
quiet at the end of the day,
gaze at the quarry

where one day
work just stopped –
with one echoing blast –
leaving this desolation.
Imagine those building blocks
becoming bridges, homes and churches;
imagine poppies blooming
out of the red heart of the rock.[3]

Jan Sutch Pickard

Notes:

1. From *Coracle*, the magazine of the Iona Community, Kathy Galloway (Ed.)
2. From *A Pocket Full of Crumbs*, Jan Sutch Pickard, Wild Goose Publications, 2016
3. From *Pushing the Boat Out,* Kathy Galloway (Ed.), Wild Goose Publications, 1995

2. The Iona Community comes to Camas

The stories of those who worked at Camas in the 1940s and '50s provide a wonderful insight into the early work of the Iona Community there. The following accounts reflect the issues and ideas of the time, and the language, theology and context of the day.

The vision of the visionary

George MacLeod is said to have stumbled across Camas whilst out walking on the Ross of Mull, and inspired with a vision, in 1943 he negotiated the lease with the Duke of Argyll. He called the Camas project *'a parallel experiment'* to the work of rebuilding the Abbey on Iona and initially he saw it as a place to accommodate and include the many men who were drawn to be part of that work.

George first wrote about Camas in the Iona Community's magazine, *Coracle*, in May 1945, in a piece titled 'CAMAS – A VENTURE FOR UNIVERSITY MEN AND SENIOR SCHOOLBOYS'. His idea was for young men, predominantly trainee ministers, to come and work at Camas to learn the disciplines of faith whilst developing practical skills and building community.

George outlined some of the practicalities of his vision for life at Camas: 'The headquarters' would be the *'four stout quarryman's houses all in a row as an annexe to our main purposes … there will be a chaplain and a cook, forbye Charles Foreman (who was the winter Abbey caretaker and fortuitously a salmon fisherman) and twenty men a fortnight is our present computation.'*[1]

Central to this plan was his decision to train the men to fish for salmon. Ever the rhetorician, and no doubt with a twinkle in his eye, George commented: *'It was not just a romantic flourish that wed us to the place – though we doubt not that Columba got his salmon here … Let the fishing be parallel to the building on the wall, demanding taut muscles and steady hand, corporate obedience and cold early work at times.'* George's idea was to *'feed the community members, and the youth groups and the islanders – and sell in the open market if there was any left to spare'.*[2]

George, having secured the fishing licence, registered as a fishmonger, and his daughter, Mary, recalled: *'What I thought was really exciting about*

Camas was that it was a salmon-fishing station, and my father had to be registered as a fishmonger in order to sell the salmon. I thought that was much more interesting than him being a minister, or him being Leader of the Iona Community.'[3]

'The net of God's Love'

The theological symbolism of fish was a vivid inspiration: '*The church desperately wants more fishers of men … and we must hook men into the net of God's Love,'* George proclaimed.[4] Formal worship took place daily in the 'Chapel of the Nets', which had been set up by Douglas Trotter and Colin Day in the 1940s. Douglas commented: '*… one thing I remember, vividly, is designing and building what has come to be called the "Chapel of the Nets", in which everything – the seats and the Communion table – is part of the fishing equipment.'*[5] George eloquently explained that, '*they are not imitation nets, nor ecclesiastical nets, nor gold and silver art shop nets that bank our worship. It is amidst the things of every day, amidst the instruments of our ordinary labour, that God comes to meet with his people.'*[6]

George ended the *Coracle* article by saying that Camas had been tidied and prepared by a group of senior schoolboys from Rugby – and with an appeal for applicants for that July and August. Alastair Porter was one of those who rose to the challenge: '*Following on George MacLeod's piece in Coracle in 1945, in which he set out his vision for Camas, and sought applicants, a group of us from the Glasgow Academy took up the offer later that summer. There were eight of us supported by Charlie Foreman, the salmon fisherman, and by the Rev. Colin Bell, our chaplain and leader.*

'*Our main daily activity was setting out the salmon nets under Charlie's guidance, but we caught only the very occasional fish, though it was most exciting when we did. The evenings were spent not only in wide-ranging discussions, but also in attempting some choral-group singing, in which Colin's fine bass voice took the lead. On Sundays we embarked upon the strenuous exercise of rowing the coble, with its six heavy oars, across the Sound to Iona. Morning service in the Abbey, led by George himself, made the journey all worthwhile … and then we rowed back again!'*[7]

'The only difference between them and us is that they have been found out'

Towards the end of the 1940s George realised that Camas would be a good place to bring what were then known as 'Borstal Boys'. These were groups of vulnerable young men who had been in trouble and placed in young offenders institutions. George was Chairman of the Polmont Borstal Visiting Committee for many years and his understanding of their circumstances is reflected in his compassionate comment that *'the only difference between them and us is that they have been found out'*.[8] Ron Ferguson, George's biographer, said: George *'used to contrast his own privileged upbringing with those of youngsters in trouble, and he would defend young people from deprived areas and backgrounds with passionate advocacy'*.[9] George's powerful commitment to social justice saw him seeking to challenge and change the circumstances from which many of the young men had come. *'He argued passionately that … it was not enough to pray with the Borstal boys: it was necessary to clear the slums and build new houses and schools.'*[10]

In 1949 Allan MacInnes took over the fishing licence and worked with his two daughters Annie and Katie, and in later years Annie ran the fishing with her husband, Bertie MacRae. Some of the young men would help out and learn about fishing, as Annie explains: *'They were very good if you wanted a hand with lifting the nets up a bit. They were good, the borstal boys: they helped us quite a lot. They were on their best behaviour.'*

Out for a swim!

Annie also paints a picture of the fun at Camas: *'Dr George would get in bed, and the boys would have a smelly old fish – a mackerel or something – hanging, and they would lower it down and torment him. So up he would get then, roaring around, and cowping them all out of their beds. And we didn't get any sleep either, because it was just one layer of flooring … He was a great case!*

'And then he would have them up early, and out: "Out for a swim! Out for a swim!" Well, he didn't get very many to go with him, but one or two would be coaxed into doing this, and he would swim away out, and he would swim back in. I mean, he was quite an old man then.'[11]

George saw the value of giving the boys an experience outwith their usual confined routines – in the open spaces and fresh air of Camas. The idea flourished and hundreds of young men benefitted, and, as George happily boasted, *'They never ran away!'*[12]

It is testimony to George's work and dedication that he continued to support many of the 'Borstal Boys' throughout the later stages of their lives.

Rachel McCann

Camas in the 1950s: Freedom, friendship and faith

These are some memories of Camas from the 1950s when, as a young student, I helped with the youth camps at Camas and on Iona.

Camas had sturdy stone-built, slate-roofed, two-storey houses in a single block, close by the rocky shore of a north-facing bay or inlet. It was sheltered from the prevailing south-west wind by a steep heather-tufted rocky hill down which flowed a burn of pure water. Nearby, on the landward side, there were unroofed, derelict cottages, only the stone walls and gables of which were left standing. A jetty roughly put together with large red granite boulders provided safe landing for small boats.

Access was by land, across the moor over planks and ditches from Ardfenaig and the Bunessan/Fionnphort road, which at that time was only partially surfaced and had grass growing along the middle. Walking across the moor in early summer, even heavy-laden, was a delight – a cuckoo singing in the distance, a fresh wind blowing and the smell of bog-myrtle in the air.

Camas youth camps were housed in the ground level of the southmost house in the block and the upper levels of three of the houses; at ground level there was an entrance and two large rooms, a half-floored kitchen to the left and a common room to the right; the common room had wooden benches smoothed by use, set against the walls round an open fireplace where freshly caught salmon or mackerel could be cooked and water boiled. Two attic spaces above the adjacent houses were used as dormitories in which camp beds were provided. At that time the camps at Camas were all-male. There was no power, no telephone, no piped water supply (water from the burn was used for drinking and washing up). Lighting was by candle, paraffin lamp or portable torch; heating and cooking by peat, driftwood or Calor gas. The Chapel of the Nets, accessed externally by a stone stair and internally by rope ladder and trapdoor, was a unique place of worship furnished with objects of a maritime nature: fishing nets hanging round the walls defined the space; the communion table was part of a boat's deck supported by two large herring barrels; a wooden rudder used to set the course of a boat at sea, now formed a lectern for the chapel Bible, source of guidance to those who read it; the group sat on small barrel buoys; lighting was by candles held in an assortment of objects found on the seashore.

One house in the block was occupied in the salmon season by Allan MacInnes and his daughters Annie and Katie. They used to catch the salmon that were swimming between the north coast of the Ross of Mull and the islands some distance offshore. Twice daily, weather permitting, Allan went out in his boat to take salmon from the nets and to clear the nets from entangled seaweed and jellyfish. When asked how the fishing was going he was wont to reply: 'Millions of jellyfish!' Allan spoke both his native Gaelic and English in gentle lilting tones. He loved Camas and although the activities of the community there must have been somewhat disruptive, he was always ready to engage, to offer information and advice, to take some of us out to the nets in his boat and, when salmon were being caught, to provide one to poach over the peat fire for our supper. He was indeed a lovely man and a great friend of the Iona Community's enterprise at Camas.

The main purpose of our work with young people at Camas was to offer all who came, whether from institutions, with groups or alone, the freedom of living in a remote and very beautiful part of Scotland, sharing the richness and the responsibilities of a basic life together in community. We engaged with the personal, social and political issues which those present raised in the context of belief and values, with a view to personal enjoyment, growth and learning.

The Borstal Boys

During July and August, Camas was open for groups and individuals to come for a holiday. Apprentices, students, young workers and members of church youth groups came from a wide variety of areas for these months. However, in the 1950s, in May and June, camps for young offenders were held at Camas and Iona. Accompanied by officers, or 'screws', they came from three different borstals – Castle Huntly near Dundee, Jessiefield in

Dumfries and Polmont, Falkirk.

Who were the young people? Each one, of course, had a unique personal story; yet certain features were shared by most. They came from all over Scotland, but most were from the larger conurbations. Some were exceptionally gifted, highly intelligent, physically robust or verbally articulate, while others were clearly less confident and more vulnerable to the external pressures and inner conflicts of their earlier years. Nearly all had one thing in common: they came from seriously deprived communities and deeply troubled families. As I got to know them, I realised that they knew much more about the hard edges of life and how to survive than I did.

Camas provided the ideal environment in which each could experience the freedom to pursue their own interests within the constraints of the group, which required them to share the responsibilities for their life together. While the confident ones took to the hills and beaches with great zest, others, at first, felt lost outside the institution in which they had spent a significant part of their adolescence.

For young offenders the focus was on freedom, self-discipline and preparation for return to life in the world after borstal. Being at Camas, where everyone was accepted and valued, enabled us all to experience the liberating and life-changing love of God in Christian community at it best.

Activities

I don't know whether health and safety regulations were in force in the 1950s or not. Suffice it to say that while care was taken of all young people, life at Camas was not without risk. Activities included exploring the Ross of Mull, climbing Ben More, swimming at Traigh na Margaidh (Market Bay), boating, fishing for mackerel or salmon, an open-air sleepover in the heather on the hilltop behind the bay, ceilidhs around the fire, attending a dance or ceilidh at Bunessan, daily worship in the Chapel of the Nets, lively discussion in the common room, a visit to Iona by foot and ferry for one or two nights for the Friday dance, the Abbey services and time to explore the island.

Imagine the sheer pleasure of roaming with friends round the Ross of Mull after months in an institution; the excitement of discovering a snake sunning itself on a stone and not knowing the difference between a grass snake and an adder, catching it and putting it in a cardboard box to take it back to Camas for identification (it proved to be an adder!); the challenge of climbing Ben More; the joy of sleeping on the heather under the stars; plunging into the sea at a nearby beach; or attending a late-night ceilidh at Bunessan and dancing with local girls, even though it meant facing the long walk back to Camas in the dark, until the midsummer sun rose as you made your way home across the moor.

Some of the people who were key to the valuable work at Camas at this time included:

Charles Hills

Of all the prison officers who came with boys to Camas, the man who made by far the strongest impression was Charles Hills. As housemaster of Bruce House at Polmont, he came to Camas on several occasions. Compassionate and humorous, he was committed to ensuring that visits to Camas should provide a learning experience for officers and leaders as well as for the boys themselves. Charles' vocation was to find ways of making borstal and its related activities more effective in the rehabilitation of young offenders. We discovered that he knew each boy and the challenging circumstances from which he came. He saw not only what each boy was but also what he might become. He recognised the strengths in each boy and sought to enhance the boy's self-esteem by supporting him to discover for himself the strengths and gifts he possessed. Charles was convinced that self-discipline was preferable to imposed discipline and that we meet our own needs in part by meeting the needs of others, so he encouraged boys to support others whose problems were different and perhaps greater than their own. After Polmont, Charles pursued his distinguished career in the Scottish Prison Service, eventually as Governor of Saughton Prison.

Tom Colvin

Tom Colvin was the Iona Community's Youth Secretary at the time, and was responsible for arranging the camps on Iona and at Camas. As a graduate in Engineering and Theology he was well equipped academically for the job; much more to the point, he was a tough, down-to-earth character with the ability to relate to young people from vastly different backgrounds. He was a special friend to those who were disadvantaged or oppressed. Through his work he promoted Christian involvement with members of the Young Communist League and was as much at home with either. At Camas he was a force to be reckoned with – distinctively dressed in kilt and string vest, striding across the heather, singing funny songs at a ceilidh or leading worship. Tom insisted that the Bible in the Chapel of the Nets should be kept open at Isaiah Chapter 53: '*All we, like sheep, have gone astray …*' with emphasis on the word '*all*'. At Camas, there was no 'them and us'. Camp leaders, prison officers and young offenders were all made of the same stuff, all equally valued by God and the community. Frequently Tom's views caused controversy but his Glaswegian warmth, his political commitment and his simple deeply held faith gave him a presence and an authority that evoked affection and respect from young people and leaders alike.

Tom Milroy

The fittest and most athletic of the Camas Leaders was Tom Milroy. He could climb Ben More and come down again before the rest of us had topped the lower slopes! Formerly a miner from Fallin in the Central Belt of Scotland, his head and face carried a deep scar from a serious mining accident, after which he moved to become a youth leader, then a student for ministry in the Church of Scotland. As miners find and extract value in dark places, Tom discovered talent in people whom many in society had given up on altogether. The earthiness of his humour, and his common sense, was matched by his strong faith, his sensitivity and his love of people. Each year after finishing his studies he and some others set up things at Camas, carrying equipment across the moor with unequalled stamina.

I know that some of us who were leaders or volunteers had contact with Camas attenders afterwards. We were sometimes asked to serve as aftercare guardians to young men who were released from borstal on licence. This involved regular monthly meetings, continuing support, home visits, occasional hospitality, even occasional appearances in court when things went wrong. Some of these men kept in touch with Camas Leaders for years into marriage, parenthood and beyond.

Stewart McGregor

Camas days

In 1958, George MacLeod invited me to come to Iona as a volunteer, ostensibly 'to help build a road' – I'm not sure where to! No road existed – and when I arrived, in early May, totally unexpected, the lovely Ralph Morton, then George's deputy, first of all put me to the task of guiding tourists round the Abbey. (I had never even heard of Iona Abbey until meeting George a few months before arriving there!)

A few weeks later, Ralph asked if I would go to Camas, as there was a need for a cook. A cook! If I'd cooked an egg in my life, that was about it. Nothing daunted, and with the confidence and arrogance of youth, off I went on the ferry – and immediately fell in love with the place – a love affair which has lasted all my life.

Camas in the 1950s was still pretty undeveloped. Only the main building had a roof. My bed was in a small room adjoining the Chapel of the Nets. Downstairs, the three rooms were much as they are now – the kitchen, the living room next door with the fireplace (the only source of heat outside the kitchen) and the dining room with the hatch through to the kitchen.

I was only there for three weeks, but I can vividly recall two of the groups who came. The first was a group of boys from a young offenders institution. On their arrival, the first sight that met their eyes was the heavy rowing boat used by Mr MacInnes, pulled up on the beach. With a shout of delight, some of them leapt in, and began hurling out of the boat all the heavy stones he kept in the bottom for ballast. I can't remember whether they actually got it into the water or not – I do remember the howl of rage from Mr MacInnes when he came out and saw what was happening.

Meanwhile, I was in the kitchen, preparing to give them a welcoming cuppa. Needing water, I asked one of the boys to fill the kettle from our usual water source – the burn flowing down beside the house. The tea made, I started passing the cups through the hatch – to be met in a few seconds with howls of 'Who put the salt in the tea?!' It transpired that the wee lad had gone out to fill the kettle, seen the nearby sea as a much handier source of water than the burn, and duly filled the kettle from the sea – never having seen sea before, how was he to know it was salt?

Salmon was more than plentiful in those days – and Mr MacInnes usually handed in a couple each day – so naturally I served up salmon at least twice a day, until the boys moaned 'Not salmon again!' – I doubt if they ever touched another salmon in their lives. But they had a fantastic time.

The other group came from Glasgow, from Church House in Bridgeton, under the charismatic leadership of George Buchanan-Smith (brother of the then Conservative MP). Their arrival was heralded by the appearance of a string of Icelandic ponies, lent to George by his brother-in-law for the week. The boys duly appeared down the track – and of course immediately saw the ponies. Whooping with delight, they proceeded to leap on the ponies, who simply stood there in stolid patience, refusing to move. I think they eventually took the boys off on excursions around Mull. George had also brought up a large motorboat – and again, they had a wonderful time. Presumably, they survived my cooking – and the salmon.

I've been back to Camas many times since (but never again as cook!), and enjoyed every visit. For me, it still speaks of the founding ethos of the Iona Community – the combination of work and worship, of rebuilding community and lives, of intimate sharing and challenging living – it helps us remember our story, and still makes a difference to hundreds every year. Long may it continue!

John Harvey

Notes:

1. From *Coracle*, 1945
2. From *Coracle,* 1945
3. From *Outside a Safe Place: An Oral History of the Early Years of the Iona Community*, Anne Muir, Wild Goose Publications, 2011
4. From *Coracle,* 1945
5. From *Outside a Safe Place: An Oral History of the Early Years of the Iona Community*, Anne Muir, Wild Goose Publications, 2011
6. From *Coracle,* 1945
7. From *Coracle,* the magazine of the Iona Community, Ruth Harvey (Ed.)
8. From *George MacLeod: Founder of the Iona Community*, Ron Ferguson, Wild Goose Publications, reprint 2004
9. From *George MacLeod: Founder of the Iona Community*, Ron Ferguson, Wild Goose Publications, reprint 2004
10. From *George MacLeod: Founder of the Iona Community*, Ron Ferguson, Wild Goose Publications, reprint 2004
11. From *Outside a Safe Place: An Oral History of the Early Years of the Iona Community*, Anne Muir, Wild Goose Publications, 2011
12. From the documentary *Sermon in Stone*, Iona Community, 1966

3. FISHING FAMILY

The salmon fishing continued at Camas, alongside the youth programme, until 1996. Here residents of Mull share some memories from the early days of the work at Camas during the 1950s and '60s.

The MacInnes family

There are clear records of MacInnes family connections on Mull, Iona and Ulva for generations. All those years ago, folk were quite mobile and often moved around by boat, so there are also connections with Kerrera and Oban. My great-great-grandfather ran the Kerrera ferry in the 1890s. My grandfather, Allan MacInnes, served in the Argylls in WWI and married my grannie during the war. He did various jobs around Oban after the war; then the family (with three small children) moved to Carsaig in 1923, with the intention of salmon fishing in Loch Scridain. It became clear that the Loch Scridain fishing was not as good as hoped for and he managed to secure the lease of the salmon fishing in Carsaig itself, which was much better. The fishing was worked by my grandfather and other helpers but principally by two of his daughters – Annie and Katie. However, Carsaig Estate was sold by the Gordons to the Grays and the lease for the Carsaig fishing was terminated at very short notice. The family still had to survive and my grandpa spoke to Dr George MacLeod, who indicated that the fishing at Camas was available to lease.

They travelled by boat from Carsaig to Camas, with nets, all the gear and personal possessions, and lived during the week in the very sparse accommodation there. The story goes that Camas was much colder than Carsaig, so they had to go back to Carsaig very soon for extra bedding! They lived on the ground floor in the area with the door second from the far end. The gear was stored and maintained, fish sorted and packed all in the part of the building next door and in the door third from the end.

It may be thought that Camas was, and even is, remote and difficult to access. However, as previously mentioned, much travel was done by sea, and to get the catch that wasn't sold locally to market, they would take the boxed fish to Iona by boat, where they would meet with the *King George V*, which would take the fish to Oban, where it would be put on the evening train to Glasgow and even to Billingsgate Market in London to be at the fish market for the early hours. In the early days, before ice was readily available, the fish was wrapped in wild iris leaves.

My mother trained as a primary teacher in the early '60s and secured the post of Head Teacher of the one-teacher school at Creich. There was a house with the job and we all moved (my mum and dad, me and my sister) to the schoolhouse at Creich. My dad started working with my grandpa at Camas, and by then, grandpa had moved to Fionnphort along with my Auntie Anne.

A lot of my summers were spent at Camas, mostly just hanging about and probably not being much of a help, but I don't remember ever being shouted at to do things! My two cousins about the very same age as me went too, so we had a lot of fun and helped where we could. Sometimes we got to stay over at Camas; this was a real privilege and a huge adventure for a small boy at primary school. There were always things to do, we were never bored, and we could sit down in the evening and listen to some of grandpa's stories beside the peat fire in the kitchen or play rummy or whist.

There were various other older cousins and uncles who would have helped work the fishing over the years too. My grandpa was really quite an old man by the time I knew him, but he never seemed old to me. He was still very fit and able to carry sacks of fish over the bog and a cylinder of gas the other way – just the same as any younger man. He was the centre of decisions but it really was our Auntie Anne that kept everything and everybody going. She was always working but always appeared relaxed and kept us all fed and happy as well.

At that time there was no internet, let alone internet shopping. There were catalogues, but the best was the draper's van which travelled around and was based in Tighnabruaich and run by Andrew and Ian Irvine. It was always a welcoming place and a bit of an event when the van was due. My grandpa always wore a tweed jacket, and his existing one had seen better days and was getting very threadbare and patched. So, he bought a new tweed jacket from the van and I think it must have been a Saturday afternoon as we were all leaving Camas for the weekend (as you could not fish from Saturday afternoon till Monday morning). Grandpa smoked a pipe and was also getting a bit deaf too, and, as was his wont, he was striding out ahead of others on his way home and wearing his brand-new jacket. There was a small breeze blowing in our faces and it became obvious to those behind that there was a slight plume of smoke rising from him! We shouted and whistled to alert him, without success, so I was sent as the youngest and carrying nothing – to run and catch up to alert grandpa. It turned out he had finished his pipe and put it in his pocket – but it wasn't completely out and had quietly smouldered and burned a big hole right through his brand-new jacket – and he was so cross! We all laughed however and never let him forget it.

Camas was a busy place with the fishing and the Iona Community folk as well but one of the entertainments was draughts – never chess as that was far too complicated – but my grandpa was really good at draughts. I often remember the draughts board set up outside on a sunny day and a big gathering around it after grandpa had been teaching the basic principles. It became quite competitive and the borstal boys would organise tournaments at which grandpa would stand to the side and referee.

My own father had an injury to his back which made it difficult for him with all the heavy lifting involved in the fishing. My grandpa was a traditionalist, so there were, and would remain, cotton (heavy and water-absorbing) nets in use at Camas. My dad had found it much lighter and easier to use synthetic nets and advocated a change for everyone's benefit – but no, this was not going to happen. So in the interests of his back, dad set up on his own, fishing back at Carsaig, which had become available, and I then spent a lot of time in Carsaig, as well as returning to Camas to help at the beginning and end of the season – and in between as well.

Sandy Brunton

Sunshine and salmon

Like other youngsters in the extended family of Allan MacInnes, such as Gregor Cameron, John Cooper, Sandy and Mary Brunton, Norma MacInnes, the Turner girls and many more, I took part in the summer salmon fishing at Camas. There was no telly, no cell phones, no computers or computer games, no record players, only the radio … and yet we were never bored or short of something to do … and of course it was nearly always sunny!

Douglas Canning

Memories of summer holidays

I have a lot of memories of Camas, having been sent to stay with my grandfather Alan MacInnes, who had the salmon fishing there, and family during summer holidays in the mid-1960s. I am not sure if that was to help my mother out or as a help to my Auntie Anne (my mother's sister). I actually don't remember that much about the Iona Community people but I remember the borstal boys, as we called them, chasing the sheep – as they had never seen a sheep before!

I was sent down from Dervaig with the men who cut the grass in the graveyards when it was Fionnphort's turn to be cut – a wee girl sandwiched between two men in the front of a van! There was always lots of jobs to do at Camas as there were quite a few mouths to feed, so there were garden jobs and helping with carrying water from the well. The well was a granite-lined spring and had to be scrubbed out every so often, and while it refilled there was a second well further round the shore. The water for washing was collected in a barrel, and I remember people had their own towel/sheet that they used for drying themselves after washing off the red jellyfish stings, which we of course were well-warned not to touch. We also carried home peats from the bog and I had a specially cut down-sack of my own.

I remember one day we wanted to make a dumpling but didn't have any dried fruit, so we decided to borrow some from the Iona Community kitchen next door. There was nobody around so we climbed down into the kitchen through a trap door from the upstairs where the chapel was!

Another highlight was the day George MacLeod came to see my grandfather and brought me my first can of orangeade. When the boat went round to Bunessan with the fish for the bus, the boys sometimes would bring me back a sweetie from the shop, or a special treat was a can of Creamola Foam.

I can't remember a single wet day!

Sheena Walker

Annie MacRae, salmon fisher

Born in August 1930 into the MacInnes family in Carsaig, Annie was the seventh of eight children and grew up in a loving family.

Supported by other members of the family, Annie and her father Allan took on the fishing at Camas in 1949. Annie described getting fires going, cleaning the place, chasing out the rats and mice – and then the rhythm of daily work during the season, with the busyness of the salmon run that came in June or July, and the organisation needed to get 126 fish caught (once in six days!) and safely away to market.

They lived at Camas during the week and work stopped at 12:00 on a Saturday, so that they could return to Carsaig, where her mother stayed, running the post office. Then it was back to work first thing on Monday.

Annie met Bertie MacRae, a merchant seaman who had family on the Ross of Mull, but who had grown up in the Falklands. They were married in 1970, and Bertie joined in with the fishing at Camas. Eventually Allan handed over to the husband and wife team, though even as an old man he would visit from Carsaig. After several enjoyable years of working together, Annie decided it was time to stop camping at Camas and set up a comfortable home for the two of them – and visitors – in Fionnphort. Bertie continued to fish at Camas with the help of Jane Griffiths.

When asked to remember one thing she loved about fishing at Camas, Annie said: 'I enjoyed it all – on a lovely day, or wet days when your bottom would get wet. Oilskins weren't so good in those days. The day I think about was not long after Bertie started with us. It was pouring with rain, thunder, lightning. We got one or two salmon out of the net. Then we put down the lines for mackerel. It was a good catch. I was as happy as happy in pouring rain and thunder and lightning. Like two clowns we were, out there!'

Jan Sutch Pickard

Life in community

The Iona Community is committed to 'the rebuilding of community', and as the Camas staff handbook explains: 'For staff and volunteers, life at Camas is more than just a job – it is the chance to experience sharing a common lifestyle, to live in an environmentally sustainable way in harmony with our surroundings. We aim to share this life and community with our guests, giving them an experience of welcome and belonging.'

Staff and guests come from a variety of backgrounds, places, beliefs and paths to work together towards a common goal. Former Leader of the Iona Community Kathy Galloway sums up this relational model: 'Camas offers a holistic and integrated community, where care for oneself, for others and for the environment are different aspects of a shared experience.'[1]

A life together

In 1975 Deryck Collingwood was appointed as the first full-time youth worker to be based at Camas. He lived and worked there with his wife Pat. The development of Camas during the Collingwoods' time was considerable; in many respects the ethos and practical work during this period laid the foundations for the Centre today.

The work at Camas was greatly supported by Graeme Brown, then Iona Community Leader. After a grant was negotiated by Tor Justad (Iona Community Youth Organiser at the time), Deryck's post was funded by social services as part of their work with vulnerable young people who came to Camas through what was then known as 'Intermediate Treatment'.

Deryck was pivotal in establishing a year-round staff group at Camas, and the current Resident Group model is influenced by this vision. At the time Deryck said: *'I look towards the development of a Resident Group, meeting daily in the Chapel of the Nets, and sharing a common life, purse and witness in a simplicity appropriate to the place, with a degree of self-sufficiency in burning peat and growing food. On a practical level a Resident Group presents a much more realistic challenge of lifestyle and faith to those who come, and a realistic basis for the important relationships with the local population.'*[2]

Deryck and Pat's commitment to community was demonstrated by their decision to split their salary with other members of the team. This enabled Mark Jardine and Graham Coulthard to join the community, followed by John Williamson and Ingrid Derbyshire the next season. Ingrid later met her husband, Paul, at Camas and they went on to be Camas Leaders. The Collingwoods had two children during their time at Camas, and Mark Jardine fondly remembers a 'young Sarah Collingwood who was then a toddler, who delighted in running around the "green" in her splashsuit testing its waterproof qualities in the puddles'. As in more recent years, having a family at Camas helped to create a warm and friendly environment for guests.

The value of community in welcoming young people was clear to Deryck: *'We aim to provide a base where young people can learn, together with the adults here, to recognise our mutual dependence upon one another and to enable group leaders to come to know their young people in an intimacy of shared living which is difficult to achieve in a place less remote and less primitive.*

'Working together for common survival is a call that demands response, often without needing to be expressed verbally. A major function of Christian community should be in demonstrating a "life together", of caring for one another. That caring and acceptance is uppermost in our life together in community at Camas. Sometimes this involves confronting ourselves and each other, but it is all part of learning to accept differences as people and differences of opinions and practice. It has been encouraging to see how many groups come as little more than a collection of individuals but very quickly learn to care for one another and develop strong friendships. We all know the value of getting city kids right away for a week together, at least in terms of developing relationships within the group; it is also encouraging to see that, away from the pressures of home, kids can still be kids.' [3]

Rachel McCann

Interdependence

In the 1980s, as Camas Leader, I was incredibly fortunate to have a small, strong and very able resident staff team. I was aware of our interdependence, and the different skills we all brought to each other. This included a sense of humour, integrity and grit, and a big heart that embraced faith and no faith. One of the biggest challenges of making Camas 'work' was finding the right balance of people for a resident community. Individuals who could not only share specific skills, qualifications and experience, but be willing and able to live 'off-grid' and enjoy a frenetic summer of living alongside youngsters with their myriad needs.

The simplicity of Camas was sometimes an issue for these young people, and the community aspect of everyone pulling together to make it work was often a sticking point. 'Chores?! What are they?!'

Sheila Bates (Russell)

I enjoyed helping with all the community tasks, like collecting veg for our tea from the garden or helping in the kitchen when we made a cake. Washing the dishes takes forever though!

Young person

Challenge and community

We focused a lot on offering hospitality to a wide variety of guests, and at the same time, paid much attention to the process of living authentically together as a community. Camas is an intense place to be. It provides natural challenges for each of us, enabling personal growth and development. The 'trick' is to be challenged and not crushed, to be stretched and supported – encouraged to go beyond our own perceived limitations. It is the same process that is lived out for both team members and guests. To respond to the challenges we need courage, honesty, openness, willingness, hope and vision.[4]

Vincent Manning

A season of life in community

Thinking about the season at Camas enables an awareness of the cycles of life and the patterns of nature. The re-creation of springtime accompanies the new season and a new team of people; the vibrancy of summer offers an environment for energy, fun and laughter for many visitors; as autumn and winter draw in we slow down and reflect: what has it meant to explore community throughout the season at Camas with staff, guests, neighbours and friends?

Building community

Camas weeks have a programme of activities, but it is often the 'in between times' – sitting in the common room or around a fire, watching the sea or walking up the track – that provide an opportunity to build friendships and create connections. The emphasis on building community is one of the things that makes Camas different to many other outdoor centres. Staff and guests join together fully in the common life; sharing meals, washing dishes and pushing wheelbarrows become places of connection and commonality. Camas relies on interdependency, co-operation and supportive relationships – everyone needs to do their bit!

In seeking to break down barriers and build genuine community, it is necessary to recognise the point where our own views and values meet that of the guests, and the places where there is tension. Facilitating a safe space takes care and commitment. For example, in enabling young people to learn about environmental issues through practical experiences of gardening, composting or recycling at Camas, it is important to be aware that many of them come from very different places than Camas, places where poor housing, lack of green space or poor food provision may be common. One reflection with a youth group from Edinburgh enabled a good and sensitive conversation around this through drawing and storytelling.

Feedback from guests has shown that the value of the community and the relationships between staff and guests is an influential part of the Camas experience for young people. Comments have included that staff set good examples of how to deal with conflict, of how men should treat women, and that young people have felt respected and safe. Professionalism and good youth work practice underpins all that happens at Camas, and this is the solid base that enables the sharing of fun, friendship and informality in the context of community.

Living as a community

A supportive and well-equipped staff team provides a strong basis for welcoming groups. Each season is a fresh page waiting to be written on as individuals from a variety of backgrounds take up the challenge to live simply and with a shared vision. During the 2000 season, we had a staff team of ten people from eight different countries. Bringing together many ideas, cultures, expectations and spiritual paths is not without its personal and collective challenges, but it was an educational and enriching experience for us all. It is not always easy to live and work with nine other people, and the long hours can be difficult; mistakes and miscommunications are all part of the process of learning how to build authentic relationships and live lovingly. It was interesting to see how powerful laughter can be in breaking down barriers of language and cultural norms! Passing from strangers to colleagues to friends enabled us all to grow. Creating an atmosphere of care and respect amongst the team is something that impacts and influences the experience of both staff and guests.

Living within a local community

Camas is part of the history and culture of the Ross of Mull and some of the people who live on Mull and Iona have previously worked at Camas or spent time there as children. It is good to remember that Camas is a community within a local community and to consider ways in which Camas can be a supportive presence. In 2000 we sought to build on the work of previous Camas staff in making Camas available as a resource for our neighbours. Welcoming local schools, the Brownies, the Mull and Iona Youth Forum (the latter bringing young people together from various parts of the island) enriched the programme and local relationships. We also took on a number of local beach cleans, and thanks to the rich harvest in our garden, we were able to swap excess vegetables with other local gardeners, and the shop and pub! We had a lovely 'Open Day' and we rejoined the LETS scheme, offering services such as baking bread in exchange for a hot bath! We continued to benefit from the ideas, support, knowledge and skill of local people on Mull and Iona and we closed the season with a party to thank them.

At a time when media and capitalism emphasise individualism and consumerism, living simply with a community approach is countercultural. This showed us the ordinary, everyday joy of connection and creativity, and it's been a privilege to be part of that.[5]

Rachel McCann

Somewhere I could be myself

Because of the wonderful welcome the people and place offered to me, as to countless others, Camas was always somewhere I felt I could fully be myself in a way I hadn't known or imagined possible before I first got involved there.

Debra Hall

I gained a sense of community I had not experienced before. I gained friendships I will deeply value. I learned about myself, others and this beautiful island.

Young person

We loved them

When I was a volunteer, we had a group from Glasgow who fought and swore and were pretty challenging for us! At first some didn't enjoy it as it was so different to their own experience, but you could see as the week went on, they settled down; and by the end of the week they loved it. I think it was because we shared community with them – we spent time with them and listened to them and helped them through. We loved them.

Mary Duncanson

Young people discover gifts and skills they did not know they had. Sharing and cooperation are essential, and our young people learned teamwork and positive role-modelling from the Camas staff.

Group Leader

I made new friends.

Young person

I learned I could get on with people from different areas and backgrounds and it was good fun.

Young person

The young people are often surprised at encountering experiences of natural beauty and community on residential, or by their own capacities for developing relationships, for trying new things, and for supporting other young people. Some have been surprised by what they have learnt about themselves and how much they have developed.

Group Leader

The power of community

One of my first weeks here last year was with a mixed group – a group of teenagers from America taking a confirmation course, mixed with a group of young people from inner-city Glasgow. The Scottish girls seemed intimidated; the American girls looked and sounded like the people you see on American soap operas, their world in so many ways so different. The environment, the weather, the wealth (or assumed wealth), the culture, the accents – how could these girls ever connect?! But they did, and they did quite quickly. The two groups gelled and found commonalities. An incredible experience of the power of community: people whose paths would be very unlikely to cross came together, and the relationships which were built will continue (even if just in each other's memories). Groups come, and they have to (we all have to) connect. The simplicity of life here means you need to be able to rely on each other for basic daily tasks and activities. One young person reflected that, 'It doesn't matter if people are different because we can all work together in a team no matter what.'[6]

Mary Ireson

I learned how to be more sociable and I learned more about the people around me.

Young person

Building community

Camas is an outdoor centre with a difference. We do all the adventurous outdoor activities here – kayaking, coasteering, climbing and abseiling – but the focus of Camas is building community, and that's what makes it different. For some people who come here, there is a lack of self-identity, purpose and community in their lives, and the work of Camas is mainly around exploring these.

The Camas experience is really transformative as it pushes individuals so far out of their comfort zone that they are forced to reflect on themselves, usually realising that they are much more capable than they thought. It is powerful when people who don't know each other that well come together to share and form a new community for the week, supporting each other through challenging and rewarding experiences. Usually when people arrive, they are a bit hesitant as it's a very different experience from what they are used to. But from arrival to the end of the week, people get more comfortable. You start to see that people become really relaxed, their behaviour changes and they start to build positive relationships, and usually by the end of the week, they have made Camas their home and don't want to leave.[7]

Barry McLaughlin

Compassion and care

Camas gives you the opportunity to work in an environment where compassion is at the forefront of what you do. You work as part of a team that genuinely look out for each other. You feel part of something much bigger because you are all there for the same purpose and goal – to create the opportunity for the people coming, to learn, to reflect and to grow in a supportive, beautiful and creative space away from all the stresses of their lives back home. It's hard work both physically and emotionally but it is the most rewarding experience I have ever had and what I have taken away from it is invaluable.

Lynsey Semple

Teamwork

The dynamic and flexible approach to our days at Camas is reflected in the staff and volunteers, and I am constantly amazed at how much people who come here are prepared to give in order to make this work. Working with volunteers and seeing them take ownership and responsibility in their role is equally rewarding to see and the community of staff and volunteers that is built over the season is, for the most part, full of humour, love, support and lots of dancing while doing the dishes!

Abbi Mason

Supportive staff. No pressure, but great opportunities for teamwork and challenge. Great to see our group cooperating well.

Group Leader

Some of the Camas staff were from different countries; they were kind and funny and I hadn't met people like them before.

Young person

The road less travelled

There is a challenge to get to Camas, trekking a mile and a half across a rough track after a long journey. But for many of the young people who come, the start of the challenge is when they make the decision to leave Glasgow, Edinburgh, Macclesfield, or wherever home is. Camas welcomes a wide range of groups, but our primary focus is working with those experiencing significant disadvantage.

Although times have changed since the 1950s when Camas first welcomed groups, the idea of it being a safe and simple place, away from the commotion of everyday life, still remains key. It is a place of significant change and new possibilities for many people. It can give people a new way of looking at what really matters and the opportunity to grow in self-confidence.

One thing that sets us apart and aids us in our goal is our community approach. We encourage young people to make Camas home for the week; they share it with staff, and we form a unique community. Living together we share common tasks such as meals by candlelight, washing up, tending the chickens, cleaning the common room. This approach highlights the individual contribution of each person to the whole community and brings people together in the process.

We create a space where people feel safe in expressing opinions; and if young people do not wish to take part in certain activities, they are given a choice. One alternative may be to support staff in the kitchen or garden. There is as much to gain from providing a meal for the community as there is from kayaking in the bay. We also offer space to reflect both as a group and individually. When people reflect on their experiences at Camas, this can often shape their subsequent actions and decisions. Building a community is based on nurturing confidence and acceptance; through this, change happens, and new possibilities are achievable.[8]

Avril Leonard

Good connections

Building community is at the heart of Camas; it is the ultimate aim of each week – for people to come together and share life. We find it helpful to do this through sharing meals as this is one of the times when groups can reflect on and share experiences. I see the best work of Camas happening through this building of relationships and community, and often the connections and friendships made continue when the young people go back home.

Davie Johnstone

A common space

Camas is based around community. The whole story of Camas is of people living together in these buildings and in this environment and sharing in a common task. We seek to offer a safe space for people, and that sense of community, of having people around you who want to care for you, that can be powerful … and that applies to staff and guests.

Hannah Blyth

We laughed a lot, the banter was brilliant and I enjoyed being with everyone – Camas staff and our group.

Young person

Its beauty and awesome staff help our young people find community.

Group Leader

A loving community

For me, the magic of Camas lies in the true hospitality to be found by all who make the pilgrimage across land, sea and track. Camas is a place where, regardless of background or behaviour, young people find themselves held in love, respect, warmth, community, fun, nature, and have a structure to their days. All of this magic created by those lucky enough to live and work at Camas enables many young people to feel safe enough to relax, breathe freely, play and be children, feel part of a loving community, conquer fears, discover hopes and dare to dream – often for the first time in their lives.

Angela Formby

Challenge and conflict

Camas is such a beautiful place because there are people from so many walks of life gathered together. Guests as well as staff. The challenge of this is that we don't always understand each other …

I think it takes a community to navigate conflict in a way that builds sustainable cohesion and justice, including the humble unglamorous justice of being a functioning community. I believe in humans gathering together to share our vulnerabilities and troubles with mutual respect and curiosity. When we encourage this in ourselves and others, we tap into a deep sense of two things: what is needed (by ourselves and each other) and how we each have something to contribute to fulfil these needs. I truly believe that learning to navigate our conflicts with each other is the key to building justice and avoiding planetary self-destructions. Camas is such a beautiful place because there are people from so many walks of life gathered together.

Kelsey Lavoie

I made friends with someone I don't usually mix with back home, me and him get on great now.

Young person

Most importantly the group enjoyed friendship and community.

Group Leader

Individual members of the group are confronted quickly with the consequences of their actions. People living together in a remote place with no electricity or TV are compelled to take certain fundamental decisions about the organisation of their lives. Because of this, and because of the experience of the Camas staff in working with our kind of young people, the weeks spent at Camas are held in very high estimation by us.

Group Leader

The bonds that have been made between staff and young people during the week were exceptional, and it is to be hoped that this support will assist the continuing work with the group.

Group Leader

Communal joys

George MacLeod famously said, '*only a demanding common task builds community*', and … we repeat this with a groan as we clean toilets or chop vegetables together. But in our hearts, we know it's true. We know from experience that the quality of relationship, of trust, of mutual respect and increased understanding is significantly different when we have to depend on others as partners in a shared venture or common cause. Real communion, *koinonia*, is only possible when we are able to be honest with one another, to admit our vulnerability and need, to share our struggles as well as our achievements, to disagree deeply and yet remain in relationship and work through our differences.[9]

At Camas, guests and staff get to know each other really well in such an isolated and small-scale living place, and they find that self-reliance and mutual dependence are two sides of the same coin.[10] Valuing the communal joys figures largely there: people discover the communal joy of working all afternoon in the craft room, chopping vegetables together in the kitchen, learning to kayak or abseil, breaking bread together in the Camas dining rooms. And in sharing these communal joys, as so many people discover, we find the confidence to share our stories, our hopes, ourselves.[11]

Kathy Galloway

Camas provides a wonderful opportunity for young people to enjoy time together, learning more about each other and sharing more of themselves.

Group Leader

I have learned a lot about trusting others and the importance of this so as not to end up isolated.

Young person

Radical hospitality

I first came to Camas as a young person. I spent a week there on two consecutive summers and fell in love with the people and place. Those memories are still special to me – full of friends, rainy days with board games, new challenges, listening to people play guitar round the fire and a surprise party on my fifteenth birthday.

   More recently I have been back as a volunteer and Programme Worker. The work that Camas makes possible is invaluable, delivering radical hospitality, love and acceptance to those who often need it the most and I am so grateful to have been a part of that. The sense of community that is built and shared in those weeks is something that I feel is unique to Camas and can stay with people for a long time after they leave.

Cat Muckart

Transformation

Camas is a place for deep relating. The integration of staff into the whole life – which means they are fully involved with the groups that arrive each Saturday, staying up until all are in bed – is part of the charism/uniqueness of this place. It generates a depth of relating that allows for inner transformation.

Ruth Harvey

Intensity

We are gathered together,
the thoughts that brought us
are laid bare.
Tentatively reaching
and trusting for healing.

There is hurt and vulnerability –
living together is hard,
feelings are raw.

We are building an overwhelming closeness,
thoughts are laid to rest for now
in the warmth of the circle.

Ruth Thomas

Connection

I love it here –
this place
where sea meets shore
meets sky meets sand
where I meet you
where we connect.

Rachel Shepton

Notes:

1. From *Living by the Rule: The Rule of the Iona Community*, Kathy Galloway, Wild Goose Publications, 2010
2. From *Coracle*, the magazine of the Iona Community, 1976
3. From *Coracle*, the magazine of the Iona Community, 1976
4. From *Coracle*, the magazine of the Iona Community, 1999, Kathy Galloway (Ed.)
5. From *Coracle*, the magazine of the Iona Community, 2000, Kathy Galloway (Ed.)
6. From *Coracle*, the magazine of the Iona Community, Neil Paynter (Ed.), 2010
7. From Camas Outdoor Activity Centre Promotional Film, 2018, Ian Moore, www.iona.org.uk
8. Adapted from *Youth Scotland Magazine*, 2015
9. From *Living by the Rule: The Rule of the Iona Community*, Kathy Galloway, Wild Goose Publications, 2010
10. From *The Sacred Garden*, BBC Scotland, 2004
11. Adapted from *Gathered and Scattered: Readings and Meditations from the Iona Community*, Neil Paynter (Ed.), Wild Goose Publications, 2006

Camas Guests

The Iona Community's residential Centres on Iona and Mull 'strive to be places of hospitality, sanctuary and challenge …'[1]

1. Youth Groups

Young people are the heart of Camas, and youth groups, schools, social work groups and community projects have visited from a variety of locations, particularly from urban and inner-city areas – the Iona Community remains committed to enabling young people from challenging circumstances to experience Camas. Strong partnerships have developed between Camas and many of the groups, with some visiting regularly for over twenty years.

In 2019 Camas was a finalist at the YouthLink Scotland Awards. CEO of YouthLink Scotland, Tim Frew, commented: 'We have seen some fantastic examples of youth work making an immense contribution to young people's lives. In every part of Scotland, every day, thousands of youth workers, many of them volunteers, are supporting young people to follow their dreams and realise their potential, and the Camas team is a great example of the positive impact youth work has.'[2]

The voices of young people and group leaders are heard in the following reflections and stories.

INTERMEDIATE TREATMENT

I.T. groups were young people who were funded to go to Camas by Social Services departments during the late 1960s, '70s and early '80s. Though the name is now outmoded, the groups were a radical, innovative and effective approach to support vulnerable young people who were at risk. The partnership between Camas and a number of I.T. groups from around the UK was mutually beneficial. Norman Alm and his colleagues brought groups to Camas for many years, starting in 1969.

The Camas experience

Tor Justad was the Iona Community Youth Organiser involved with Camas at that time and was looking to expand its use. I was just setting up programmes for young people in trouble in Dundee, which were more involved than social work supervision but did not involve removal to a residential school, and I thought Camas would be an ideal base for us to take groups to for a week at a time. And so it turned out. This type of intervention was called 'Intermediate Treatment (I.T.)'. (Intermediate between supervision and residential care – but one critic said it meant 'between one offence and the next one'!) Dundee was one of the first such schemes to get started, and as it happened, our use of Camas led the way for I.T. groups from all over Scotland to get the benefit of the Camas experience.

The way we ran our groups in Dundee was to get the young people, as far as possible, to take responsibility for the running of them (decor of the building, programme, enforcing any codes of conduct, chairing meetings). Camas was perfect for our yearly camps because it was remote, primitive (chemical toilets at that time and no electricity) and quite beautiful, with a range of activities which that age group (14-17) enjoyed. All this brought out everyone's behaviour in high relief, and invited reflection on it by them and the rest of the group. Interestingly it was often our adult volunteers who had more difficulty coping with the very basic lifestyle at Camas than the youngsters.

We used Camas because, having tried various types of camping and residential experiences, we found weeks at Camas were the most useful for increasing group cohesion and encouraging the sort of interaction we looked for in our groups.

The isolation of the place meant that every group there became a little world of its own. Personalities came to the fore and small incidents sometimes loomed large. There was obviously a negative side to that in that there was no escape from each other, and crises did develop. But it was precisely those that were focal points for group problem-solving and discussion. We aimed to create challenges for the group and for individuals to rise to.

The style of the staff at Camas and their approach accorded with our own and complemented it. This showed the value of giving attention to individual young people, finding fun in ordinary events and having adults who can be zany but also stable and reliable.

We must not forget, though, that for many of the young people 'roughing it' was a way of life in the city. We took more than one youngster to Camas whose home was without electricity and homeliness due to poverty. For them, Camas was a place of warmth and comfort. Sensitivity, preparation and follow-up was very important with the young people we took to Camas.[3]

Norman Alm

KIBBLE EDUCATION AND CARE CENTRE

'Kibble supports at risk children and young people (aged 5-26) across the UK. Many of the young people we care for have experienced significant trauma in their lives and Kibble offers dedicated care and support to help them move forward. This includes residential and community support, as well as dedicated schools and well-being services. We provide a safe, stable environment that is both nurturing and therapeutic.'

From the Kibble website[4]

Kibble brought groups to Camas for ten years. Despite the challenges the young people faced in daily life, they always brought a sense of fun. The first year they visited, one young man, who was anxious about coming, refused to travel without his bike, so the Kibble staff brought it, though it lay unused at the foot of the track for the week. By the end of the week, he said, 'I wasn't going to come as I didn't want to be without my Playstation and TV and bike, but you realise you can live without them – there's loads to do and it's not scary either, everyone is really nice.'

Here, a former Camas volunteer writes about Kibble's 'Games Evening', which they organised as part of the 'Camas Challenge'. The Camas Challenge happens on the last night at Camas when visiting groups are challenged to take responsibility for the evening's meal, entertainment and reflection.

My island reckoning

I stand on rugged Scottish soil as an idiot volunteer at a youth Adventure Camp on the Isle of Mull. It is the Camas Challenge night and our guests, the Kibbles (adult caseworkers and their charges from a residential school in Glasgow) have cooked up a series of competitions.

Dot, in her usual all-black with a pink scarf threaded around her neck, cries, 'The games are about to begin!' Kibble and Camas have a long rivalry, and we both take this very seriously.

Mercy me.

The Glasgow lads, 13- to 16-year-olds, nudge each other smugly, their thin arms crossed over their shallow chests. The gnarly claws of dread scrabble at my heart, and the odour of unwashed bodies mingles with my own wilted-lettuce smell of cowardice.

Kibble caseworker Billy nods and continues: 'Each team's first challenge is to construct a free-standing sculpture using only what can be found on the beach. No wood or glue allowed.' His Scottish burr is as thick as a swarm of midges.

Both teams ragtag it to the beach. I schlep along, craving a swallowing hole.

Leading the Camas contingent is engineering student Tim, with adult volunteers Izzy, Adrien and Jenny, gardener Helen and prehistoric me. Our squat tower of turquoise polyester rope, cardboard and disinfectant bottles quickly collapses like a sack of wet groceries. We lose to a motley crew of kids, who congratulate themselves boisterously as though they'd just dog-paddled across the English Channel. On their last evening, they seem supercharged.

Our next challenge requires flinging a Wellington boot backward, the winning team being the one that throws it the farthest. Resignedly, when the scuffed old wellie is handed to me, I hurl it over my right shoulder so hard I nearly dislocate it. It sails a few feet and plops down in the straggly, sheep-chewed grass, appearing aggrieved and disappointed in me.

Kibbles win by a toe – actually, more than that. They again clap themselves on the back and high-five each other. I yearn for my duvet and a good book!

Our next challenge is to skip a stone over the water. 'Not without divine intervention,' I mutter. Near the islet we probe for small flat stones in shallow water. Before we get started, the opposition gives me 50 extra points, presumably because of my antiquity. Trembling inside like a leaf in a storm, I concentrate on Tim's instructions. We each get three tries. On my first try, the ginger-coloured pebble plunks to the sea bottom, but on my second attempt – I skip a stone for the first time in my life! It hops merrily over the shimmering sea like a song. The Kibbles' jaws drop. Dot says I skipped the stone 'most elegantly'.

Then Billy shouts, 'Football on the beach!' Panic, thick as syrup, washes over my vitals. Tall, stalwart Izzy, purple-haired Helen and I try weaselling out, but Dot insists that we all give it a go. When it's my turn to play I slink onto the marked-off playing beach. Close by, a seabird squawks over the Atlantic, urging me to get off Mull, but it is too late.

The sand sizzles under a remorseless white sun. The young, crazed and vigorous crowd wallops the ball off to the far left of the beach, and I am abandoned, eyes stinging, in the fine dust of the kicked-up sand. I edge back uncertainly toward the spectators, feeling like a wallflower at a cotillion.

Then another miracle happens. A little-known, compassionate Celtic sports deity with Kryptonian powers picks up on my distress signal. The black-and-white ball, whistling in the air just a few short minutes before, suddenly rolls daintily in front of me, like a rotund cosmic gift. The unprotected goal winks at me only a few feet away, while everyone else is sprinting back from left field. All those years as a soccer mom finally payoff: I bend it like Beckham and kick the ball as hard as I can into the net! Momentarily, the planet wobbles on its axis, and then everyone – spectators and players – whoops it up, either in disbelief, consternation, or jubilation! With shining eyes, my team hugs me and thumps me on the back.

The Challenge finally over, I glow red as a berry, self-conscious and delighted, as I move forward to receive my jumbo candy bar from Billy for being Camas' most valuable player.[5]

Susan H. Evans

THEGKEXPERIENCE

Focusing on well-being, confidence, self-esteem and resilience, theGKexperience is a Glasgow youth work charity founded on the belief that young people are brilliant and that they all deserve the same opportunities in order to enable them to reach their potential. Youth workers and young leaders work together to support amazing young people facing challenges in their everyday lives.

We build positive relationships with young people, on their terms, and this means being involved on a regular basis in their communities, offering – in partnership with existing local projects – opportunities for their development and growth. We have a strong belief that young people from Scotland's most disadvantaged communities are some of the most gifted, talented and brilliant people, having skills and qualities exclusive to them.

We offer residential experiences in beautiful and remote locations in Scotland, including Camas, which model community living, developing positive, respectful relationships, and use the arts, cookery, development of life skills and issue-based working, as well as exciting outdoor activities.[6]

Martin Johnstone, former Chair of theGKexperience, commented: '*Allowing the outdoor residential and wilderness experience helps young people to soar … [They] love the outdoor experience, even if it is a bit scary. It helps them to bond, to trust and to thrive. A significant percentage of the young people … could easily be dismissed as "problems", "no-hopers" … And yet … their strength, their potential and their capacity to make a difference shine.*'

A young person explained that the residentials were for '*young people who don't get the best in life … letting them get away to somewhere they can meet new people, doing something that they've never tried before*'.[7]

A solid and valuable partnership has developed between GK and Camas and the feedback from young people emphasises the benefits of their visits to Mull:

'The Camas trip was good; we were away for ages and there were loads of people, so I made loads of friends. The leaders at Camas were really good, they were really nice and that, and it's a nice place.'

'It's a great chance, it's an amazing thing to do, you have loads of fun and you meet great people as well.'

'Camas was brilliant; by the end of the week, people had experienced a good time, and getting away from some of the tough stuff in their own home.'

'It's a bit out of my comfort zone, going away with a group of random people, and then needing to adapt to certain ways and rules … but aye, I never expected myself to do it, to be quite honest.'

Dolphins jumping into the sunset

This week we had some wild weather! During one of the kayak sessions it started to thunder. This made the atmosphere quite exciting. We continued even when it started to rain (we were wet anyway) … It was a quite spooky session on the water. Towards the end there were flashes of lightning. That's when we made our way back to the shore. While the kayakers just got wet, the climbers were trying to stay dry in the group shelter. They played games and had hot chocolate while waiting for the rain to die down. Later in the evening, we went up on a little outcrop and watched the sun set. Just then, the dolphins appeared and jumped into the sunset.

From the Camas blog[8]

The expedition story

The plan: take six boys from different schemes in Glasgow on expedition and walk for one and a half days, heading from the Glenmore Pass car park down the valley towards Lochbuie, then along the remote coastal path to Carsaig. There we would be picked up by the beautiful *Birthe Marie* skippered by Mark Jardine. From here we would continue our journey by sailing-boat around the Ross of Mull, visiting stunning white sandy beaches, climbing crags and the rocky shore of Ulva. We would finish at Fionnphort pier – just in time to jump on the coach home. Four days in total.

The staff running this expedition had all worked at Camas sometime over the past 30 years: Mark in the late '70s and early '80s, Neil in the '90s and me, Avril, in the present day. This really helped when trying to bring the sense of community that our guests feel at Camas to the expedition experience. There is so much that can be gained from this community approach, building confidence through the supportive atmosphere it can create.

The group arrived at the starting point. On a clear day the view down the valley is spectacular, looking over the three lochs. But it had just started raining and the mist was coming down. Fortunately, spirits were high despite the weather, with a mix of excitement and anticipation. Neil had met with the group previously in Glasgow to go over some expedition preparation: packing, food, appropriate clothing, etc. As a result, when they jumped off the bus, we were pretty much ready to go, just a little bit of extra kit waterproofing was needed.

At this point everyone was raring to go, but it is important that everyone sets off with an understanding of the aims of the expedition. Not just where we are heading but what is expected of us, our behaviour and attitude. How are we going to move forward positively? In order to build community, we need to respect ourselves and others around us. On expedition respecting our equipment is also essential, to keep ourselves safe. So, we got into a team huddle, set out some group objectives to help us achieve our aims and then headed off into the mist.

For most of the team it was the first time carrying an expedition rucksack and for some of the younger boys the walking was quite hard-going. The group were split into pairs, one older boy, one younger, the elder acting as a mentor for his partner. The boys took their roles seriously, offering support and guidance when needed. The pace was great with only a few stops for snacks and the occasional refusal to move, which was handled by the team really well. With such a supportive atmosphere everyone was encouraged to keep going to our first campsite. When we got through the rough terrain and met the smooth path, there was a sense of elation among the group knowing camp was near. The 'Quote of the Day' had to be when one team member said, 'I feel successful.'

Getting into camp was when the routine of our day really started to build. For the next three days cooking meals, pitching tents, drying kit, washing pans all needed to happen. One thing we do at Camas is to share in common tasks; this is also true of time on expedition. On the first night two of the boys were taught how to pitch a tent, with the knowledge that tomorrow they would in turn have to teach two others how to pitch *their* tent. While this was happening, two cooking teams were formed – two boys in each working with staff members. For some of the group, this was the first time they had ever cooked. It was a bit wet and a bit midgy, so after eating and clearing up people were swift to get into their tents, knowing that in the morning we still had a good amount of walking to do before we met up with Mark and the boat.

Journeying makes you think about your resources, so in the morning we helped young people in some more dry kit preservation, as the rain still hadn't lifted. We were working on a 'helping you to help yourself culture'. This meant that the young people felt supported and cared for. At the same time, they were given the opportunity to take what they had learnt and to start to do things for themselves; this is where confidence can begin to grow. All packed and ready to go, we added the next section of our routine, reflection. Reflections happen every morning and evening at Camas and this is also the case on expedition.

Onward with the day, we started to walk. The pace was great and the thought of the *Birthe Marie* waiting for us at Carsaig kept morale high. Walking alongside each other gave us the time to chat and get to know one another. The group really started to form. There was a point on the path where the terrain got rough and hard to pick out. Mentors really looked out for their partners here, but at times tiredness and uneven ground caused some to get disheartened. There is always the stage on an expedition when you realise that it's really hard, but the only option is to keep on going. At this point people show themselves what they are truly capable of. They delve inside themselves and look for the support around them, get up and move forward. It's at these times that journeying acts as a great metaphor for one's personal life journey.

About halfway to Carsaig the sky cleared, and we took in the view. However, it was still slow-going. But everyone was helping each other, sharing kit. The sense of achievement that came when we saw the boat and headed down to the pier was amazing. Everyone was so proud of themselves.

The wind was low, so the sails were down. Mark taught some of the boys how to steer and the others enjoyed the view of the Carsaig Arches while having a well-deserved sit-down. Everyone was keen to fish but as seasickness was apparent among the crew, we headed to our second camp spot, Eilean Dubh. The white sands and clear waters were beautiful, and it was dry – which was much appreciated after the previous night. Kit-drying lines were set up; our budding tent experts taught two more boys how to pitch. Then they joined a cooking team and got that new skill in the bag. Others collected wood for the fire. With onesies on and the fire going we reflected on how far we had come over the past two days. It already seemed like an epic journey, and with two more days of fun and challenge to come.

The expedition routine was now in full swing: everyone got up in the morning, some people got breakfast ready and some packed away tents. It was amazing to see how boys who needed support with a lot of things on the first day were packed, ready to go and with a smile on their face. After some time spent reflecting on what each of us brought to the group, we were ready for the next challenge, and that morning had a little break from the boat and went climbing just around the corner from our campsite. Working together, some great leadership came through and the bonds between us became even stronger.

After lunch we sailed up the Sound of Iona. The group wanted to do some fishing, so we stopped for a while and Mark gave us a demo on line-fishing. Before he could finish explaining, he had a bite – and pulled out three mackerel. Unfortunately, the rest of us weren't so lucky. After a while we gave up and continued on to our final campsite, Ulva.

Journeying can bring things up for people that when at home can be pushed down. For some group members tiredness and having to look at our own actions proved tough. But the bonds that had been built over the previous few days helped. It's not easy sharing a tent, common tasks, a small boat and 24 hours a day together but the satisfaction of coming out the other side made it all worth it.

On the last morning people were slow to rise – it had been a long few days. As we headed for a visit to Fingal's Cave, Staffa appeared out of nowhere from the mist. After a good bit of awe and wonder on Staffa, we made our way to the Bull Hole (just around the corner from Fionnphort). Safely attached to Mark's mooring, we took a bit of time to look back over our journey together. A map showing our completed trip was set out in front of the group. We looked at what we had achieved, our shared experiences.

In turn, we said what had been hard, what we had learnt and what we would be taking away with us. The honesty that came was incredible. One of the younger members of the team said that previously he had been scared of the older boys at home on their scheme, but now it felt more like having a 'big brother'. At the end of the reflection each member was given a limpet shell necklace to keep as a memory of all they had shared together. At the pier it was hugs and smiles all round; everyone had a look of pride from their accomplishments. Onesies were donned for a sleepy journey home. They then had six hours ahead to reflect on the last four days together and the community they had built and were taking back home.

The young people learnt how to rely on themselves and to support others in the group. They progressed so far that they attended a week-long residential – challenging, but successful – and now they regularly participate in youth group activities, such as cooking and sports. It's made a world of difference to them.

Avril Leonard

GLASGOW WOMEN'S LIBRARY – LESBIANS IN PEER SUPPORT
(LIPS)

*Camas is a place of welcome for all LGBTQ+ people. LIPS were a group of
young lesbian and bisexual women who were part of Glasgow Women's Library.
They enjoyed their weeks at Camas, despite some initial anxieties. They came
with their Development Workers to experience Camas activities and to undertake some workshops on drug awareness and harm reduction. One of the young
women wrote this about their trip:*

LIPS Mull things over

The recent trip to Camas on Mull by members of LIPS has to go down as
one of the most incredible experiences I have had to date. I had more than
my fair share of apprehension before we got there, as I am not really a
'sporty' type!

But there we were on the train, twelve of us, all laughing and joking,
and I began to feel more confident about the trip. One of the best things
was the way we all seemed to gel as a group very early on, even though
some of us had hardly known each other before.

The Camas staff were wonderful too, and I think during the week everybody somewhat opened their minds – LIPS members as well as Camas staff.

Our first afternoon was one of my (many) favourite memories. A bunch
of us went for a swim in the bay. It was freezing but we all loved it anyway!
One of our members became a regular sight there at 7:30 in the morning,
but after that first day she was there by herself! The rest of us contented
ourselves with swimming later in the day, with or without costumes!

Time slowed right down at Camas. Days were full and busy, but not
rushed. Every day we did chores on a rota after breakfast. The worst of
these, I thought, would be the toilets, but washing up is the worst thing to
do – especially when twenty people have just had porridge for breakfast!

At the beginning and end of the day we had a quiet time to come
together for reflection. This was held in a lovely place called the Chapel of
the Nets. As the name implies, it has fishing nets strung from the rafters
and great piles of nets to sit on.

Somehow in between all this we did all sorts of activities, including gardening, crafts, abseiling, kayaking and workshops. We also visited Iona and camped for a night. I'm afraid to say I disappeared into a deep, hot bath whilst everyone put up the tents (it wasn't deliberate, honest!). I had a great night at the ceilidh and disco too. We went in a boat to Staffa to see Fingal's Cave the next day across a choppy sea!

Leaving Camas was unspeakably difficult. There were some tears and lots of promises to return, which I certainly hope I will be able to keep.[9]

'K'

What   I   remember   most   was

the   coruscation   of   the   setting:

our anxious feet,   eating fresh,   paths

into cool grey earth,   black rain-kissed   rocks that

we climbed   in someone else's   boots and the

hearts that we drew with sticks in the hot yellow sand
on the night we went to Market Bay

Ely Percy

CRE8

Cre8 is a local charity which has been doing work and providing services for young people in Macclesfield for many years … We provide an innovative service to young people and their families which we hope supports and enables people to play a full and active role in their neighbourhood.

Cre8 is a community based on Christian values of care and compassion, social justice, generosity, forgiveness, honesty and trust. Many of our employees and volunteers live in and are part of the neighbourhood we work in, which we think is very important.

Cre8 runs a wide range of activities and services for young people (usually aged between 8 right up to 25) and their families, from the Moss Rose Estate in Macclesfield, including clubs, two social enterprise businesses which employ local young people, music groups, residentials and a sustainable food-growing project. Our work is aimed towards empowering young people and adults in the local area to make change happen for themselves and also for their local neighbourhood.

The vision is for people to be able to free themselves from things that hold them back, like poor health, damaged relationships and unemployment, and to get access to good things like friendship, education and training, work and fun.

We work locally to achieve profound change as part of a wider movement for social justice and equality.

From the Cre8 website[10]

Cre8 have been coming to Camas for almost 20 years and a strong reciprocal relationship has developed between the two projects, with a number staff and volunteers working at both places. Here are some snapshots of their time at Camas.

Fun and friendship

It was lovely to have the Cre8 crew back at Camas – we felt like friends right from the start. They were keen on the 'Iron Man' challenge and it was amazing to see the young people standing by the shore, supporting each other and cheering each other on. Lots of fun every morning! We had games and songs in the common room at night, and some of the young people who weren't convinced at the start joined in later in the week and seemed to appreciate what Camas had to offer.

From the Camas blog

Cre8 at Camas

We took a group of 16 young people aged 11-16 – some of whom had not been away from home before – to Camas. The trip was incredible. Some challenges, lows and difficulties that come with living together away from

home and having to learn to get along and take part in everything –
including the chores to keep the community running smoothly (like
washing up and cleaning the loos). Some big highs as well: coasteering
around the bay, sailing, swimming, bog-jumping and being in the spectacular Scottish wildness. Memorable moments included: a grumpy hike in
defiant dressing gowns (perfect outerwear for a hike in Scotland!), being
stopped on the road by large Highland cows ('Are they real?'), charging into
the sea in pouring rain to escape horrific midges, and sitting up till 2am
trying to persuade angry young people to go to sleep instead of fighting.

Sharing food

Everyone eats together at Camas: visitors, volunteers and staff. The anchor
is rung, we gather upstairs and the meal is opened. We all share the same
meal, cooked by one of the Camas team, sometimes with young people's
help. Vegetables and fruit might come from the Camas garden, everything
else is brought down the track in wheelbarrows. Yesterday we ate the fish
we caught. Hattie, a Camas volunteer, made amazing fish cakes with vegetables, followed by fruit crumble and custard; she cooked for thirty-five
of us. We think Hattie is a superstar!

'Iron Man' Awards!

Tonight we will have our 'Iron Man' Award presentation at Camas; there
are eight winners this year: two girls, three lads and three leaders. To win
this prestigious handmade award, young people and adults have experienced the pain and exhilaration of swimming in the sea at Camas, wearing
only a swimming costume, before breakfast, i.e. before 8am. This year, the
sea was particularly refreshing, especially when it was raining and there
was no water for a hot shower afterwards.

Camas Challenge

Getting ready for our last night. This afternoon our community are cooking
a three-course lamb dinner, decorating the rooms, planning a reflection
and organising games. Tonight we will play Capture the Flag and Mafia.

Not just fun and games

It's not all fun and games. It might seem as though it is … just fun and games, but it's not. There are things that happen on residential that shouldn't, and sometimes we come close to arranging for someone to be sent home. Youth work is about dealing with the unwelcome things that come along, while keeping your eyes fixed clearly on the goal. Not the short-term goal, but the thing that you are trying to create, maybe over months or years. The goal in Cre8's eyes is to live well in community, just as God calls us to do. To do this we know that we have to live in love and peace with each other – this is not always easy when you are living with sixteen teenagers four hundred miles from home.

Teenagers nearly always have their own personal 'stuff' to deal with. It doesn't matter where they were born or what their life experience in childhood has been: teenagers all have 'stuff'. But in addition to this stuff, which gets in the way of being happy and getting on with growing up, many of the young people involved with Cre8 have other hurts. These can lead to anxieties and other symptoms which can make living together volatile and difficult. As leaders and volunteers, we try to keep everyone feeling OK. We do our best to keep the young people looking beyond their own individual selves, looking outside themselves and towards the needs of each other and of living together in a positive, supportive and loving community. This is not easy when squabbles (or worse) break out. This is when the going gets tough, when all our skills are called for and when we work together as a team; we have to – good teamwork is essential. Constantly, we put our efforts into 'being with' the young people; to encourage, celebrate, challenge, guide and console them. Being quick to challenge them when they aren't 'good' with each other; and being quick to encourage and thank them at other times, when things are good and smiles are everywhere. Fun, laughter, helpfulness, kindness, consideration and compassion. Fun and games, not always, but more than sometimes.

From the Cre8 website

The story of building the Camas shed

Years before becoming Programme Director at Cre8, I had been inspired by George MacLeod's story of the rebuilding of Iona Abbey; as a joiner I easily related to the idea of the sacred work of our hands. I had always been keen to get young people involved in practical work – I knew it could be fun: the teamwork, banter and satisfaction gained from building stuff were not new to me. At Cre8, we've always built projects; some of it stands at Camas, and also on Iona in the shape of the restored beach hut.

It must be more than ten years ago that we built the now-famous green hut by the road at the top of the Camas track. There had been an iconic blue plywood box at the top of the track since we first started coming to Mull that was used for the storage of vegetable and grocery deliveries together with the all-important post. The precious cargo of post and parcels was always eagerly awaited by the Camas team.

But Mary, the Camas Coordinator, wanted a hut. This top-of-the-track development should be designed big enough to store the increasing fleet of staff bicycles. Mary knew we could build a hut: some years previously Cre8 had built the pavilion in the Camas garden – and that was still standing.

We pulled up at the top of the track in our beaten-up old transit van after a ten-hour journey. We were loaded up with young lads from Cre8, together with sleeping gear, tools, concrete mixer, shovels and rock-breakers. Mary had given us a tough job: we had to site the hut in between a fence and the stream on boggy ground, as this was the only space available. When we arrived and saw the space, we realised we had to build the hut *into* the stream!

I had previously asked Mary and Emily, the Camas Programme Worker, to measure the space whilst I was on the phone. It was a comical conversation, with pouring rain and breaking phone signals and me trying to imagine the descriptions, metric and imperial getting in the way of our calculations. I was sure the hut they wanted would not fit in the space, but we agreed to give it a go anyway.

That first evening before we even set foot down the Camas track I got the lads to get the mixer going. They threw stone and cement into a mix whilst two of us rolled boulders down the stream to form the foundations.

'Build your house on a rock,' He said. We made a rough formwork and poured a concrete-capping onto the boulders, all within two hours of pulling up. Then we cleaned out the mixer and carried our gear down the track for a sound night's sleep. Some of the lads had gone down the track earlier as they were going to build a chicken run, which still stands in the garden.

The next morning we set off up the track early. I got the lads to fire up the mixer and we started laying blocks. We only had three days to build the hut and we hadn't even got a base to build from. By lunchtime we were ready to pour concrete, but we had a problem. Our base was to be partly over the stream, supported by the retaining wall we'd built from concrete blocks, and I knew we would need reinforcement in the base, otherwise it was sure to crack. But we had no steel. I pondered on getting some from the local building supplies company but knew we had little time. I looked around and wondered where we could find steel. Then one of the lads pointed out two rusty mountain bikes lying in the grass nearby, padlocked to the fence just outside the track. We jumped through the bracken towards them, sussed out that they'd been there for a long time and their owners must be long gone. The lads soon had the locks off, and we laid the bikes down, straightened out the handlebars and said, 'These'll do.' We dropped the bikes into the still-fluid, six-inch concrete base, but there was hitch – the pedals stuck out of the concrete. We dragged the now-heavy bikes out, dripping in wet, setting concrete; I hit the pedals flat with a sledgehammer and we threw them back in; they still had their perished tyres on. This time the bikes disappeared. I sometimes wonder, when that base gets broken up, what people will make of the prehistoric bikes that were cased in concrete. Maybe they'll think they've discovered a crime scene!

Whilst all this was going on, two of the lads had started laying out the timber for the hut. The next morning we cut and nailed the frames. We had no plan; we didn't need one. The sides went up, the roof timbers went on, the onduline was fitted to the roof, but we discovered we had no door. We hadn't ordered enough timber to make a door and it was now too late. I set off on the scrounge and found an old door down the track at Camas. When I returned the lads had cut Cre8 Trinity symbols for the eaves' ends to finish off each end of the roof. I was really chuffed. With deft skill we altered the door to make it fit – and the job was done.

That first winter Emily phoned me to say that the stream had become a river; floodwater was spilling over the bridge and was flooding the hut. Would it be OK? I hoped so – and it was fine. The hut dried out and no lasting damage was done. I guess those concreted bikes are going to be there for some years to come.

Rob Wardle

Each winter the Camas staff go 'on tour' to visit groups who have come to Camas; this is both to follow up their week and to reconnect and talk about future visits …

Camas reunion

Last night we had a 'Camas reunion' at club! John and Abbi from Camas came down and joined us for the evening, and a few of the Cre8 leaders that went to Camas came along, as well as most of the young people who went on the trip. We looked at photos projected on the wall of the church and remembered all the things we did – kayaking, playing guitar, boat trips, 'King of the ring', cooking and sharing food, and fishing. Lots and lots of good memories.

We presented each young person with a framed photo collage of their time at Camas. Each young person came up, shook our hands and received a big round of applause from their peers.

Then we sat down and shared a 'Camas-style' meal together. We had homemade sweet potato soup, homemade bread and homemade apple crumble and custard. All made that afternoon with help from some of the older young people that came with us to Camas this year – we have never peeled so many apples! And then we did our chores – we washed up together.

Thanks to Abbi and John for joining us for the evening, and to everyone who helped cook and prepare for the night. Good to remember and a great atmosphere – it felt just like it did in the summer at Camas. We are a group that has shared an experience together and that will stay with us.

From the Cre8 website

MUIRHOUSE YOUTH DEVELOPMENT GROUP (MYDG)

MYDG have visited Camas for over 20 years and some of their group have also volunteered at Camas.

'Our mission is to be an anchor in the lives of young people and to support them throughout their personal journeys. Providing opportunities that make a difference to the lives of young people in Muirhouse will enable them to have a positive sense of their own future and the world around them.' (MYDG mission statement)

MYDG is not a simple youth work programme … It is an indigenous organisation, committed to its own longevity; working with and through its local community; with young people finding and making their places within it as they grow up, as they gain independence, and as they become able and capable of being increasingly responsible for steering MYDG and ensuring that it creates opportunities for others who come along after themselves.

MYDG could be described as a process of social change, or 'a quiet revolution', which has empowered several generations of young people from North Edinburgh. MYDG is never top down; it is always about relationships; it puts young people first; it is there when they need it and there for them to return to …

MYDG began in 1997. The local social context was characterised by extremes – family breakdown, loss of traditional employment, drug and substance misuse becoming more widespread, domestic violence – but interspersed with people who wanted to make things change for the better. Young people in Muirhouse and adjacent areas of North Edinburgh had nowhere to go in the evenings, no activities, no focal points, no voice. Organic, unstructured, peer- and volunteer-led, MYDG began to take shape, and welcome support came from local agencies who provided premises and resources, with a strong community commitment. MYDG was small and low profile, yet determined, and was hugely successful in the ways in which young people benefitted – from being listened to, from forming relevant and constructive relationships, from having new experiences, and from others believing in them.

MYDG engages young people with a focus on the following four areas of work:

– Health and well-being
– Life transitions
– Training, accreditation and volunteering
– Arts and creativity

From the Muirhouse Youth Development website [11]

One of the young people from MYDG said this about his time at Camas:

'It's brilliant. I keep coming back. It's good to get away from city life and be by the water. Nae big tall buildings, nae pollution. At first you think "ah it's pretty rough, nae electricity, nae TV and things", but once you get here and you realise it's a nice place, it's excellent. You just get on with it and don't really miss the electricity.'

Another young person commented:

'It's a safe place where we can be free. No one carries knives – you don't have to be on your guard all the time. People treat us with respect and I can relax and have a laugh with everyone.' [12]

'Vintage!'

Last week was very special – we welcomed MYDG from Muirhouse in Edinburgh! The group consisted of young adults of varying ages with two leaders. They arrived late on Saturday, weary after a long trip and were hungry. After some lovely food, there was a reflection on the history of Camas where everyone sat spellbound by the stories of these old buildings. After this everyone was just pleased to get out and have a little swim around the islands.

The next day the group took part in rock climbing and kayaking. The older ones all made it to the top of the quarry; their speed and movement was breathtaking. The kayaking team also displayed awesome abilities out on the water, while exploring some of the lovelier parts of Camas Bay. The group were always there to motivate and help each other through their activities.

The group then headed to Iona, and made their way to the beach at the north end, where they had a lovely picnic and played games. After this they made their way to the Abbey and explored its weird and wonderful areas. On the ferry back they saw dolphins leaping alongside the boat – it was truly magical.

The Camas Challenge was on the last night. The reflection was chilled out and quite moving as everyone picked up something from the beach that would remind them of their time at Camas. They also wrote down something that they would like to change in their life back at home on a piece of paper, which they then cast into the fire. Everyone felt closer than ever as a community at this point. The night ended on a massive high as everyone huddled up to each other in the common room and belted out the words to 'Three Little Birds', by Bob Marley. It was the perfect end to a perfect week, and the Camas staff were so proud of the group's achievements. They tried everything, were always so helpful and permanently had 'vintage' banter. It was a week that we will never forget. 'Vintage!'

From the Camas blog

Camas and us

Camas is the sort of place that creates memories that are shared rather than individual. Even though I spend a lot of time sitting on the bench outside the kitchen lost in my own thoughts, I am aware of the sounds around me, like young people running the length of the games room and the Chapel of the Nets, or washing up and cooking!

I brought MYDG groups to Camas for many years and they often found the very different environment challenging and difficult to begin with – but by the end of the week they didn't want to leave.

I sometimes bump into young people I have taken to Camas, some of whom are now in their late 40s, and they still remember the place. Although they remember some of the activities and the daft things that happened to them, like mucking out the toilets, it seems to be the *feelings* they recall the most. For example when they managed something that they thought they would *never* do; this is usually to do with tasks they didn't like doing, or the sense of achievement when they abseiled.

I have not taken a group to Camas for a few years now, but I have taken my two teenage sons on a number of occasions. We have joined other groups; and a few years ago they organised some adult guests to play 'Capture-the-flag', a game the boys had learned the previous year from Camas volunteers. I witnessed the feelings of pride they had in getting those adults to join in and play.

We love going to Camas as a family – me and the boys! In a world where 'Xbox detox' is a need in itself, I am glad that I can share important experiences and feelings with the boys without forcing it on them. The Camas journey for me is a deep one. For some it is one-off, while for others, we can't get enough – and keep coming back!

Peter Johnson

POLMONT YOUNG OFFENDERS INSTITUTION

The link between Camas and the young people of Polmont was re-established in the mid-2000s. Iain Campbell, the Iona Community's Youth Worker at the time, wrote: *'It's been quite some time since the days of the "borstal boys" visiting Camas with George MacLeod, but one of the most exciting parts of the Iona Community's work has come full circle.'*

A gifted artist, Iain ran creative arts workshops at Polmont and visited regularly as part of the preparatory work to bring them to Camas. Some of the young men were undertaking their Duke of Edinburgh Award and Camas was seen as an ideal venue for a residential expedition.

Iain reflected that *'going to Camas was a very important experience for me. Spending time with the boys outside the prison context created an entirely different relationship with them; joining in with activities that neither I nor they had taken part in before brought a real sense of equality – like being just as scared as some of them going over the cliff edge to abseil down the Camas quarry wall. The idea that there is an "us and them" disappeared in that context.*

'Many of the boys would say that spending time with the Camas staff and volunteers was a "life-changing experience" for them. People treated them with dignity and respect, as fellow human beings, who had a laugh with them and

demonstrated to them beyond words that there are good people in the world who are willing to give young offenders a second chance.'

Iain continued to work with the young men after the Camas trip, and commented: *'Working in prison has given me so many glimmers of hope: relationships have been built, imaginations fired up, mustard seeds of faith nurtured. Not only have my preconceptions of prison been erased and my youth work skills sharpened, but this work has made me care more deeply about the social context which creates the circumstances through which people end up in jail. It has given me a greater concern for the underlying social justice issues involved, such as poverty and unemployment.'*[13]

Rachel McCann

Some comments from the young men at Polmont about their visits to Camas:

'We were supposed to go abseiling, but it was too windy, so we sat on the mountain and ate scones … it was brilliant. Later, at night, we sat round a big fire and all the guys had their guitars out and we were singing. It just felt like being normal again. It was a good experience.'

'It's the first time I felt like a normal person in five months.'

'We were apprehensive, but after a while we settled in and nobody had a bad word to say about it.'

'You felt freedom again cos you weren't being locked up and told to go to your bed. Your door wasn't locked. It was just brilliant, the whole thing. I enjoyed it. I will always remember it. I will never forget it.'

'We did a lot of activities. The biggest thing I did was climb Ben More. It gave us such a sense of achievement.'[14]

UNIVERSITY OF CUMBRIA

Second-year Outdoor Education students from the University of Cumbria wended their way to and from Camas on a self-directed journey. Towards the end of the journey, they were challenged to stay up all night on a static solo experience. The Camas team tended a hearth for them from dusk until dawn, in a reoccupied shieling in the heart of the Ardfenaig township. The next day they amazed us with some reflective presentations based on their lived experience of a week at Camas. The following is an extract from one group presentation, on the theme of 'Challenge'.

Challenge

'Challenge' is used in Outdoor Education as a tool for personal development. This can be a physical, emotional or mental challenge. Barnes and Sharp say that Outdoor Education heightens awareness and respect for ourselves through the meeting of challenges in the natural environment.[15]

We are going to consider different perceptions of the challenges that we have faced and explored through our time at Camas. Starting with a poem:

The challenge of time

Time is a challenge for me.
It's taken me Camas to see
how so often I rush
with no time for hush.
How can that possibly be?

Time is a challenge for me.
Oh how I long to be free
of the ever-repeating days
and such linear ways.
Oh how can that possibly be?

Time is a challenge for me.
New sequences are the key

for our true human self
to come out from the shelf.
Oh how can this possibly be?

Time is a challenge for me,
to follow a new trajectory
instead of moving so fast
and skimming the past.
Oh how can this possibly be?

Time is a challenge for me.
I can finally be free
to spread from the pack
and get back on track
with what nature intends us to be.

Lucy Allan

> *'Given that we as humans are as natural as anything else, what might these archetypal patterns – the rhythms of Sun and Earth – suggest about how human life is meant to unfold?'*[16]

These natural patterns do have slight repetition, but not always the same each year. The shifting dance between nature and culture is one of the dynamics that makes us human. Yet a lot of people have lost the balance and have become controlled by a linear time structure in our days, e.g. getting up for work at 9am every day. French philosopher Henri Lefebvre believes that the rhythms of our culture and society are unhealthy for us, and are oppressing us. We need to be freed!

My challenge of time at Camas has allowed me to embrace a more relaxed time structure, creating a better balance between my natural and cultural time pattern.

Going without …

Challenge is needed for personal development, and one of the challenges we faced was that we had no electricity at Camas. We had to do without appliances and lighting that we usually take for granted at home. It was a new/different way of living which opened my eyes. This is something I will take back home with me: I won't be using electricity just because it is there. As Roger Greenaway says, *'new skills of any kind open up more choices and chances'.*[17] Not using electricity as much is a new skill for me and is definitely as valuable as the other skills I learnt on the trip.

I would now like to explore how the absence of challenge can be what challenges your perceptions. I have found that Camas has not necessarily been a place where I have faced and explored *too many* challenges. They have been present, but for me Camas has been a place that has allowed me to develop by finding a way to learn how to feel comfortable with what I may have already known about myself, and particularly about my preferred approach to Outdoor Education. To me the outdoors is a place to 'be', and the act of 'being' might itself be enough. This, in some ways, reflects my background from *friluftsliv* in Norway:

> '*Friluftsliv means spending time outside and experiencing nature first-hand … [It offers] the possibility of recreation, rejuvenation and the benefits of increased physical activity and reduced stress levels through a connection with nature and quality time with friends and loved ones.*'[18]

Since moving to England two years ago I have found myself introduced to a more activity-centred approach to the outdoors. One benefit to a residential is the opportunity to fully immerse yourself and give yourself time to consider an approach that might be new to you. The Camas approach to me seems quite similar in many ways to the *friluftsliv* approach, compared to what I have previously been introduced to in the UK. Immersion into the programme here has helped me to challenge, and find peace with, my personal preferred approach. Wurdinger comments: *'For some the challenges of everyday life might be enough to discover untapped potential. It is not necessary for people to overcome physical challenges to discover their inner strengths.'*[19]

Challenge is necessary for personal development. But, whilst challenges can be found in the outdoors, the outdoors can also be used to face, and deal with, not just physical but inner challenges. Colin Mortlock, in *Beyond Adventure*, talks about his *'journey inwards'* and how he used the outdoors as a facilitator for this journey.[20]

Challenge and change

Camas didn't provide me with the challenges I faced during my stay, rather I brought my challenges with me. Camas – the incredible outdoor space and the community I was able to be a part of – has allowed me, and provided me with, the opportunity to face and deal with my already existing challenges. I often find my mind is haunted by the big questions: 'What is the meaning of life?', etc. I arrived on Friday with my thoughts bogged down by these very questions; the questions I have come to reason with whilst being here.

The opportunity Camas has given me is one of freedom. The opportunity to be fully present and surrounded by the tranquility of nature has allowed me to understand and accept that the answers to these questions are fluid and will change. Just like the challenges we all face will also change. But right now, we are here, acknowledging our different challenges and this very moment and thanking them for allowing personal development to occur.

Lucy Allan, Emilie Selby Ebbestad, Ellie Green, Abbey Charlotte Connelly, from the Camas blog

ABERCORN SCHOOL

Abercorn Secondary School in Glasgow caters for young people with additional support needs. It provides 'a nurturing environment and a belief that all young people deserve to be successful, confident individuals who can effectively contribute to our world … Our school community strives to put achievement, respect for others, fairness and honesty at the centre of our school life.'[21]

The young people who come to Camas face many challenges in their lives, but always bring laughter and kindness. Derek and Jane, the two dedicated teachers who brought the group, have become firm friends of Camas.

Twenty years of Camas trips

Jane and I brought pupils from Abercorn to Camas for 20 years or so. Camas has been such a wonderful place for our kids to enjoy. When we first went to Camas, there was no electricity at all and no toilets, save for a bucket and bracken! There were no showers, and I well remember dunking my head into a large sink full of freezing water each morning! This was however somewhat tempered at night-time when we would sit in front of a wood-burning stove, listening to stories and enjoying a hot chocolate.

A good number of the children that we have brought to Camas down through the years had never been out of Glasgow before, so the journey to Camas was something of an adventure. Camas allowed our kids the opportunity to find a peacefulness and serenity that would be difficult to find anywhere else. In all of the years that we brought children to Camas, never once did I hear anyone say that they did not enjoy the experience.

Jane and I would like to take this opportunity to thank all the Camas staff that we have met and befriended down through the years. The staff have been excellent role models for our children and have never failed to leave an impression on them.

Derek Robertson

From the Abercorn School newsletter

The pupils had a fantastic time abseiling, canoeing, hillwalking, peat-digging, swimming and doing a host of indoor activities. They were fortunate enough to be basking in bright sunshine for the week!

This was a great opportunity for pupils to develop deeper friendships with one another, and they were excellent at helping each other through the day's activities. All the pupils enjoyed the experience and discovered what it was like to live together as a community. The pupils were a credit to themselves and to Abercorn, and it was a joy for Miss Campbell and Mr Robertson to lead.

Fun times with Abercorn

This week Camas was visited by one of our longest-running groups: Abercorn School from Glasgow. It was a week of high-fives, arm-wrestling, cook-offs and 'made you looks'.

Everybody had a great time. Two of the group performed at the Iona ceilidh and almost everybody had a dance. It was a hoot of a week, full of work and play and sunny days and starry nights.

From the Camas blog

An oak tree in the garden

One highlight of the 2017 season was when our longest-standing teacher visitors came for their final week with Abercorn School in Glasgow in September. Derek and Jane have been bringing groups of young people with additional support needs for 20 years! Derek is retiring and so this was his last visit with a group – we had a great week and planted Derek and Jane an oak tree in the garden to celebrate their time with us.

From the Camas blog

HEBRIDEAN ADVENTURE CAMP

The recent Hebridean Adventure Camps reflect the old Open Camps, in that they welcome individual young people from a variety of backgrounds. This is the moving story of one Adventure Camp in 2018:

Dropping into natural time

Drawing inspiration from my apprenticeship with Mark Morey from the Institute of Natural Learning in North America, we set off with the aim of a self-reliant adventure into the unknown. We practised routines of listening to the birds and of recognising animal tracks and signs; we shared skills of navigation, self-care and the art of staying warm and dry. We walked on deer paths and skirted remnants of Atlantic rainforest, while passing old fortifications and shielings, and shared the wonder of the beauty of lichen on ancient standing stones.

It was nightfall by the time we made camp. The rain cleared and a fire was struck, kindled from plants collected and dried on the move.

The next morning heralded a surprise, as the *Birthe Marie* entered the bay. The group boarded and headed off into lumpy seas with the sails raised. Later they found shelter in a nearby cove, cast lines and fished for their evening meal.

As they rounded the point and entered Camas Tuath, the conch sounded to welcome their return – and a great cheer erupted from the boat.

Around the shieling fire that night, the young people revisited their intentions for the journey; and claimed their learning both in their journals and in a magic wand crafted from hazel …

'A crucial element to any expedition is nap time, and we were able to do this in a beautiful remnant of Atlantic rainforest. I loved how the canopy of leaves broke up the light; and as I lay back to appreciate this, I thought about how we had all gotten there – scouting our way past houses without being noticed, stopping for flapjacks at a solitary standing stone. I felt grateful to the young team for their infectious energy and enthusiasm for the trip and lucky to be having this adventure with them.' (Cat, Camas volunteer)

Pirates

Six nights in, and it was a calm, contented evening at the Camp of the Shieling. The old stones, tarpaulin and bracken provided shelter from the light breeze and a fire flickered from the hearth. Within the enclosure, the teen Bracken Clan laughed, told stories and sang songs about the day whilst whittling their spoons and weaving cordage for fishing line from foraged nettles. It felt like home.

Suddenly a fisherman, clearly distressed, emerged at camp and cried out: 'Help! The pirates are coming into the bay – they're going to destroy everything!' The Bracken Clan rallied, donning camouflage and courage, and headed off in search of a solution to the fisherman's plight. A tale of challenge, invisibility and the transformative art of hospitality ensued, as they sought help from the ancestors, woodland fairies and items from the landscape to complete their quest.

By the end of the night, both heroes and foes were shaking hands and toasting health, as the larger clan danced around the fire …

'We spent a long time getting into character, dressing up, drawing on tattoos and creating pirate personas. As we waited for the kids to arrive, we floated around in our canoe, fully in character, singing pirate songs. As soon as they arrived, the action began – we jumped ashore and gave chase; their eyes lit up as the world of make-believe became real and three swashbuckling pirates chased them through the bracken.' (Joey, Camas volunteer)

Soloing

Nature does not give her teachings away, wrapped in a processed bun and served on a plate. Learning has to be earned. Experiencing cold, dark, soil on skin, hunger, midges and being alone can provide a powerful encounter with yourself. One element of Hebridean Adventure Camp was soloing: spending a night out alone.

Individuals donned a mask over their eyes and were led to their site where they would stay through the night – alert to the sights, sounds, nuances and timelessness of the landscape. Paying attention in nature often means tracking the inner as well as outer landscape. And the strategies and tools young people use in response to these encounters can yield potent metaphors for their journey and the direction they are moving towards with their life choices.

Time passed … the sun set … and rose again … and in between experiences were had …

The conch blew to signal the return, and as the young people entered the red granite walls of Camas their hands and faces were wiped clean with warm water and sweet oils, as we welcomed these wild creatures, and their wide open sense of peace, calm and connection, back into our human community. We were hungry for their stories …

'When they returned, I was struck by the powerful sense of quiet, contented calm they carried with them, alongside their sleeping bags. Their faces, although tired, radiated a deep sense of achievement. They had left camp the night before with a clear intention for their solo journey. Each and every one of them had survived the night, along with midges, frogs, creepy-crawlies, cold, dirt, wilderness and their own thoughts for company. Beyond survival, I sensed a significant shift. Somewhere between dusk and dawn they had become ever

so slightly different people, and I was lucky enough to witness their eyes now shining that little bit brighter.' (Angela, Camas volunteer)

Wrapping the bundle

For the final phase of the camp, we invited parents to join the Bracken Clan to experience what their children had been up to. The young people spent the day teaching their parents crafts, how to make a fire, how to pay attention, how to play games in the outdoors.

The family camp was about integration. Ropes of connection to the environment, others and ourselves that were woven during the week became stronger. In reflection on the final evening, we emphasised that these ropes can become strong baskets that contain life. The parents and young people spent time setting goals for themselves to help strengthen their home community, strategised who would hold them accountable to their resolutions and identified strands they wished to weave into their lives when back at home.

'In some ways, the whole week had been leading up to this opportunity to integrate the experiences of our week. Hearing the young people share about their week showed the unique power of stories. Not only did the young people have an opportunity to craft and create these stories, but were also able to share them with the people who love and care for them most.' (Joel, Camas volunteer) [22]

Rhyddian Knight

COMMUNITY KIDS WEEK

Each year, young people who are children of Iona Community members come to Camas for a week, whilst their parents gather for Community Week on Iona. This is always a popular week, where rich, often lifelong friendships are formed.

I have co-led Community Kids weeks several times and know that Camas is a place of sanctuary for the young people, who have been struggling with things like bereavement, loss, change and the challenges of being a teenager. The Camas week has provided them with community, support and friendship; and a number of these young people have gone on to work at Camas as volunteers and resident staff members.

Rachael Yates

Freedom and joy

I remember, in 1974, walking down the track with my wee brother Neil. The track seemed interminable, but at the end of it we discovered that there was 'another' Iona Community, this time on Mull – and the glories of this micro-community first unveiled themselves. We were six and four, on a day out with Dougald, a wonderful Iona volunteer who'd found freedom from inner-city Glasgow. Camas is an inclusive, wild place where those on the margins, like Dougald, find a home and a sense of belonging.

In 1982, as one of the first groups of Community Kids, we, a collection of 4-16-year-olds, welcomed our parents and other Community members to Camas – they scrambled over Goat Island from the boat; we washed their feet as they arrived, with George MacLeod in the lead. Then we fed them lunch. A truly liturgical moment.

All three of our girls, Maeve, followed by Freya, then Sophie, have been formed and re-formed by the magic of Camas each year during Community Kids Week, and by the staff who pour themselves out, body, mind and spirit, to make these weeks, and all weeks, transformative. Our girls' sense of belonging to the Iona Community, and its vision and commitment to a just and peaceful world, through Camas is intense, as is their joy in an outdoor life – relishing mountains, sea, gardens, the environment and off-grid living.

Ruth Harvey

Maeve, one of Ruth's daughters, wrote the following piece when she was 14, after being asked to write about her 'perfect place' for school …

My perfect place

To be woken up by the singing and laughter of my closest friends and family, the bright sunlight streaming through the open window. A brand-new book, crisp and untouched, waits by my bed to be opened and the story of romance or adventure to be uncovered. The smell of fresh pages overpowered by the saltiness of the sea. This is my perfect place.

Memories and good times are created and had; on the sand, on the water and in the water. Laughter is constant, happiness is constant, and love is constant. Continual clicks that are the sound of some of my happiest moments being preserved within a machine. Occasional beeps that are the sound of passing time being recorded, to be remembered and laughed at in future years. This is my perfect place.

Shrieks of mirth echo around the isolated building, out to the Atlantic Ocean and up to the deserted quarry as our meal is announced. Up the uneven steps like a herd of elephants, chatting to our heart's content, the prospect of a warm, hearty meal is music to our ears. Cackles, snorts, chortles and giggles are heard from all around; the sense of community is overwhelming. This is my perfect place.

A secluded bay on the west coast of Scotland, an occasional dolphin or basking shark out in the teal blue ocean for everyone to marvel. The fear of being stung by a jellyfish when swimming in the salty sea is far out-weighed by the fear of not having enough fun with your friends. Meagre fishermen's huts transformed into chaotic dormitories, snug sofas sur-rounding a cosy wood-burner and a room for you to express yourself in art but at the same time have friendly matches of table tennis or pool. Two deserted islands standing out in the bay, sometimes connected to land, sometimes cut off from all people; always a danger. This is my perfect place.

Always working together as one to complete a task. From cleaning the toilets to wiping tables to washing up, everything is done as a team. What may seem like a chore or a burden is altered to become a Taylor-Swift-singing, people-splashing, friend-making, bad-dancing, all-round amazing experience. Cheers and shouts as everyone reaches the top of the vertical cliff face: support is all around. Every other person is another block, helping you and comforting you and telling you that you can do it and that it is possible to conquer your fears. This is my perfect place.

Long and lively chats, lasting well into the night. Discussing everything from Harry Potter to Hercules in as much detail as we feel necessary. In-depth deliberations round the dinner table; there is talk of Japan and Jeremy Fisher. Cracking a joke as we hike up the treacherous gully, over to the sandy white beaches of Market Bay to laugh our nights away under a blanket of stars. This is Camas. This is my perfect place.[23]

Maeve Austin

The spirit of Camas

Camas has been a part of my life, a part of my soul, from a young age. I have been blessed to experience this magical place both as a youth at Community Kids Week – learning to live in community, face my fears and connect with Mother Nature – and as an adult volunteer – witnessing time and time again the spirit of Camas seep into the souls of those who come here. Although ever-evolving, that beautiful bay and its ancient teachings will always have a place in my heart.

Mairead Spangler

Best two out of three

The Community members sent their kids to Camas while they had a week on Iona. Now, these guys were AWESOME! We did all sorts of fun things. We did the typical abseiling, kayaking, raft-building, hillwalking, etc. But they also went camping on the Camas lawn, and then we played manhunt (which is a glorified way to play hide-and-seek, actually it is the best way to play hide-and-seek). We also took a trip to Market Bay, which was like none other I have ever been on! While at the beach, we had a massive wrestling match – and it was guys vs. gals! And let me say this … boy, was it close. We had a big rope circle around us, and the deal was you had to push all the opposing team out of the circle, and it was best two out of three. And I think, if I am right, that the girls ended up winning! But we all expected that anyway, right?

We really like those Community Kids – and we look forward to having them back for more fun next year!

From the Camas blog

From Community Kids … to Camas crew

An interview with Keir Aitken, Doug Birley and Immy Reeves, who attended Community Kids Week and were members of the Camas team in 2021.

Rachel (McCann): Can you tell me about when you first came to Camas? What brought you there, and what were your first impressions?

Doug: I had been quite excited to go as I had heard a lot about Camas from my sisters who had been before. It lived up to all the hype and was a really fun place to be – Community Kids week was something that I looked forward to every year.

Immy: I came the same year as Doug (2009) and I remember being really nervous and quite quiet, but really enjoying it.

Keir: All the years are a bit of a blur in terms of which was which, but I remember it was something I looked forward to throughout the year and it was really cool to have this group of friends that kept coming back, and we would be straight back into our friendships. Even if we didn't see each other in between Camas trips, relationships were easy to pick up each year.

Rachel: I get the impression that the Community Kids Week seems to develop strong bonds, and friendships seem to develop as you get older?

Keir: Yes, we were lucky in that we are all a similar age; my sister has it too with some of her age group who have been to Camas. We have managed to continue our friendship post-Camas and then back at Camas.

Immy: Yes it's a really intense and really loving bond where you all support each other even though it's just once a year, when you come together in community. I don't have any other friendships quite like these ones.

Rachel: What did you think of Camas as a place when you first came? Did you feel OK with how basic and how close to nature it was?

Doug: Something I have always really appreciated about Camas is the fact that it was more basic, and I have had experiences that my friends back at school didn't, in terms of being away from technology and knowing that that's possible for me. A lot of friends did just not understand that that was something that could happen, but being here I knew that was something I could do.

Keir: I feel like a bit of a grumpy old man when I say this, but now that some people get a phone signal at Camas … I kind of wish that wasn't the case, because I remember really appreciating the time away from it. I need the complete restriction of not being able to go on my phone, rather than having a choice.

Immy: I liked knowing that I could go to this place that didn't have any signal or Wi-Fi, and knowing I could have those breaks, especially when I was in high school. It also gave me a lot of perspective in school, like if there was drama or stress; the Camas week was really good to balance that out with a different group of friends in a different place.

Doug: Yes, that rings true for me, having friends outside of school who I knew were going to be my friends regardless of what happened at school. So when things weren't good at school or my friends there were doing things I disagreed with, I didn't feel as much pressure to do those things because I had my Camas friends who I didn't need to prove anything to. I love and cherish those friends and they love and cherish me regardless of what I do.

Rachel: That's wonderful to have those bonds and connections. So how did you three end up being here at Camas together today, volunteering and as staff members?

Doug: We didn't really plan to all be together this year. We all wanted to be here for our own separate reasons, then it just turned out we were here together.

Keir: Thomas Bunting, another Community Kid, was here earlier in the season; and we had all said when we were younger that we would come back and volunteer here. I applied quite late, after calling the others and hearing about their experiences, as they had all done seasons before, and their reviews on their experiences convinced me to apply.

Rachel: I think it's lovely you are all here together and giving back to the place you enjoyed when you were younger. How have you found this season?

Doug: It's been really special; even with Covid restrictions it's felt very much like the same place it's always been. It's a wonderful place that brings wonderful people and it hasn't failed to do that this year.

Immy: I am really happy with the staff team; everyone gets on so well and is quite close and that's really impacted on my experience. It's been a really great summer; I can't fault it really.

Keir: It's been exactly what I needed at this point in my life. I have come away and don't have anything specific to go back to, and I needed somewhere to reflect upon what my next steps in life were going to be. I have played artistically here and I don't think I would have been able to achieve that in the city or many other places. So I am grateful that Camas has provided me with the space and time to reflect. It has provided the space for me to be creative. I have created work while I have been here. I am going to be running a 'Creative Week' at Camas – this is a perfect place to bring creatives at all stages in their careers together to work in response to the environmental consciousness and community living aspects of Camas. I give credit to Tom [Wardle, Camas Coordinator], because when we pitched the idea, he said, 'Let's do it!'

Rachel: It's great that you can all share your gifts and experiences here. Just moving on to the groups that come, how do you see them benefitting from their time at Camas?

Doug: I know it changed my own life. Without a doubt, my life would be very different without the experience of coming here. But some of the young people, when they first come, will find it a very strange place to be – for a lot of them that results in them acting up in various ways and that's often very common at the start of the week; there will be bickering and fights and problems arising around the place. The focus on creating a community and the intensity and doing things for the first time often puts people in a vulnerable position, but it is a really powerful way of helping them feel like they are together and that they have to look out for each other.

There is a distinct change between the beginning and end of the week and it's often only noticeable on the very last day when people realise that it's coming to an end, and they realise it's something they have really cherished, even if they didn't realise that at the time.

Also, seeing people come back year on year, you see the progression. Obviously all that credit can't be given to Camas; a lot of the young people come from youth work projects who work with them over a long period of time. But residentials like Camas are a fantastic tool for those youth workers to really have a turbocharged week of really getting to know those young people and seeing the difference in them.

Rachel: Yes, that reminds me of what you said about bringing The Barn youth group to Camas when you were a youth worker with them …

Doug: Yes, with some of the people who came with The Barn, I didn't have much to relate to them with, before coming to Camas. They would get into a lot of difficult situations at home and in the local community in the Gorbals, but during the week at Camas, there was a transformation where they weren't trying to prove anything to each other; they would just have fun and run around and play as teenagers – that was something that was really valuable and special to see.

After Camas, to an outsider, it may seem like they have regressed back to how they were, but the experience and memories of Camas stay with them forever. It gave me an extra connection with them, and if I brought up a story of our time at Camas, I could see something in their face just change as they remembered it, and they valued those memories and experiences.

Immy: The fact that the Camas team has volunteers who have been here as guests – Bridgid from Litchfield and Keelin from theGKexperience – shows the impact it has had on them. Also the GK week this year – though it was a bit chaotic with Covid and they were stuck here due to isolation rules for eighteen days and couldn't do all the activities and it was mentally quite hard for some of them – they are coming back next week and looking forward to it; that tells you a lot.

Keir: Some of the 'little' things really matter, like at the beginning of the week, some of them have never played a board game before, or never eaten vegetarian food as a choice. But at the end of the week to hear them say 'I love board games', or 'vegetarian food is actually quite nice' is amazing. They don't believe us when we tell them the vegan chocolate cake is vegan because they don't think vegan food can be good! Just in those very small ways being opened up to new experiences is important.

Rachel: It is really valuable. Thinking about the future, is there anything you would like to see in terms of Camas being developed or changed in terms of it moving forward?

Keir: I like the idea of a longer residential; we saw some benefits of the eighteen days that GK had here. Also, I would like to see more thematic weeks, for example peace and justice weeks. So that rather than groups that come from a shared geographical location, it's groups who come for a shared belief or interest.

Immy: It would be good to have more diversity in the team, as most of us come from similar middle-class backgrounds and we are all white. A lot of the groups that come up are very different to us, so it would be good to have more diversity amongst staff and volunteers.

Doug: Yes, there are loads of people who come with a group and want to come back to volunteer, but for a lot of people that is a seemingly unachievable goal for a variety of reasons, like the things that are going on in their lives at that point. But what has happened more this year is that people have come for 'taster sessions' of volunteering and that has come from the young person or their youth worker being proactive. But I think that's something that should be more widely available and more formally developed by Camas – to create opportunities for young people who are a bit older who have experienced Camas and are phasing out of their youth groups. Camas is a really good stepping stone from being a young person to being an adult.

Rachel: Thanks so much to all three of you. It's been a real privilege to listen to your thoughts on Camas and it's wonderful you are taking care of the place now and into the future. Is there anything else you would like to say?

Doug: A really common piece of feedback I hear as people are leaving and going up the track is that Camas is 'the best thing they have ever done' in their life, that the week they have had here is 'the best week' of their life. One comment that really stuck out to me was from a person in his 40s who had been here for two nights and three days. He had done quite a lot of things in his life, and at the end of the week he said, 'Yes, this has been the most fantastic thing I have ever done in my life.' And it really struck me how much of an effect such a short time in a place like this can have.

Keir Aitken, Doug Birley, Immy Reeves and Rachel McCann

YOUTH FESTIVAL

Youth Festival comes to Camas

In 2018, when the Abbey Centre was closed for refurbishing, young people who would normally attend the annual Youth Festival on Iona decided to come to Camas …

'Over the course of an amazing week, we were able to try so many new things. It was a great opportunity to get out of my comfort zone while surrounded by supportive and helpful people. One of my best memories is going kayaking for the first time.' (Ciera)

During a sunny week in July, a group of volunteer leaders and young people from Glasgow and beyond gathered at Camas for Youth Festival – a week of activities, workshops and discussions, of sharing spaces, good food and lots of fun and laughter.

We began the week together with a long journey from Glasgow. Most of the folk who came hadn't met each other before; some were involved in youth groups in Glasgow who regularly go to Camas, some were from across the UK and from as far south as London, and so had already travelled a long way before we came together. Bringing together a mix of people with different experiences has often been one of the most powerful things about Youth Festival – enabling folk to build connections and relationships with those that they would not normally meet in their daily lives. This week was no different.

We arrived at Camas, greeted as usual by the fiercely welcoming and warm Camas staff team, as well as a hearty shepherd's pie and generous helpings of chocolate cake. Folk began to settle into each other's company, and that night we began our programme.

Through a series of small-group clan sessions, workshops and discussions, over the week we explored the theme of 'identity', looking at the different experiences, values and identities that make us who we are. The group started to think about how an identity that they shared – that of being a 'young person' – is stereotyped in different ways, and presented their ideas through a series of interactive sculptures using Camas objects (which included Martin Johnstone, our Member in Residence for the week, being 'mugged' with a whale bone). Sculptures were made which showed the potential in young people, and their power to change the world for the better, possibly more than previous generations ever have.

We moved on to look at gender identity and sexuality, challenging binaries and stereotypes that dictate who people are or 'should be', before more widely looking at how society is structured in ways that discriminate and privilege people based on aspects of their identity. A Youth Fest banner was painted, with a crest designed by the clan groups to represent how their different identities came together to form our festival community; and folk wrote on this one action that they planned to carry out in their own communities back home.

Interspersed through all of this were, of course, the usual Camas activities: kayaking sessions with epic games of kayak polo, abseiling at the quarry – featuring great shouts of encouragement from those enjoying tea and scones at the bottom – coasteering, trips to Market Bay and many games of 'Woosh'!

A particular highlight of the week was an Open Space session on the Thursday night, in which each person was given a minute to share anything they wanted with the group. Folk read poems, danced, shared their passions, their stories. It was an hour that came to represent the whole week – the passion and brilliance of young people, and the need both to create space so that they can speak, but also to relinquish it so that they can be heard. Here's to next year!

'I'm grateful to organisers of Youth Festival for helping someone like me understand more about life, and for the opportunity to meet wonderful people.' (Lawrence) [24]

Hattie Cooper Hockey

Just how inspiring so many young people are

I had the privilege of spending a week at Camas as a volunteer at Youth Festival with a spectacular group of young people, including some utterly outstanding young leaders. Amid all the laughter and banter, as well as using muscles that have lain dormant for a long time, I was reminded (again) of just how inspiring so many young people are. I want to join them in their passionate hopes for a better world, rather than simply imbue them with a burdensome concern for the institutions and organisations I hold dear.[25]

Martin Johnstone, Member in Residence at Youth Festival. A Member in Residence is a member or associate of the Iona Community who volunteers to help at Camas for one week.

Joe

Joe originally came to Camas with a group from Grimsby. With a wonderfully wild spirit he created some memorable moments and found a sense of belonging at Camas. He settled in Oban and made many friends there.

Sadly Joe passed away all too soon. This poem remembers him:

Lights flicker in Oban Bay,
always the same,
always in change.

Joe meets me,
the same wide grin on his face,
only this time his hands are softer,
his hug more tender,
and the scars are healing.
He has a new home now, he announces – his home.
Pride guides me around the kitchen:
cupboards full of food and plans to decorate.

He says he never meant to scare me
the first time we met when
he waved a big knife.
I laugh and tell him
I knew from the off he was a teddy bear.[26]

Rachel McCann

Notes:

1. From *Living by the Rule: The Rule of the Iona Community*, Kathy Galloway, Wild Goose Publications, 2010
2. From a YouthLink press release (www.youthlinkscotland.org)
3. From *A Measure of Diversion*, Dr. N. Alm, National Youth Bureau, April, 1981
4. Kibble website: www.kibble.org
5. From the *Christian Science Monitor*, August, 2016
6. From theGKexperience website: www.thegkexperience.org.uk
7. *I Wasnae Expectin' That: Stories of theGKexperience,* theGKexperience. See https://www.churchofscotland.org.uk/__data/assets/pdf_file/0016/21337/thegkexperience_stories_2014.pdf

8. The Camas Diary: http://thecamasdiary.blogspot.com

9. From *Glasgow Women's Library Magazine*, 2000

10. Cre8 website: www.cre8macclesfield.org

11. Muirhouse Youth Development Group website: www.mydg.org.uk

12. Quotes from young people from *The Iona Community: Today's Challenge, Tomorrow's Hope* (DVD), Wild Goose Publications, 2001

13. Quotes by Iain Campbell from *Coracle*, the magazine of the Iona Community, Ruth Harvey (Ed.), 2006

14. From *The Sacred Garden*, BBC Radio Scotland, 2004

15. See *The RHP Companion to Outdoor Education*, Peter Barnes and Bob Sharp (eds.), 2004, Russell House Publishing, p.2

16. From *Nature and the Human Soul: Cultivating Wholeness and Community in a Fragmented World*, Bill Plotkin, New World Library, 2008, p.14

17. From *More than Activities: A Practical Handbook on Work with Young People*, Roger Greenaway, Save the Children, 1990

18. From www.visitnorway.com – Quoted in 'Stark correlations between the changes within Norwegian *friluftsliv* and British outdoor practice', Sam Johnston, *Horizon*, Summer 2015, Issue 70

19. From *Philosophical Issues in Adventure Education*, Scott D. Wurdinger, Kendall/Hunt Publishing Company, 2007, p.84

20. See *Beyond Adventure: An Inner Journey*, Colin Mortlock, Cicerone Press, 2001

21. From the Abercorn website: www.abercorn-sec.glasgow.sch.uk

22. From *Coracle*, the magazine of the Iona Community, Neil Paynter (Ed.), 2017

23. From *Coracle*, the magazine of the Iona Community, Neil Paynter (Ed.), 2015

24. From *Coracle*, the magazine of the Iona Community, Neil Paynter (Ed.), 2015

25. From *Coracle*, the magazine of the Iona Community, Neil Paynter (Ed.), 2015

26. From *Gathered and Scattered: Readings and Meditations from the Iona Community*, Neil Paynter (Ed.), Wild Goose Publications, 2007

2. Adult Guests

Camas is also a place of welcome and acceptance for adults. Over the years, visiting groups have included people from homelessness projects, former prisoners, army veterans, students, those living with HIV, refugees, women's groups. Themed weeks have included peace and justice weeks, creative arts weeks, work weeks, garden weeks and an annual week for new members of the Iona Community.

THE ARK – a story of hope

On a dull day in June six young men and five volunteers (all full of bacon rolls) set out from 'The Ark' in Edinburgh in a minibus for a journey to Camas. The Ark was a breakfast café and resource centre for homeless and former homeless people. We were able to accomplish this trip thanks to the generosity of many folk who had donated money, equipment and several other kindnesses.

Apart from one young man who was disruptive (and who left on Tuesday) the lads took to Camas like ducks to water! All the chores were done without complaint, even cleaning the loos. They missed their bacon rolls for breakfast, didn't appreciate some of the vegetarian dishes, but didn't know Laura's cottage pie was veggie. They loved the grilled veggie burgers and the special hot chocolate.

Willie's aim was to get rid of the 'skunks' (minks). Jimmie discovered that a cairn can show the way, as well as be a memorial to someone – so he built cairns on every walk he took. There is still one on the island opposite the kitchen and maybe several on the way to the quarry.

The kayaking was a great success, and the group built a raft from plastic drums and looked as if they were going to set off for America! Perhaps the abseiling was enjoyed most. They have treasured photos of each one descending the cliff. They didn't want to walk much – they do more than enough of that around Edinburgh. They liked fishing and just sitting with the staff and volunteers, chatting and drinking tea. Jimmie made some wonderful rolls for the last evening meal, with some help and laughter from Laura.

For us it was a bit of a Kleenex-tissue-week, and very sobering at times.

Think how you might feel if you were at supper and one of them said, 'We are socially excluded; we haven't had a meal like this before where we all sit down and eat together.' Reflection time could also be very moving: they loved having candles (you can't have candles in hostels). One young man, holding a sponge ball, said: 'We must absorb everything that happens this week so that we can remember it back in Edinburgh.' Another, on being asked to talk about a favourite place, said: 'I haven't got one, all I know is care homes, young offenders projects and prison' – and yet that person entered into the life of Camas as much as, if not more than, any of the others. One person painted a picture of Camas with the island and cross, a kayak and an abseiler. One lad, who said he had no good memories before, now has – and sat with tears streaming down his face on the last evening.

After walking up the track on the last morning, we had a special Camas reflection, led by David, where a ball of wool was thrown across to each person with a spoken memory of the week. At the end of the reflection there was a web of wool and we were all connected, as we had been during the week. Then, because we were going our separate ways, the wool was broken and we wound bits around our wrists to remember our ties. (When I next saw the lads in Edinburgh they all had their wool around their wrists. 'We will never take it off, Viv. And can we go next year?')

Going back to Camas three weeks later I found ample evidence of the lads in the dormitory, where they had painted 'Old Edinburgh Boys' on the rafters – they have left their mark.[1]

Viv Davies

Receiving (A poem for John)

A closeness to nature and sense of community creates a nurturing environment at Camas. It offers a safe and sacred space for stories to be shared. For people who struggle with mental health difficulties, Camas often seems to bring a sense of peace and belonging.

John (not his real name) came to Camas with a group of homeless people. I had been very busy during the week, and was worried I wouldn't have the energy to be fully present to our guests, something which was important to me. Listening to John was a privilege, and a gift. He told me his story of life in the army, followed by a breakdown and the loss of relationships at work and home. It was also a story of hope – of the courage he had to survive; of his creativity and skill, particularly in woodwork; of his compassion and desire to help others in similar situations.

The conversation with John was a place of grace, and reminded me that we are all able to teach and learn, to give and receive.

Shyly showing me your smile,
slowly sharing your heart, your hope,
as close to you as the lifeblood
and as precious as the air.

I hold it in my hands,
anxious I may drop it, crack it, or even crush it
with clumsy words and tired mind.

I listen ...
the poetry of your passion
leads me through the landscape of your dreams.
And I know you will go there – waking to see, as I see,
your strength in world-worn eyes,
your tenderness in work-torn hands.

I listen ...
above the clamouring voices,
sometimes religiosity,
above demands and worries
that today feel heavy on me;
you whisper of the Mystery:
the leaves who are your sanctuary,
the stones who keep your soul.

I listen ...
and with what you risk to give me,
I am renewed.

Rachel McCann

NEW MEMBERS WEEK

As part of a two-year programme to join the Iona Community, new members come to Camas for a week of practical work, building community, theological reflection and fun. Former Iona Community Leader Norman Shanks notes the significance of this week: 'Camas occupies a special place in the hearts and minds of many Community members, largely because of the very rich experiences they have had there during the New Members Week … With its closeness to nature and the open, honest relationships it encourages, there are ways in which the idea of spirituality comes specially alive …'[2]

In the beginning …

There are several imaginative legends about the origin of New Members Week at Camas. I can attest to the fact that it originated in 1978, initiated by then Leader of the Iona Community, Graeme Brown. In the same year when I was joining the community, so were Pat and Deryck Collingwood, who were then living and working at Camas. The New Members Programme at that time involved four weeks of being resident on Iona. Pat and Deryck could not leave Camas for more than two weeks, so the new members of 1978 spent one week at Camas instead. Rather more prosaic than some other explanations but there is no doubt that its value was recognised, and Camas has figured regularly in the programme ever since.

Margaret Stewart

Two stories spring to mind

The New Members Week at Camas became a really valuable part of the programme and though it was a time for learning and reflection it was also a great deal of fun. Two stories spring to mind: the first when Ron Ferguson decided to release the Camas goat into the women's dormitory! The second when I went kayaking for the first time in my life, and rapidly capsized into the water. I looked around expecting a helping hand, but instead I saw all the new members rushing to get their cameras to get a picture of a soaked Leader of the Iona Community spluttering about in the sea!

Graeme Brown

Space to grow and be still

New members are a very diverse bunch, from all kinds of backgrounds and with varying experiences of life in remote parts of the west coast of Scotland like Mull. And although they may be completely different in age from the youth groups who normally visit, they share many of the same anxieties and questions about coming to Camas. Will it be very cold? How will they cope with sleeping in a dorm? What clothes should they bring?

As with any group, the first evening at Camas can feel awkward as people adjust to this new group of people, and to a very different environment. But gradually through the week a new rhythm takes over. Coming to breakfast in the morning you see people standing on rocks gazing out to sea. Conversations over a mug of tea in a corner of the common room. Hilarity over the dishwashing. Music and stories around the fire at night. Camas is a wonderful setting to build community – warm, unhurried, with space both for relationships to grow, and to be still. Away from pressured and demanding lives, people can explore their faith and their journey into the Iona Community together and have space for themselves and each other.

Christian MacLean

Nature and nurture

Arriving at the beginning of the track for our first week of the 2015 New Members Programme I thought, 'What on earth am I doing here?' At 72 it seemed both an honour and a little strange to be journeying on another of life's adventures, although in my heart I felt it was the right 'path' – an exciting culmination of many years increasing association with the Iona Community. We were to be here for one week, together with the 2014 new members.

We walked to the buildings, with the cheerful, positive staff helping us by carrying our luggage in wheelbarrows, and by the time we arrived we felt we knew each other and were at home.

Our first-year programme was explained to us during the week, and we thoroughly enjoyed ourselves, helping out wherever possible. Necessary tasks were written on a board for us to choose. My contribution was collecting the eggs and daily vegetables, some gardening and helping in the kitchen.

A walk to Market Bay and a swim in the sea was stunning, a good exercise in teamwork along the way and fun – and the sea felt wonderful.

To be together with the 2014 new members gave us an insight into what was expected of us, and hearing about their new members' projects inspired us. It showed us how we can live out our commitments within our own communities and make a change. Knowing there were other like-minded people doing the same, I no longer felt like a round peg in a square hole.

What a place to peel away the constrictions of modern life, to feel and touch nature and to get to know people very quickly as themselves – amazing friendships have grown from this place.

For anyone thinking of becoming a member of the Iona Community, I would say please apply. It is the most life-changing way of life, and to feel part of this community is a treasure.

Jean Belgrove

Building bridges

Camas is the perfect place to experience what the Iona Community is all about. The two weeks I've spent there so far on the New Members Programme have given me the opportunity to experience life in community: learning by doing, learning by being, learning with each other and from each other.

I was particularly blessed on the second occasion when an accident in the garden on my first day kept me indoors for the rest of the week. This really was a blessing because it gave me the opportunity to have some extended and deep conversations with whoever was working or relaxing in the building at the time, mostly in the kitchen preparing the next meal while the rest of the group were outside working or on some adventure or other.

Those conversations – sharing our stories, what had brought us to Camas and to the Iona Community, what we would be going on to or back to, what was really important to us right then – were significant for me and I think for my new friends as well. Intensely personal but very relaxed, profound but free-ranging, those conversations will stay in my mind for a long time. Longer, I hope, than the embarrassment of being pulled out of a ditch in the garden, although that particular event has been preserved for posterity in the form of 'Bob's Bridge', admirably built by then Leader Peter Macdonald and Stuart Fulton, which now links the compost bins with the garden.

Bob Thomas

The noise inside my head

There is a focused sense of activity around me as I rake sheep poo with my fellow Iona Community member Ian. He chuckles softly at the situation, as we lean on our rakes and brushes and gently take in our surroundings. We are at Camas for the week as part of the New Members Programme. After finishing the poo, we collect seashells for Ian's congregation back home, and then I walk the labyrinth alone. I wonder at the noise that has been living inside my head … over the last few days it has been getting quieter.

Thursday night is the Camas Challenge and we go shopping during the day to collect some ingredients for the meal we're preparing. We make kale crisps – which are fun to do and delicious! The dessert is one of my favourites – cranachan – and this is made even better with fresh raspberries from the Camas garden. This meal, and helping to make and serve it, was a real highlight for me. I do not have a family of my own and this felt like being part of a big loving family.

Before going to Camas I had been working for three weeks without a day off and the thought of going to Camas – cooking, doing the dishes and other tasks – did not gladden my heart. I also dreaded the shared bedrooms, the cold showers and the Girl Guide camp feel that I had unfairly assigned to the place. However, I feel God moved in me that week and that I am a better person for it.

The noise in my head was almost completely gone by the end of the week, and when I went back to work I felt revived – and even arrived an hour early! My boss was very pleased – and suggested that I go to Camas for the week every year!

Susan Lindsay

GSDs

The week at Camas taught me a lot about the restorative power of work and structure. I felt physically and mentally healthier by the end of the week, having experienced some of the hardest physical work I have ever undertaken. The most physical days were those spent 'stomping the bracken' to create a clear path through which to build the deer fence that will surround the new woodland. I also spent mornings nailing boards and chicken wire down in an attempt to fix the track and working in the garden. Besides these larger tasks, GSDs (Getting Stuff Dones) were a part of the structure of the week. From dishes to chicken-feeding to cleaning toilets, GSDs were an invaluable way to affirm self-worth, challenge us and bring us together as a group. Whilst I still believe that working hard won't win you a place in heaven, I do believe that hard work can be an integral and important part of a healthy community (and individual!) life.

Alex Clare-Young

Lots of fun too

So, here's a list of everything the new members did: Some of them spent hours making mountains of new pillows and cushions for our common room, a group of people repainted the common room and kitchen, a lot of rubbish was cleared. There was much track maintenance, the Chapel of the Nets was totally cleaned out, all the windows were washed (inside and out), there was lots of help cooking, a massive amount of peat-cutting, a fire pit was rebuilt, lots of work was done in the garden, and lots of wheelbarrow runs for food and firewood.

We had lots of fun too. We went abseiling, hillwalking, kayaking, and the best bit was on the last day when the new members made dinner. Oh my goodness, it was amazing! They did a lovely reflection for us, and then my favourite part of the evening was when they decided to entertain us with 'Camas Has Got Talent'. There were loads of performances – from singing, to skits, to accordion-playing, to lots of jokes, and the final act of the evening was when Rosiadh from the Isle of Skye busted out her bagpipes and played us all a few reels – to the roaring applause of a happily tired team. Then we bid them a very fond farewell … Thanks for all your help, team!

From the Camas blog

Camas

Green-checked tea towels
hung patiently in a row
and dancing in the stiff breeze.

We too have come
to be blown through,
renewed in wind and warmth;
and returned refreshed,
ready for service.

David McNeish

Camas reflection

Give me some more of these silences.
The kind that are filled with the sounds of creation.
Like the constant ebb and flow of the sea,
or directionless noise of the wind and rain,
or the solitary cry of the oystercatcher, echoing against granite.

Give me some more of these silences.
The kind that just hang in timeless security,
enabling the mind to drift into uncharted places,
so comforting, so reassuring – the moment never needs to end.

Give me some more of these conversations.
Like the ones I've had along the track,
by the sink, in the garden, round the fire,
building shelters, sewing tents, painting signs, digging earth.

Give me some more of these conversations.
The kind that help gain understanding,
break down barriers, challenge assumptions.
The kind that inspire me to move beyond conversation, into action.

Give me some more of this friendship.
The kind that allows me to be vulnerable,
valued, accepted for who I am,
away from familiar constraints and expectations –
where an idea is quashed, maybe goes unnoticed.

Give me some more of this friendship.
The kind where a hug is never far off
and tea for twenty is never much hassle.
Where there's plenty of music and singing and laughter
yet where raw edges can't be ignored.

Give me some more of this simple lifestyle.
Where wholesome food, heart-pumping exercise
and pure, clean air just make so much sense.

Give me some more of this simple lifestyle.
Where the absence of comforts like electricity, hot water and flush toilets
doesn't really matter.
Where all our rushing around, work deadlines,
heavy meetings and stressful phone calls
seem so unimportant.

This simple lifestyle frees the mind, lifts the spirit,
gives space to think, relaxes my body, feeds my creativity,
gives life a new perspective.

Give me some more of this life together.
Where, in this special place,
so small, so secluded,
yet so connected to the world,
we find a spiritual meaning in the rhythms of our day.

Give me some more of this life together.
Where the depth of our relationships
is carried in our hearts
and our experiences go beyond this place
to inspire us and challenges us
and fill us with hope.[3]

Neil Squires

New Members Week

The space – and time and distance
vast and open and free
sea and sky, clouds and stars
the track across the moor
reflective welcome.

The silence – welcome too,
sheep bleating
gulls shrieking
oystercatchers piping
people laughing, talking, snoring …

The work – 'not the track again,
please, no – the lazy beds?'
or muddy ditches in the rain

and dishes, dishes and toilet-cleaning
fatigue – always happy (almost).

The people – come and go
in my mind so vividly
a wonderful procession
of new members – motley,
challenging, committed – and the staff

the depth – of their commitment too
the costly offering
the common task
'something understood'
the Chapel of the Nets – candles, communion
deep and lasting – at Camas.

Norman Shanks

EXPLORING CREATION WITH KATHY GALLOWAY

Kathy ran 'Exploring Creation' weeks at Camas for over twenty years, exploring what the Celts called 'the Big Book' of creation and focusing on ecology in its broadest sense – the connections between people and place, and what Kathy terms 'theological geology'. The weeks involved creative and practical projects, exploring the culture and history of the Ross of Mull, outdoor activities, trips to local projects and sites of interest and ceilidhs around the common room fire. They were tender weeks of healing, sharing and learning. As one guest put it: 'Camas is a safe place to dance with our shadows.'

A number of poems in this book were created during these weeks, and the following pieces of writing show the rich inspiration that flowed.

The common life and autumnal colours

Kathy Galloway hosted another adult week at Camas. We welcomed fifteen folk from all over the UK and beyond. They contributed to the common life and enjoyed the autumnal colours of Camas. They explored nature and the environment. Some got the full sensory experience – plunging into the sea for a swim! Others took to the water in kayaks and got up close to the lichen-crusted coastal rock. Others took on the rock and abseiled! Folk were encouraged to pick up paintbrushes and pens and make art. Evenings were spent in cosy conversation. The end of the week was celebrated with a delicious curry night; we were entertained, and then had a final, thoughtful reflection from Kathy.

From the Camas blog

Blackberry-picking and selkie stories

We had a group of lovely people from all over the world and with lots of different experiences. We went blackberry-picking in the pouring rain while others enjoyed tea in the polytunnel and dug spuds for dinner. This was also a week of trees and their fruit; the plum tree gave us some beautiful plums, which were made into an amazing dessert.

We went on a few day trips, one to Ardalanish Weavers, where Aeneas told us the story of the how they became organic weavers and why he thinks his Hebridean sheep look handsome and happy! We also went to the tidal island of Erraid and, after lunch and selkie stories at the lighthouse observatory, walked to the seal colony to see if there were any sealskins on the shore.

Our last night was filled with good food, songs, comedy and wonderful poems!

From the Camas blog

Sacred simplicity

One of the most memorable and sacred experiences I have had was a simple communion led by Kathy Galloway at Camas. Sitting around rough wooden tables, we broke homemade bread and drank wine – no fancy chalices or golden plates – just basic Camas crockery. The wind and waves could be heard outside, fully illuminating the stories of Jesus and his fishing friends. We sang and said prayers for places and people where God's love was needed. The gentleness, grace and friendships experienced during the week were embodied in our community communion on our last night of the week.

Camas guest

Camas poems

Harry throws fire at midnight
on the green
and we are drawn from sleep
into an ancient dream of midsummer

the dark sea moves ceaselessly
its ebb and flow
is the ebb and flow of my blood
and is constant

far out in the bay under the moon
the *splish splish* of the paddle
is the sound of a sea creature
coming home

leaning against the stone walls of the house
in the time between
which is not day but is light
and is night but is not dark
we are bonded by our silence
silver threads of stillness weave us
into bright patterns of stars
shining on rocks and water
and shadows on the hill
and peace laps our souls

on the high cliff
our feet springing off heather and root
looking out over the sea
higher than the wheeling gulls
we are like gods
we might fly …

under the rafters
in the glow of candlelight
we break bread
and the word

to live is this[4]

Kathy Galloway

Stone heart

… but I came to love my solitude, and
ranged across wide, empty hills, with heather
springing rough beneath my feet, barren land
of bracken-hidden tracks that led whether
they would, regardless of my choosing, till
the only way was down towards the sea.
I came there under a grey sky, and still
the leanness of the land delighted me,
seeing the stripped-back beauty of the bones,
the wind-whipped water and the stretch of sand,
yellow mosses, salt-damp, time-polished stones;
a stone-hard, soul-surrendered place to stand.

The shock is not that of invaded place,
but recognition of the cost of grace.[5]

Kathy Galloway

Nearly smiling in Camas

Sometimes …
Sometimes …
Something happens when I'm present in Camas:
normal thought is replaced by an older,
wiser, calmer brain.
This mind is unimpressed by
new cars, bank balance,
handsome looks,
sinking the 'long putt', skiing the 'black run' well.

It is fashion-challenged
and cares not a jot
what you think of me.
It is slow breathing
with pinpoint perception.

It nearly smiles,
lives in my body as well as my head.
It talks in tingles and luminous non-words,
can orchestrate songs … or sadness,
it sees that I am, and offers this to the heart,
without comment.
It is neither sad, nor happy …
It just is.
If I was religious
I'd call it 'endlessness',
'nearly smiling endlessness'.

Stuart Barrie

Pulling bracken (A song written for the Camas Challenge)
(*Tune: 'Pulling Bracken'*)

Chorus:

Tending trees, aching knees
Pulling bracken, pulling bracken;
Planting leeks, Camas weeks,
Full of fun and friendship.

1. Twisted carrots, giant marrows,
    Grow in great abundance;
    Bramble pie and rowan berry
    Make us all feel merry.

Chorus

2. At the mill, the old looms rattle
    Warp and weft together.
    Weave the colours of the land,
    The rock and sea and heather.

Chorus

3. In the fields, the sheep and cattle
    Brave the wind and weather;
    So do we, on track and beach
    And walk the earth together.

Chorus

4. In the house, the fire burns brightly
    And the soup is warming.
    Conversation, song and laughter,
    Signs of friendship forming.

Chorus

Kathy Galloway

A WEEK FOR WOMEN

When Lesley Orr and I spoke about the need to create spaces for women survivors of gender-based violence to network, the most obvious place that came into our heads was Camas. Where else could women who had experienced injustice and abuse, particularly in institutional settings, feel safe? We wanted such women to be able to share their experiences, their hopes, their longings and their vision – but for part of their time together to be a holiday. We believed that women who had endured so much that was painful deserved some light in their darkness.

Camas was perfect. There is something about the rhythmic lapping of the waves on the rocks just outside the kitchen window that is washing and healing.

The first days were difficult – hairy, even – as we didn't know each other, nor how to broach the experiences we knew we had in common. How should we begin to speak and to share? In that awkwardness, we turned to the sea: a walk to Market Bay where some swam and dolphins joined us briefly. Kayaking, coasteering, splashing, throwing sticks and stones into the water to be taken away by the tide …

It was the end of the season and so there were few staff, and they kept in the background at first, as Lesley and I had asked them to do. How were we to navigate around them too? But by the middle of the week they were sitting with us in the evenings, and it was no longer uncomfortable. There was a sense of sisterhood and solidarity within our group, and the Camas staff and volunteers were sensitive and 'with' us too.

For all of us, it was a week when there was transformation (even for the fluffy white dog that fell into a boggy puddle and came out black).

These are some comments from two of the participants on the week:

My time at Camas was at a period when I was at the lowest I've ever been in my life. So it was somewhat of a challenge – but I loved it, and continue to tell anyone who will listen what a wonderful place it is. Lovely people who could not have done more to make us all welcome and cared for. That first night – looking up at the clear skies, seeing the stars and the Milky Way – was a spiritual, enlightening time for me. Only now do I realise just how big an impact it all had on me. (*Anita*)

As the only woman who wasn't Scottish (or living in Scotland) and the only Muslim, as well as the fact that I knew nothing about Camas, to say I was nervous would be a slight understatement! That week turned out to be amazing and full of so many firsts for me and several other women. As dramatic as it sounds, there is something magical about Camas (despite the initial trauma I experienced as a townie!) – everything from the tranquility of the location to the ecological and spiritual ethos of the staff and volunteers made it all so very special. I will never forget everyone I met that week, all the amazing experiences and Camas itself and can't wait to go back! ('S')

Helen Douglas

GRAMNET

Iona Community member Alison Swinfen/Phipps, UNESCO Chair in Refugee Integration through Languages and the Arts, has initiated trips to Camas for the Glasgow Refugee, Asylum and Migration Network (GRAMNet), which 'aims to bring together researchers and practitioners, NGOs and policy makers working with migrants, refugees and asylum seekers in Scotland', and is funded by the University of Glasgow. Camas has also welcomed groups of refugees and asylum seekers.

Time and space to explore

We all know the feeling you get from a holiday or a refreshing break away. The freedom that comes from being far away from the worries that keep us up at night, wake us up in the morning, or follow us around all day. The comfort that comes from switching off your mobile phone, going on a long walk, or spending time with loved ones.

Last weekend a group of academics, activists, practitioners and artists who work with refugees, asylum seekers and migrants in Glasgow (and beyond) came together in a remote corner of the Isle of Mull to share methods of self-care, and to practise it in the process.

The people who came together are usually incredibly busy and (over)committed, concerned with the injustice of the world and the people affected by the UK asylum process and associated border controls. In Glasgow, this group normally gathers through a series of events to discuss changes in the asylum system and other serious issues, or to think deeply about a relevant film.

We went by train, ferry, coach and foot, down the track to Camas. This physical and mental distance allowed people to disconnect with everyday worries and technologies and to find the time and space necessary to explore the theme of self-care in playful and creative ways. Some people in the group were already good friends, but many were complete strangers, and it was striking how easy it was to be open and vulnerable here in the presence of strangers.

Being on Mull was a much-needed reminder of the connections that exist between us – the GRAMNet network is always there, even if the lines of connection in the network sometimes seem faint or you cannot communicate them in one language. There is a strength that grows from knowing that what you do, you do with others.

Many people expressed the feeling that they carry a weight of responsibility on their shoulders to do justice for others. There is a pressure to keep phones on and to check e-mails constantly. However, after five days with my phone switched off the only thing that happened was the absence of 'e-mail apnoea', where you hold your breath before reading another anxiety-inducing e-mail. Instead of carrying around this weight, we should be mindful of the connections we share in the network and of the people and places we can go to for support.

Thanks to all the people who organised the trip, the residents and volunteers at Camas and the people who couldn't be there, but who make up the rest of the Glasgow Refugee, Asylum and Migration Network.[6]

Bridget Holtom

A conversation without words

I cannot tell you the *real* story of the GRAMNet trip to Camas.

I cannot tell you because not only was the experience so unique from one person to another, but also because it is impossible to describe: the kind of pedagogies in practice at Camas cannot be reduced to language. It felt as if we were engaging in a conversation without words – a rare treat for those used to the busy daily routine of the university.

GRAMNet sponsored sixteen of us who are researching, teaching or working in personally and politically charged topics to visit Camas, and join in the community there.

Our story started when we arrived in the pouring rain to walk one kilometre along the rickety and muddy path to the Camas Centre. Sam, the youngest member of our group at nearly fifteen months old, travelled in comparative comfort in his buggy, protected from the rain and strapped into a wheelbarrow with bungee ropes in a makeshift sedan chair. For the rest of us, getting absolutely drenched and windswept was the beginning of a process of stripping off the layers of city life which build up over time in the concrete metropolis where we normally dwell. These invisible layers, which continued to be shed over the three days on Mull, represented individual casings of resilience, protecting us from the busy and hyperstimulating rhythms of the city.

No electricity, no phone connection and sometimes even no hot water made us appreciate the little things: like warm homemade scones in the morning; the subtle changes in light as dusk sets in; or simply a cup of tea and a seat by the wood-burning stove in a candlelit room …

Helped along by reflections and challenges set by the friendly residents and volunteers, and by an Augusto Boal Theatre of the Oppressed workshop given by Isabel Harland from the Govan and Craigton Integration Network, we opened ourselves to being vulnerable to each other, to being willing to take the responsibilities and risks which community and discovery depends upon.

This relationship between vulnerability and resilience was explored in a workshop delivered by Nina Murray from the Scottish Refugee Council, which concluded in an exercise asking: How can Ph.D. research fulfil political goals, and be communicated back to research participants and wider audiences with impact and integrity, with the potential of contributing to policy or social change? The kind of sensitivity and care for how we conduct research was also reflected in the way in which people shared the space together on Mull, and will hopefully continue to make ripples in our ongoing Ph.D. projects, and beyond.

For outdoor activities we split into two groups – half the group went kayaking on the eerie salt marshes and around the beautiful pink granite formations of the coastline, to float in the evening sun, and the other half went wild-walking over bogs, meadows and rocks, with the two groups swapping over the next morning. On arrival at the sandy-white beach over the hill, some people jumped into the cold sea, as others drank hot chocolate.

On the last night, we sat around a fire in the roundhouse, as a thunder and lightning storm brewed overhead. While reflecting together on our time at Camas, one of the volunteers told us that such an experience of community spirit and relationship with nature that we had at Camas is not an exceptional episode to keep as a memory, but an approach to life …[7]

Poppy Kohner

A safe place: Welcoming refugee groups to Camas

In 2018 we welcomed two refugee groups. The first was United Glasgow, a football team dedicated to using sport as a way to enable refugees and bring people together. This group of football fanatics were 'unlucky' enough to arrive at Camas in the middle of the 2018 World Cup. Throughout the week there were constant games of football on local beaches and lots of dancing in the common room in the evening. We even borrowed a TV from Iona and were able to spend one celebratory afternoon catching up on the World Cup.

Later in the year, we welcomed a group of Kurdish refugees, who had all met at a refugee camp in Dunkirk. The group leaders were four inspiring women who'd met the group while working in the camp. One year later they'd taken on the mammoth task of organising a reunion at Camas with their Kurdish friends, who had since been placed all over the UK.

The group made themselves at home instantly and got to work in the kitchen making delicious Kurdish treats – which didn't seem possible to create with our ingredients. There was much laughter and a mix of Kurdish and Scottish ceilidh dancing in the evenings.

This was a powerful week where deep friendships were made. Some of the group members stated on the last night that it had been the greatest experience they had had since coming to the UK. The week ended in a beautiful moment with us holding each other, swaying and singing in the Chapel of Nets, sharing what we had learned from one another. The unique and diverse style of hospitality that Camas provides means it is a place that can meet the needs of a wide range of people. This year I have learned what a powerful place it can be for those who have been displaced from their homes. As the refugee crisis continues, surely Camas can continue to be a safe place for those who need it.[8]

Barry McLaughlin

A Camas thank you

We rolled up on time, a sleepy huddle
of coffees and rucksacks
in Queen Street Station's morning tangle.

A train then a boat then a bus took us west,
under widening skies,
to meet the sea. We
unwound
as we went, snoozing, swapping
names and food, showing
some of our colours: a skein
of travelling stories.

Across a lark-sung moor we threaded,
a bobbing line
bearing drums and bagfuls of questions
to Camas:

How to stay strong? How to keep
growing and caring while working with pain
on a scale we can't change?

Camas: there
a bell marks the tides, a garden grows
improbably, stuff gets done
despite no electricity, worries unravel
in nests of knotted net.

It seemed we let loose into trust; uncoiled
the threads each carried until
we wove the days into delight.

It seemed we made words into tapestry: revealed
the patterns of strength, the tones of hope
that shine when stories and songs are shared.

It seemed we found no answers, but sealed
an unspoken pact to keep asking good
questions, and gather again.

Then we
left – back
on the moor, the road, the sea, the track
towards high city windows,
dispersed.

But the tapestry grows in my head, its thread
long like the road to Camas, its weave
strong like the roots of a tree leafing out
in a crack between rocks.

You strengthen it too. Thank you.[9]

Esa Aldegheri

The springline

We cross the springline
from north
to south.
The larch turns from bare brown
to fresh green.
Snow lies on the hillside above
but the river is serene.

Yet my heart does not
gladden to see the sap rising
or the leaves unfurling
or the May blossom
bejewelling the
hawthorn in the hedgerow.

I am held still
by the blood-red
of the rowan berries
in autumn, by the amber
of the beech, the damp decay
of the leaves
after the storm subsides,
and the river reveals
the remains of the flood.

This springtime
we have turned the migrating birds back.
We have destroyed their nests,
burned down the trees
where they made their eyries.
The fish cannot swim north
to their spawning grounds.
This year we will not allow
the salmon to leap,
or the swallow to swoop

to her nest beneath the eaves,
or the curlew to tell us
of journeys held
in the sharpness of his song.

In my hands are northern seeds,
for planting in a ground ready
and waiting
in the land to the south.

The best hope I have of harvest
is crossing this line,
this springline,
but with a heart tethered
by the enduring hopelessness
of the cold calculations
around the lines of flight
which mean all our springtimes
and harvests are held fast
by the cruellest winter.[10]

Alison Swinfen

NEW CALEDONIAN WOODLANDS AT CAMAS

New Caledonian Woodlands was a charity and social enterprise with two primary aims rooted at its core: to encourage environmental sustainability and to support people to improve their mental well-being. Sadly the project had to close due to funding issues, but the burgeoning woodland at Camas remains a testimony to their contribution there.

First contact

I first encountered Camas when Becky, then Resident Gardener, came to a forestry course I was running at Fyvie Castle in Aberdeenshire in autumn 2011. I gave her a lift back to Edinburgh, and on the journey south she told me all about Camas. It sounded amazing.

Six months later, in May 2012, my partner Tuula and I were on our way to Mull to stay at Camas for a few days. At Camas I put my time to good use by writing a short woodland management plan for the Camas woods and potential woods. I was excited by what had been achieved so far and the potential to do more. Little did I know that I would be back six years later, bending my back and planting hundreds of little trees in the new woodland across the track.

Meanwhile, on our holiday, we stayed in a lovely little red yurt in the woodland, emerging each morning to join the Camas folk and explore our surroundings. I remember thinking that Camas would be a great place to bring a group from New Caledonian Woodlands. I was one of their leaders. One of the things we do is take groups of conservation-minded people from all walks of life away for weekends, roughly once a month, to do worthwhile conservation activities.

And so, we have been coming to Camas ever since – and everyone has loved it!

A typical visit

We usually come to Camas in September once the youth and outdoor recreation season is over. In 2018 we also came for five days in March to help with planting the new woodland.

We pick everyone up in the centre of Edinburgh, near Princes Street, at 9am and drive to Oban, stopping in Tyndrum at the Green Welly or the Real Food Café for some great fish and chips. Then it's onto the ferry – we haven't left anyone behind in Oban yet (but very nearly). The sail over to Mull always seems very quick, barely time to get into cruise mode, then it's off on the wacky races of the singletrack roads. I really like driving on singletrack; it keeps you on your toes and there is an old-fashioned sense of chivalry in pulling in or letting a faster vehicle go past you. Excitement mounts as we travel through the heart of Mull and along the much more human-scale Ross of Mull.

After Bunessan, there it is, journey's end: the Camas shed and track end. Newbies are underwhelmed and rub their eyes in astonishment, especially if it is getting dark and murky, which it usually is. But wait, here comes the Camas wheelbarrow cavalry, always in good spirits, to give us a hand with all our gear. Then along the boardwalk, that rite of passage, along the track which appears to go on forever, then dipping down towards the sea and the first glimpse of Camas, now with woodland on both sides of the track. It's nice to be back.

What we do

Our work is usually in the garden and woods, pruning paths, pollarding the alders, digging French drains, hauling seaweed or gravel up from the beach, letting light into the woods, improving the shelter by weaving sticks into the fence, pulling bracken, rabbit-netting the dyke and, of course, planting trees. How many tasks do human beings do where the results get better after you complete the task? Planting trees is something we all need to do at least once in our lifetimes.

I believe that Camas and New Caledonian Woodlands have the same values and philosophy. We respect people and we respect the planet. We try to create the conditions where both can prosper, at least for a while, in a wild rocky place at the north-western edge of Europe.

Donald McPhillimy

WORK WEEK

Beautiful setting, warm welcome

Work Week at Camas, and a group of willing and eager volunteers make their way down the track to help prepare the centre for the arrival of a new season of guests. For some of the volunteers the week represented a return to a place of fond memories, whether having attended previous Work Weeks or having worked at Camas as a volunteer. This was my first visit to Camas – and immediately I was struck by the beautiful setting, warm welcome and abundant enthusiasm of the Camas staff team, not forgetting Tawhai who had settled into his role as Camas top dog.

Work Week guest

Memories of that week will be forever with us

At the end of a day of fresh air and hard work the log fire provided welcome relief (or a blazing inferno depending on who was in charge of keeping it going!) from the coolness of the starry night outside and the perfect setting for evening reflection, some music, reading and even knitting lessons by candlelight! A walk to the top of a nearby hill was also a magical moment as we watched the sun setting over the islands. On the final night we looked back at our week together – and what a week it was. I think that I speak for all of us when I say that there are memories of that week that will be forever with us. Thank you to everyone who made it so special.

From the Camas blog

A Camas day (Work Week poem)

Wheelbarrows,
ditches,
windows,
stitches.
Painting,
patching,
mending,
making.
Bread baked,
logs stacked,
wood chopped,
floor mopped.
Got a hammer?
Where's the spanner?
Work Week,
hide-and-seek.
Weeds out,
screws in,
washing up,
lying down.
Sleep
work
eat
stretch
play
pray.
A Camas day.

From the Camas blog

GARDEN WEEK

Thank you to everyone

The saying 'many hands make light work' was put to the test this Garden Week at Camas. We had a huge mixed group of people from all over the world – including USA, Germany, Italy, Poland, Switzerland and two groups from Glasgow and one from Edinburgh, all come to help us put our gardens to bed for the winter. With nearly 40 hands on deck we were able to combine garden and track work with climbing and kayaking sessions, ensuring lots of work and play mixed in equal measure with bundles of cake!

With such an enthusiastic bunch we had many garden projects happening simultaneously and managed to accomplish a huge amount of structural maintenance, as well as giving the garden beds the attention they needed after a long and productive summer. The real beginnings of this work started with a group of volunteers from New Caledonian Woodlands who came for a long weekend and lots of hard graft.

Walking through the garden now, it is clear to see how much effort was put in over these last few weeks. In no particular order, our list of achievements includes: finishing the dry-stone wall around the roundhouse; laying the hawthorn hedge behind the fruit cage; digging out the drains around the fruit cage and laying a French drain through it; creating steps up to the pavilion shed; clearing out the brush from the woodlands; clearing around the fruit trees to let in more light; clearing the woodland pathways. All garden beds were weeded and cleared, adding a layer of compost, topsoil, seaweed, and covering this with weed matting to all rot down nicely over winter. We have made our winter supply of green-tomato chutney, harvested and preserved sorrel, nettle and mint for winter use and are continuing to eat fresh food from the polytunnels. Thank you to everyone.

From the Camas blog

Connecting

I really enjoyed cutting and stacking peat. You can see how, over the years it's been used, there has been very little impact on the land and ecology, because it's done on a small scale. It was fun and physical, but it also felt like connecting with a traditional craft and way of life. It was a rewarding and skilled task.

A Garden Week guest

Between wilderness and not

We had a great team for a few days of bramble-bashing, stone-picking, bracken-composting, weeding, digging, mulching, mucking, and much besides. Potatoes (lots and lots) were planted in truly scrumptious compost, while on the wild side we saw the return of cuckoo flower, vetch, tormentil, silverweed, bluebells, ragged-robin, buttercups and daisies. It was an opportunity to reflect on the garden as something between wilderness and not; a chance to get the lazy beds in order for the growing season, while mostly letting be the untamed fringes of the Camas garden. Nettles, brambles and bracken still reign but a little bit less than before!

From the Camas blog

Notes:

1. From *Growing Hope: Daily Readings*, Neil Paynter (Ed.), Wild Goose Publications, 2007
2. From *Iona: God's Energy: The Vision and Spirituality of the Iona Community*, Norman Shanks, Hodder and Stoughton, 1999, second edition, Wild Goose Publications, 2009
3. From *Iona: God's Energy: The Vision and Spirituality of the Iona Community*, Norman Shanks, Hodder and Stoughton, 1999, second edition, Wild Goose Publications, 2009

4. From *The Dream of Learning Our True Name*, Kathy Galloway, Wild Goose Publications, 2004

5. From *The Dream of Learning Our True Name*, Kathy Galloway, Wild Goose Publications, 2004

6. From the GRAMNet website: https://gramnet.wordpress.com

7. From the GRAMNet website: https://gramnet.wordpress.com

8. From *Coracle*, the magazine of the Iona Community, 2019, Neil Paynter (Ed.)

9. From *Coracle*, the magazine of the Iona Community, 2019, Neil Paynter (Ed.)

10. From *Coracle*, the magazine of the Iona Community, 2019, Neil Paynter (Ed.)

OVER THE YEARS

Over the years much at Camas has changed and much has stayed the same. Work with young people has remained a constant, and is emphasised here in both profound and humorous anecdotes and reflections …

1960s

Building positive futures for young people

In the 1960s the Iona Community was at the forefront of exploring ways of engaging with young people and addressing some of the significant social challenges of that time. The initiatives took place in Community House in Glasgow and in different locations across the UK through Iona Community members and allied networks.

The 1960s was a period of change in politics, music and society locally and globally. Inspirational and novel projects were developed in the East End of Glasgow, and in the South Side area through the work of the Gorbals Group. Further afield there were initiatives in Bathgate, Edinburgh, Aberdeen, Liverpool and Bristol, usually involving young people between the years of 15-25, nearly all from working-class areas and disadvantaged communities.

Those who were involved in this work offered an 'informal meeting place' for young people. The Iona Community Youth Secretary ran '214 Club', an 'open door' youth club attracting young people from various areas of Glasgow. The Youth Secretary was also responsible for organising and coordinating the youth programme on Iona and at Camas.

In the very early '60s, youth activities on Iona and Camas were mainly during the Easter period and the summer months of late June to early September. Around 100 young people went every week to the Iona Youth Camp Programme and much smaller groups came to Camas. Many of the summer camp participants on Iona and at Camas were recruited through Iona Community members working in inner-city parishes, new towns and large outer-city housing estates across central Scotland and parts of England.

Responding to the challenges – an emerging rationale for developments at Camas and Iona?

In the early '60s, government working groups in both Scotland and England were reviewing educational experiences for those leaving school at 15 years of age. The following, extracted from one of the reports, offers evidence of the analysis being undertaken then and some of the challenges being identified:

'The experience of living away from home for a short period, in a fairly small and intimate group, and in a novel environment, is especially significant for pupils. This is variously achieved through school journeys and expeditions, camps, or residential courses of different types. We do not doubt their value for all pupils. By introducing young people to fresh surroundings and helping them to acquire new knowledge or try their hand at new skills, they provide a general educational stimulus … And in residential activities, even more than in other out of school activities, pupils and teachers enjoy a closer companionship.'

It was against the above backdrop that the Iona Community began further development of its work with young people and 'educational programmes' on Iona and at Camas. Approaches were made to schools inviting cooperation and partnership-working. The Iona Community requested that the young people selected by the school would be those likely to leave school at fifteen and those finding school life less than comfortable or challenging. Given the government emphasis that such innovative learning experiences should be developed, the full cost of the Iona and Camas programme weeks was not a difficulty. Thus began a development process across a number of schools, mainly from Scotland but also England, which resulted in one month being added each consecutive year to the Iona and Camas programme during the mid '60s.

The big match

The specific activity programme each week was usually developed in cooperation with each school and group. An important aspect was to introduce the young people to the work and interests of the Iona Community in Iona and Mull and on the mainland. Special attention was also given to include learning more about the lives and interests of those who lived locally on the islands. For many of the young people this was a major culture change and huge learning experience. The Camas experience in the '60s was usually constructed around three aspects: outdoor and adventure activities, a self-selected education project or a project contributing to the improvement of Camas, and discussion groups relating to young people and the challenges they faced in their day-to-day lives.

Camas also ran weeks for young people from Polmont Young Offenders Institution. This week reflected the special concern, interest and commitment of a good number of members of the Iona Community. A special event and highlight during the Polmont Group week was the 'annual' football match, Camas vs. Bunessan. The build-up to the match was an important aspect of the process: training on the beach, considering how the game would be played. The match always proved to be competitive and exacting for the 90 minutes, but the additional highlight was the hospitality of the Bunessan local team and social engagement after the match. This always had a huge impact on the group – to be accepted and welcomed by the locals on Mull.

Follow-up work was undertaken with the Polmont Young Offenders Group. This involved offering 'aftercare' support: advice about accommodation, jobs and offering contacts and introductions to youth groups linked to Iona Community members and allied networks.

In the '60s the Iona Community also had very close working links with chaplains working in industry, and this resulted in programmed weeks at Camas for young apprentices, as part of their training. This initiative brought young people together from workplaces and industries on Clydeside, in Central Scotland and in Teesside, NE England.

Jim Robertson

1970s

The whole way

I first went to Camas with George MacLeod, who invited me to come and see the place and to meet the young people known as 'Borstal Boys'. I enjoyed the trip and the conversations and the boys seemed glad of someone taking an interest in them. The boys would often go over from Camas to Iona for the weekly pilgrimage around the island, and in 1976 or '77 there was a young disabled man who wanted to take part. The boys didn't want him to miss out, so three or four of them carried him the whole way. This profound act of kindness and service is something that has always stayed with me, as does the joy on the boys' faces when they earned rightful praise and thanks.

Graeme Brown

A life-changing experience

I joined the early Camas community after a year working in the Abbey.

1975 was the start of the Social Work I.T. groups funding. Our focus as a small staff team was to enable and include each group of young people in the experience of community living in the amazing place that is Camas.

Bringing two babies into the world with no electricity, telephone or plumbing was a challenge but the daily white nappies blowing in the wind and clearing the stones from the small beach are two treasured memories. My children learned to walk at Camas and I learned to share family life with others. I was very grateful for offers of help carrying babies across the moor and still chuckle at sheltering in bushes as the wild winter winds almost blew us away. I remember the tractor battery that enabled us to listen to the radio and 'Playschool' cassettes.

There were some tough times, but I wouldn't change it. I learned so much about life in my six years living permanently at Camas – building, labouring, digging, planting, cooking and living within an ever-changing community.

After we moved to Edinburgh, I was sitting in the doctor's surgery and noticed a young man watching me. I smiled at him and he asked if my name was Pat. He said, 'Camas changed my life when I was a 14-year-old bad boy.'

Oh yes! Camas also changed my life. Forever in my heart.

Pat Collingwood

'Another place'

In the late 1970s, when I volunteered at Camas, many groups continued to come to Camas from the inner city. Often, they had never been away any-where and were sometimes quite disorientated on arrival at Camas with the lack of electricity or home comforts of even the most basic sort, as well as the cows or sheep wandering around. Yet there was never a concern as, if anyone *did* run away, there was nowhere to run to – all the hills and rocks looked the same and the sea was a boundary one didn't begin to question. With so little of anything in the house, there was nothing to steal. I think the worst that happened was when the Camas bicycle was thrown into the sea.

Yet, by the end of the weeks, it was wonderful to see the appreciation and respect that had grown in those young people both for the care and attention given to them and of creation around them. It was a privilege to be alongside them in discovering the joyful simplicities of life, sharing their confidences and seeing them learn to trust each other.

Camas was 'another place', a time out and completely away from the usual business of life, where so many expectations and empty traditions could fall away, and one could discover the real stuff of life and relation-ships that really matter. It was a place where real friendships were made while we washed the pots, or hiked over to Iona once a week for the camp concert or the village ceilidh. The fun that we had in being together and finding out how few material things we actually needed to live was such freedom.

Sally Denton (née Bolton)

1980s

The three-week course adventure

In the early 1980s as resident staff, we designed and ran an extended 'course' which was a three-week programme which built on the usual one-week experience. This really immersed the young people in a way which was not usually achievable in a shorter time. We were able to build on the standard activities and with the extra duration we could get to know each other a bit more and explore the challenges and rewards of being together at Camas through thick and thin. Camas Leader Deryck Collingwood drew many strands together as he oversaw this pilot, and the course was funded for several more years. Part of the deal was that we fed back to Social Work Services an appraisal of how things had gone, progress we could see and positive outcomes that could be found from the Camas experience. These were intense weeks of hard work for the staff and there were the usual minor crises to be dealt with – but there were many amazing moments and a real feeling of something more lasting having a chance of being forged.

However, one of my longest days at Camas came on the day of my 22nd birthday, when I was at the Nuns' Cave near Carsaig with two other leaders and a group of youngsters during our first three-week course. We had spent the night in the cave and as part of this trip the group was going back out 'over the top' via the Nuns' Pass, which is a very steep ascent but which would make a round trip with amazing views and a return to Loch Scridain over the uplands.

I was going back to Carsaig itself to pick up the Land Rover and drive it round by road to meet the group at the beach. One of the lads was not quite fit enough for the ascent, so he walked back with me and came in the Land Rover. I noticed that, despite the consistent very sunny weather we had been having, there now appeared to be a bit of fog coming in. By the time we arrived at the beach the lad had fallen asleep and I got out to see if there was any sign of the group.

After a while I was alarmed to see my colleague Graham arrive alone – and in a hurry. He had been running and was not only looking very hot but also quite dirty by his usual standards. He explained to me that while they were resting at the top of the Nuns' Pass one of the lads had dropped a match while lighting a cigarette and had not realised the seriousness as a tiny patch of grass instantly went on fire. It should be explained that for weeks prior to this there had been a heatwave and all the grasslands and moors were tinder-dry. The fire, fanned by a fresh breeze, quickly got totally out of control. Graham made the decision to send the group back the way it had come, with the other leader, and to try to run ahead of the fire to raise the alarm; and also to inform me that I would need to go back and pick up the group at Carsaig. No mobile phones in these days!

I left poor Graham on the phone to the fire brigade and police at the nearest house and hightailed it back towards Carsaig. I eventually met the group near the cave, safely off high ground. We took a shortcut across the sandstone flats, as the tide was low. While traversing this area, I slipped off balance and went over on my ankle and was aware of a slight cracking sound. Equipped with a stick, I made it back to the 'Landie' along with the group. I was the only driver, so I did my best, with one leg definitely not feeling comfortable. Walking down the track that afternoon felt a lot longer than it had the day before.

We made the Scottish news, as 10 square miles of moorland went up in smoke and the local fire squads fought it for a couple of days. The police came down to Camas to interview some of the boys and we had an embarrassing time of it locally that summer. I finally took my boot off at eleven in the evening and my foot blew up like a balloon. Needless to say, my role had to be changed for the rest of the course as I simply couldn't walk at any pace or for terribly far. It took about two months to heal fully.

Mark Jardine

'God must exist!'

I remember taking a group of children from Roystonhill (one of many such groups) to Camas. We brought them up to Oban in our minibus and the Camas minibus was to meet us at Craignure because our minibus was needed in Glasgow that week for other things. But for some reason the Camas minibus ended up stuck in Oban, and the last service bus across Mull was long gone. There were Camas staff on the ferry and we had enough adults to pair up with the children for us to hitch across Mull in twos.

I remember walking across the Camas track with Stephen, aged 11, and him thinking we were heading into the middle of nowhere and being quite scared – he'd never been out of Glasgow. As we came to the bend where you can look down and see Camas Bay, he stopped in his tracks, and I could feel his sense of wonder. Initially he was utterly speechless and I don't remember his exact words when he found his voice but it was something like 'God must exist!'

Linda Hill

Goat's milk and Christian care, a visit to Camas in 1984

Though the Pilgrims' Way across Mull to Fionnphort ferry is now tarred, the cows couldn't care less about cars with impatient horns. Haunches caked with mud, they amble along through a landscape that can't have changed much in 1000 years, passing the stones that still stand as part of the ancient series of signposts to 'the sacred isle'.

Between Bunessan and Fionnphort, a track on the right cuts across the moor towards the coast. Don't be surprised to see young people with wheelbarrows! They're not part of a chain gang but are taking stores to Camas Adventure Camp.

When I arrive, a nanny goat and her kid come trotting in welcome; hens are having dust baths. A white cross is painted on the door and young people are everywhere. The legend regarding the Iona Community's involvement in Camas is that Lord George MacLeod, visionary founder of the Community, was walking in that area during the war and stumbled across Camas. Thinking it would make a good camp for young people who had got into trouble in the depressed cities, he asked the Duke of Argyll for a lease, and began to bring groups of 'Borstal Boys' to Camas.

Camas has a simple lifestyle: the young people help to unload the boat, catch mackerel, and help to cook it; they drink the milk they draw from the goats. 'The Lifestyle is the Adventure' is the motto. But how do these young people adapt to this way of life? Ingrid Derbyshire works at Camas and has a background in social work. She says: 'A few are surprised to find there's no entertainment here; a very few can find it frustrating, but anyone who hangs back is soon brought into the group and shown opportunities for involvement and interest.'

Paul Derbyshire, Camas Leader, explains: 'We have group weeks when young people come through social services, and we have Open Camps when individuals can come.' During the open weeks, young people come from a wide range of backgrounds, though Paul says that many of the young people have 'a whole history of family background problems, plus truancy, crime and the social problems caused by unemployment'. These are all handled with care and sensitivity at Camas. The needs of the group are always balanced with the needs of individuals. Paul continues: 'A lot of social work departments have all sorts of people who don't fit in well with established programmes and the open weeks provide an opportunity for individuals to meet and mix with others. So this can mean that young people from disadvantaged areas can be mixing with young people from a private school.'

'It's hard and you've got to work at it,' Ingrid admits. 'One of the lads here recently came from a special educational needs school and one of the girls called him a "spoiled brat"! By the end of the week her attitude had changed.'

Justin, on his second visit to Camas, is helping in the kitchen. 'Put it this way: Camas is a change from Glasgow, isn't it? All you're doing in Glasgow is walking the streets. There's not much hope of a job there, especially when you're a 16-year-old and just left school. You come to Camas to meet new people. I would like to come more often.'

I ask him if he finds the lack of modern facilities a big change from Glasgow. He rounds on me: 'We've not got running hot water and we've got an outside toilet. It's a room and a kitchen with three of us living there; my granddad's disabled and they've been on the housing list for 40 years.'

Paul explains that Justin is being paid for by the social work department, but that this is limited, and that Justin will soon have to return home, though Camas will continue to welcome new young people.

'You hear of people who've never forgotten the week they had at Camas,' Ingrid says; and Paul adds proudly, 'We're now getting people whose older relatives have been here.'

Despite the ongoing challenges of funding, Paul and Ingrid are deter-mined to continue to welcome young people to Camas. 'Camas can teach people to work together, whatever their backgrounds, and our success is the best reason for Camas continuing,' says Paul. Justin nods solemnly in agreement, as he goes off to help Ingrid with the lunch.[1]

Lorn Macintyre

Snapshots of life

Simply life-changing, Camas was and is. My words alone can't adequately sum it up: thoughts and feelings which defy description and the confines of vocabulary. So here are some snapshots of life at Camas during the '80s ...

* They say teachers always remember their first class. My first group, as cook and general helper at Camas, was from Greenock and included a girl – only just a teenager – identified as 'at risk', having stolen shoes for a younger sibling. She'd be a 'young carer' now. A genial leader with that Mearns Centre party provided me with vital translations of their Glasgow banter.

* Recently graduated in law, I was introduced to the practical realities of the criminal justice system by a group of teenagers from Cornton Vale. Camas continued to host these groups, a link with the early days of Pol-mont Borstal camps, for several years but, despite the best efforts of the governors, government policies on young offenders eventually led to the cessation of these weeks.

* Games of 'sardines' in the most inaccessible corners of the camp with the Mary Slessor Centre community group: such patience and concen-tration – such silence! Fundraising activities with them back in Dundee. Great sing-songs led by Ricky Ross. Now, whatever happened to him?

* A range of folk with different backgrounds, qualities and needs coming to Camas in varying capacities. Innovations being tried, professional risks being taken, often because Camas lies outside, a bit separate, different, offering opportunities, ahead of the curve. 'The lifestyle is the adventure' is a phrase that pops up in all sorts of guises.

* Through Glasgow Social Work, a trio of teenage girls leaving care for independent living came to an Open Camp. Camas wasn't quite what they expected. After we had helped them with their suitcases, they searched for sockets for the hair driers we had just lugged down the track. Eyes became wider and more disbelieving as we briefed our rookies. Their reaction? They laughed – and rarely stopped laughing all week. Neither did we. What fantastic lasses they were, encouraging younger campers and good-humouredly battling the midges, which seemed to find them particularly tasty.

Paul Derbyshire

Camas recollections

Like a lot of volunteers, I discovered Camas gradually via Iona, and also my mother occasionally took schoolchildren to the youth camp on Iona. I spent a week on Iona as a teenager and recall the spiritual liberation of attending the Easter morning service in my wellies! At this point Camas was this 'other place' still waiting to be discovered …

I finally arrived there one day in May in the early 1980s, in the very best of weather with the turf warm under my bare feet. It felt like coming home. I resolved to return as soon as I could! It took a while, but in the spring of 1985 I was offered three months as cook, and in the autumn of 1985, I was appointed Team Leader. I don't know how many people applied for the job, but I was over the moon to be offered the chance. It was empowering and humbling in the same breath.

My first trip to the Nuns' Cave would have been memorable for its scramble across the boulder beach alone. Excepting team member Peter Reid, it was the first stay there for all us staff as well as the young people, and involved big learning curves! At this time Tavool House on Mull was used by the YMCA. Unbeknownst to us, they were also heading to the cave! Yep, double-booked! While we were still trying to gather driftwood to make the fire for our bangers, beans and mash, the YMCA teenagers set up camp along one side of the cave and proceeded to cook their tea in orderly groups of three, using a small gas stove. Less sleep than usual was had that night as friendly insults ricocheted across the cave walls. But we did manage to relax for a while together around the fire beforehand. The Nuns' Cave remains to this day etched deep in my being.

I have always loved big open spaces of moorland, sea and sky, guddling around in water and being in nature. This connectivity and sense of belonging saw me through some of the tougher times at Camas. I felt very at ease in this environment. Learning to share this with the many, sometimes vastly different, groups who came was emotionally demanding. The historically strong relationship with social work departments (especially in and around Glasgow and Dundee) brought many kids, some more than once. Maybe their memories of Camas resonate positively yet with them too.

One of Camas' strengths is that it can highlight our inner strengths. And if this gives young people a little more confidence in themselves then that has to be good. There were many leaps of faith with some of the groups and their ability to cope with the isolation in a safe manner. A group of young people with learning disabilities came once. One young girl in this group had suffered from selective mutism from a very young age. She had not uttered a sound for years. One evening she was at the fireside with a few other folk and to our amazement she released, just once, what can only be described as joyous sounds lasting about a minute.

Another group of young adults came all the way from Germany by bus! It was a brilliant success and the language barrier simply melted away during midsummer barbeques on the beach and a lot of laughter. This was community at its best.

A group of young men from Glenochil Prison being given the trust of all that space and freedom for a week by their enlightened prison officers was one of the most positive weeks. The dedication of the leaders was superhuman at times. So many of the guests we welcomed were hemmed in by circumstance and primarily only on the receiving end of life.

It would seem the biggest challenge during these years – with funding changes and other priorities – was simply how to keep Camas open. Though I knew it was time for me to move on, it totally broke my heart to be leaving. It is good to hear how it has evolved into a place I would have loved to have brought it to. Trying to explain to three young lads what it meant to me to be out on the track cutting peats, one fine May morning, might be easier today!

Sheila Bates (Russell)

1990s

Sacred composure brought down to earth

When a friend of one of the Camas volunteers visited us, this is what he wrote about his experience:

'Sacred composure of this place,
emotions tremble laid naked to the bone,
where reason has no words and illusions have flown,
the silent embrace to this music the soul awakes.'

At Camas, my emotions have trembled and my illusions have occasionally flown, but this has usually been due to such factors as sticking a twenty-foot pole up a pipe full of excrement or trying to explain to a group of teenagers why placing a jellyfish down each other's pants is not a particularly healthy activity to indulge in!

Camas offers a basic lifestyle. But the lack of home comforts is a temporary shock to groups who soon adapt and usually enjoy sharing in the opportunities and surprises it allows. The groups who stay for a week have usually spent large parts of their lives in residential care or in areas of poverty. As such, the *'sacred composure'* is brought down to earth. I remember being amazed by a bird cracking open a small snail's shell by holding it in its beak and smashing it on a rock. Victor from Glasgow was less than over-awed. 'So what! In Govan they use can openers.'

For others, being so close to a virtually unspoilt natural landscape can arouse great curiosity and wonder. Far from the city, for many, getting up for the toilet in the middle of the night can be the first time they have experienced complete darkness or complete silence (depending on who is sharing your dormitory!).

At the start of the 1990 season, Camas was used by Nottinghamshire Education Department for six weeks, who brought school groups on field trips. Since June, a variety of groups have visited, including a group of young homeless people, a group from a school for young people with special educational needs, and some people in their twenties and thirties who are living with HIV. We also had a church group, new members of the Iona Community, and the children of Iona Community members staying with us.

No escape routes

For many of the young people who have stayed with us, the experience of living every day closely with others their own age and older can be a time of growth in confidence. The approach of the staff at Camas means that groups can relate in a relaxed way. Many close relationships are built between staff and groups, a feat that, in such a short time, is both remarkable but also so ordinary, in that it happens every week without fail. Camas also provides a good opportunity for group leaders to show and share what they are like outside their formal role in the youth project or social work office.

Confidence is also gained by being able to do sometimes simple, but valuable, tasks, such as chopping wood or washing dishes, and this can be fun, rather than laborious – though of course no one will admit it! The skills learnt from outdoor activities are not the only, or even the main, point, but rather they are a chance to be creative and challenged and there is self-worth gained from this.

Of course, you can never be sure what people will gain from such a mixture of work, adventure, leisure and informal chat. Often we're surprised by phone calls or letters from 'Camas-sick' visitors – young people who want to let us know that their time here *was* worthwhile.

People also find that at Camas there are no escape routes. If you want to steer clear of someone or avoid washing the dishes, there aren't many places you can run away to. Problems and people are confronted and rarely avoided – that goes for staff and guests equally. This is just a reminder that living in community is rewarding, and sometimes, a pain in the neck. If work is a shared task and something needs to be done, then you just have to do it. This aspect of community life was explained during a reflective time at Camas. After hearing from the group that God, having created the world, rested on the seventh day, our cook then explained why God took the day off: 'Because God didn't live in a community! So, make sure you do your chores, OK?'

For all its human challenges, living closely with other people is good fun and more often than not gives a glimpse of what life can be, and sometimes is, in other places.

Maybe I should give the last word to someone who came as a group leader to Camas: 'I was constantly amazed at how well the group got on, despite wild weather and all the unusual and unexpected that constitutes Camas. I saw sides of people's personalities that I hadn't witnessed before. The atmosphere at Camas allowed them to be themselves, as well as to give of themselves. It allowed them to be creative, to do new things, to make new things and to show what they could do already.'[2]

Bryan Evans

Moments and memories from 1990

- It would have been a day like any other except for Julie being with us. We were hiking over the hill to the spectacular beach at Market Bay. From in front I heard, 'I wanna buy sweeties.' From behind, 'All we ever do is f***ing walk.' From my right, 'These bogs are manky.' But from my left, a song had sprung up, 'Mud, mud, muddy, mud, mud' and a laugh. It was Julie, sunk knee-deep in the peat.

- As we arrived, I yelled at Stephen: 'Aren't you going to …?!' Too late! He wasn't 'going to change' and, still wearing his jeans and boots, he stood without expression, knee-deep in the sea, watching the waves go by.

- Then there was Harry. He was sitting on the ground, sheltering a younger boy from the wind and rain. The latter was afraid of a spider on his coat, but Harry placed it gently on the grass. A contrast to what we had been told about him being 'very difficult and unruly at school'.

- Apart from teaching paddling and playing games, as kayak instructor, I liked to give groups a feel of the vastness and restless life of the sea, and the beauty of the coastline. We would coax groups to the edge of the bay, particularly at sunset, and let them sit a while. One evening one boy who had been aggressive was with us. At the end of the week, his group leader commented that he had never before seen him so still and attentive to his surroundings, and that he had been much more settled after that evening.

- We took a group by bus to Kintra, some five miles west of Camas, to another beautiful bay. The challenge we set was: 'Here is a map. Lead us home.' One of their leaders said, 'What if they go the wrong way?' 'It will take a bit longer' came the reply. We asked questions and set problems now and again to encourage them to organise as a group: knowing how many people there were, not losing any … the usual sort of thing. The young people were freed from the usual patterns and expectations, and their leaders were stunned by how much their group achieved.

- Another group were challenged by the rainy weather. Teamwork and technique safely negotiated the first fast-flowing stream, but it was the second stream-crossing that made us retreat from the Carsaig coast: even if we crossed one way, getting back might be too hard. We returned to Camas, dried clothes and decided to get wet again. We focused on kayaking skills on one day, so we could then go on another trip. I received a letter a couple of weeks later: 'You remember that kayak trip? And the seals coming to say hello like alien beings? Now I am back, when it all gets too much, I remember that day and am glad to be alive.'

- In the evening reflection, I liked encouraging the groups to talk about what had made the most impact on them during the day. Clare said, 'I've never chosen to do washing-up before today!'

We also talked about God's love for each of us, and James said, 'You mean God loves me?' When I replied, 'Yes, of course,' his smile lit up the Chapel of the Nets.

It was John who left me speechless, when he said, 'At the beach I heard God saying "enjoy the world."' … The Wild Goose had flown by again.

Mike Mineter

Youth work in 1999

The youth worker accompanies another person on their journey, without any requirement to solve any problem, and without any requirement to fix another human being. The youth worker should actively avoid problematising a person. If we are not alert, the use of labels lulls us into a false familiarity with the other person whereby we think we understand them because we have decided upon a label which 'explains them'.

At Camas, the young woman or young man that you are chatting with as you prepare the potatoes for the pot, or as you sit around the campfire, may be experiencing some things that they describe as problematic, and they may share some of those issues with you, but this is a person sharing their problems, not a problem person. This is a young person navigating her way through young adulthood.

Youth work is firstly about relationships, and the quality of our relationships depends upon our capacity to open ourselves to others, with honesty and authenticity, and in turn, be open to whatever it is they may reveal to us about themselves. All relationships, if they claim to be based upon mutual respect, require this capacity for sharing and mutual vulnerability.

I most enjoyed my time at Camas when we received groups of young people that were considered 'hard to reach'. When I hear that label, I take it to mean that, historically, the young person has failed to comply with the expectations of authority figures, be they parents, teachers, police, social workers, etc … Often, 'hard to reach' will be accompanied by the 'challenging behaviour' label. However, I always begin with an assumption that the young person labelled as having 'challenging behaviour' has had good reasons to resist the expectations of authority figures in the past. Although their behaviour might not necessarily be expedient or wise in terms of the longer-term outcomes that any caring person might want for them, their past 'protest' and noncompliance were for good reason. If a young person is consistently in conflict with those around them, the main failure, the historical responsibility for that lack of peace that characterises their lives today, rests with the adults that they have been failed by. We adults have failed them. And they will have developed their own strategy for survival, using the resources available to them. These young people have often learned how to survive, learned a kind of necessary resilience, in response to personally abusive and socially oppressive circumstances.

The youth worker's task is to accompany this young person, with all their unique circumstances, as they learn how to take responsibility as a young adult for the choices they make in response to the conditions and circumstances of their life, past, present and future. Youth work provides an opportunity to encourage them to be the best person that they can be. It is a time to recognise the uniquely beautiful qualities in each person and to thank each one for sharing the gift of themselves with us. For many young people it may be the first time that they have been recognised and accepted as they truly are. Accepted as fragile, flawed people, always growing and learning.

It is precisely these young people, those that might be excluded elsewhere, that Camas welcomes. I was there to encourage them. To invite them. To reassure them that if they risked the adventure, they would have a good time, and that they would learn. That the Camas experience would help them to grow as people.

What I encouraged at Camas was for each member of our team to engage in meaningful ways with these young people. To create an environment of trust and respect, and form relationships of mutual learning, so that each person can discover more about themselves and the world around them. This encouraged them to make choices that are more likely to achieve the outcomes, personally, relationally, educationally and spiritually, that they would choose for themselves, if they were afforded the support, opportunity and freedom to do so.

Vincent Manning

2000s

School trip smiles

Twelve children in their last year of primary school: eight girls and four boys. Arriving down the track and seeing the sea, most just ran straight in fully clothed. No tumble dryers here, you know, but clothes dry the old-fashioned way, and it's a good start to have all that excitement.

Most details have faded but I hope never to forget the smiles of the boy who carried a bin bag instead of a rucksack, and who always looked gloomy in school. Two photos with huge grins – one at the tiller of Mark's boat; the other, more surprising, when washing up (I had to promise not to send that one to his mum).

The same child delighted to be allowed to wheel the barrow full of groceries down the track, being careful not to spill anything or bump too much – not a chore to him at all.

Liz Gibson

2010s

Children at the water's edge

Camas is full of those who live for community; those who live for the sea. Those who live to tell stories and sing in the firelight.

Ph.D. students – whole groups of them from that university on the hill in Glasgow – clattered their way here on the train, through forests and lakes, past Tarbet and Arrochar. Maybe they came via the fish shack in Oban, stopping to pick up a crab-meat sandwich, as fresh as you can get, where the air smells of salt and engine oil. Clever about so many facets of science, sociology, medicine and music but ready to leave their cars at the top of the track and be children again at the water's edge …

Chatting with teenagers from the concrete streets. Sharing stories. Finding common ground …

A platoon of kayakers, back for their annual holiday, helping with the paths in the garden. Early-birds see otters plop into the water. To and from the kayak shed, sharp eyes spot the eggs perched on a hard nest of stones built by the persistent plovers, or the more successful hatchlings of the oystercatchers on their teeny rock …

One young visitor was constantly looking for something to do or someone to talk to and when walls were around, he would bounce off them, or drive his teachers up them. Out in the bay, towards the island, he found himself a great place to sit and lifted a rock up to hit it onto another on the ground. He put a small rock between and had soon devised his own rock-crushing factory, of which he was very proud. He asked to go and sit there many times. The hills echoed with bashing, clashing rocks and it was maybe not the quietest pastime, but it focused him completely. In his concentrated task in the bay he was absorbed into the wider landscape: the roll of pebbles and the suck of the water as the sea sighed over the shore and the wide sky reached down to the far horizon. As the sky turned pink, we heard him talking up to the setting sun. He said that he knew a girl who had passed away and now he imagined talking to her in the sky. So many sounds that fill up the bay over the week and are washed away again …

Rosie Gibbs

A conversation with Jon

Jon Lloyd reflected on his time as Camas Coordinator, 2012-2016, with Coracle *editor, Neil Paynter …*

Neil: Jon, any time I've ever heard you talk about Camas, at an Iona Community AGM or a plenary, you've always told stories about the people who have come – and that's what I've always found powerful and moving: the humanness of those stories – about how people have explored Camas, explored community and themselves … grown, transformed. When I say that: 'stories about people at Camas', who comes to your mind?

Jon: I think there are a few people that stick in my mind … There's a lad who comes from Provanmill, who was quite often reluctant to come, but *did* come, on expeditions a couple of times with GK and residentials. He found it really difficult to interact with the group. He'd been excluded from school and he found it really, really hard to stay in class and he used to explode and that sort of thing. But he came to Camas, and what he really loved was going out fishing, and he loved going out walking; and it was a real privilege to hear his story. His story was pretty sad. He'd been walking in the woods near Provanmill and he'd found this guy sleeping rough in the woods, who was an alcoholic and was pretty down and out. He chatted to this guy. And then came back, a couple of days later, and actually found the guy had passed away. And he had incredible guilt about that. And he contacted the police, and the police had had him in a van and he was being interviewed –

Neil: So he actually found him dead?

Jon: Yeah, he found him dead. And, you know, that was an incredibly traumatic event for him – and that was on top of all the other stuff that he was dealing with in terms of his background and where he lived and difficulties and relationships in schools and things like that … But I guess one of the privileges for me was actually being able to be there, go walking with him and hear his story. Just to be able to listen to what he had to say and be able to take him out fishing and give him something positive. Something that really lightened his life up just in the few days he was at Camas.

And since then I've heard that he's actually gone to college. He's found the environment there much more conducive to him getting on with life, and they treat him in a different way – and he's just blooming. I think the support that he got from GK and people actually working with him was really positive.

Neil: Brilliant. Anyone else come to mind? I'm sure lots of folk do.

Jon: Yeah. There's another lad, around 12 years old and very hyperactive. He wouldn't sit down for more than about two minutes. He came several times. He came on expeditions with GK and with Castlemilk as well. You know we do the opening night reflection in the Chapel of the Nets. And we were sitting there and he'd come in and plonk himself down and he'd start muttering to himself. And then he'd get up and walk off. And he'd come back again, then walk off. And, yeah, his first reaction to anything that you asked him to do was 'Na, I'm not doing that, I'm not doing that. No.'

I remember that he really liked playing table tennis, so I used to play table tennis with him. And I remember another time. I think the group was off rock climbing: 'No, I'm not going rock climbing.

I'm not doing that. No.' So I said, 'OK, just sit in the common room and do something else or come and help me in the kitchen.' I was in the kitchen making lunch. And he was sitting in the common room, and we've got the hatch that goes through to the kitchen. I had some music on, and so every time a song came on I'd pop up through the hatch and sing him a song *(laughs)*. And then we got him in the kitchen, and he was helping chopping the onions up and making lunch. Serving lunch to everyone. So that was really good.

And then at the end of the week, we ask people to strip the beds. And so we're in his dorm just making sure this was all getting done. And he was in his dorm and he was muttering: 'Oh, I'm not doing this. I'm not stripping my bed – this is stupid. I'm not stripping my bed.' And as he was saying that he was pulling the duvet out of the sheet *(laughs)* and piling it on the floor.

Neil: So he *was* doing it.

Jon: Yeah, yeah. So that was really nice.

Neil: So much about Camas is those one-to-one connections: making people feel welcome and listening to their story, and that goes a long way in a world where not enough of that happens.

You were talking about GK – Camas works with *so many* groups. Who are some of the groups you work with the most and how do you connect in with them?

Jon: Well, I think over the time I've been at Camas we've been really lucky in that we've had the same groups coming back year after year, especially with the Priority Area[3] time, which is in the summer holidays.

Neil: A lot of the same people too, so you're building relationships, trust.

Jon: Absolutely, yeah. We see the young people come. And when they come, quite often in their early teens or eleven, twelve, they're very boisterous and noisy and shouting and things like that. And then you see them get a bit older; and then we can encourage them, with the youth groups, to take a mentoring or leadership role with the younger ones, because they've been there before. So you can say 'OK, well, so you show them around, and you tell them what's OK. You can encourage them to get involved with things.' And sometimes we've seen the older ones come back as young youth leaders. And so they're actually taking responsibility for the whole group.

Neil: So they've really grown.

Jon: Exactly. And I think a lot of the youth groups have that model. So especially St Paul's do that, over at Provanmill, and GK, and we've had it with The Barn down in the Gorbals, and SIMY, who operate out of Townhead. And it's what I see as Camas' role: actually supporting the organisations and the people who do the work, week in, week out, in the weekly youth group. You know, they're building those relationships and that gives people a stability in their lives which is quite often lacking, and structure. And I think people build up a sense of security from the peer relationships they get in those situations as well, which just enables them to have a positive experience in their life, even if it's just once or twice a week. And maybe that's the influence which stops them from going finding friendships and relationships in a gang culture, for example. And that can have a real cascading effect throughout the community. And I think in Blackhill in particular, where Neil Young has developed St Paul's Youth Group and Bolt FM, that's made the difference between it being actually quite a violent culture of young people ganging up against each other and having fights and getting involved in drugs and alcohol, and something which is actually quite positive. And those sort of influences are pushed out to the fringes because they're not welcome in that community any more. And that's made a massive difference …

Neil: The Camas garden seems to have really come on over the years.

Jon: Yeah, we were really lucky the first year I was there, we got a lottery grant to bring in a new polytunnel, put in new French drains and more trees round the outside. And that was incredibly hard work for Becky, who was the gardener at that time, and then Abbi, who's taken it over now. It's made the garden much more accessible for young people. So quite often we now have chores in the morning and in the evening in the garden, so we're encouraging people to get in there. And what we really want people to do is to eat the fruit directly off the plants. So a morning reflection quite often will be to go into the garden and get into little groups and then find different things that you can eat, and to share the different experiences – we have the 'sour grape test': you have to eat a sour grape without moving a muscle on your face *(laughs)*.

Neil: A challenge!

Jon: Which actually a lot of the groups are surprisingly good at – it's just horrendous. And eating flowers, all the different things that can be found in there. So they've got that direct connection with food and the earth.

On the expedition side, again that's something we felt that we could offer because we had the skills. And also because Journeying is an amazing tool for developing self-reliance and initiative with young people. So GK were the ones who started it – they really wanted an expedition. And basically we've run probably half a dozen expeditions where we're out for three or four nights. So typically we spend a couple of days walking, going to some of the most amazing remote beautiful beaches on the south coast.

Neil: Places people don't get to … In Journeying is there a bit where people go out by themselves?

Jon: We have done that, yeah. We've done 'solos' with the Phoenix Group. So as part of that programme they'd come in for a week doing expeditions, and the next week they'd come in and do more self-development things. Part of that self-development was to go out for an afternoon and spend time on their own. And then sometimes we'd go and chat with them for a while. But, yeah, just getting that time by themselves. You know, young people very very rarely have time by themselves without some sort of stimulation, whether it be the TV or whatever.

And we've been doing more Duke of Edinburgh stuff as well. We started off with SIMY coming up and doing some practice expeditions with Neil Pratt. And then we developed the residential section of the Duke of Edinburgh Gold Award as an open course. So last year we ran that and had twelve people come from England and Scotland to do a self-development week, and that was really great as well: just bonding a group of people together and actually challenging them in a different way than they normally are challenged. I think that for those sort of youngsters, doing the Duke of Edinburgh Gold Award, the challenge is academic. But this is actually asking them about how they feel about different things and their relationships; it's something very different. Hopefully it gives them pause for thought.

Neil: Jon, if I asked you about what you see as the spiritual side of Camas being about – you know, it's not a churchy experience, obviously – how would you answer that?

Jon: I think one of the things that we try and do is stimulate people's sense of self and sense of environment through doing reflections in the morning and evening. Kathy Galloway talks about the 'big book' of Christianity. And the 'big book' is there, you know: it's creation; it's the sky and the sea, the environment and the beasts. And that's in your face every day because Camas is an outside place. You can't stay inside: you gotta go outside to go to the loo or you gotta go outside to get to the kitchen. And whatever weather and things that are there, then they are directly with you. And even if it's a dark and grey day there's an intense beauty in that environment which is incredibly nourishing; and I think actually the shape of the bay at Camas is incredibly holding as well. You know, you're just nestled in between a couple of headlands and slapped down in the valley next to the water.

Neil: Encompassing.

Jon: Yeah, it is: it's the feeling of being held, which is really important. And you know sometimes we'll do a reflection where you're going out and looking for the most miniscule things and trying to get different colours on a card with a bit of glue: and you see all these tiny bits of yellow, gravel and pink granite, pink flowers and things like that. And then sometimes you have the sort of smack-you-in-the-face type of beauty …

And then we had the aurora borealis a couple of months ago – and it was just magical. Magical is the only word that could describe it. And then yesterday, we stepped outside and there were five seals right down by the beach – I've never seen five seals right there all at one time. So, yeah, that interaction with nature I think is intensely spiritual, and it's very nurturing, it's very holding and I think it connects you with something bigger than yourself.

Neil: And people from the city come and take that back with them … Who are some of the adult groups you've welcomed to Camas this year?

Jon: This year we had Faith in Throughcare, which is a group of adults who have just come out of prison, supported by the Church of Scotland. And these guys come out of prison and they get stuck in a little flat somewhere. You know, they're separated probably from their community, they quite often have addiction issues. They're completely isolated; and just to get them away, to get them to Camas was an amazing experience for us because we were able to hear their stories and they were able just to hang out and be recognised and heard and not be judged, and it was brilliant for them. They described it as a 'mountaintop experience'. But then, at the end of the week – this is one of the issues that we talked about with Faith in Throughcare – they come back down and they're in the same situation that they were in before, and actually that's almost worse, because now they've had a positive experience and their hopes have been raised, their spirits have be enlivened, but now they're back in the same situation …

Neil: I guess part of that is, you've been talking about how you're connecting with some of the same groups through the years, so you're building relationships. And people come to Camas and have that mountaintop experience but you're connecting with them again down the road, maybe seeing them on the mainland?

Jon: Yeah, and some of the people from Faith and Throughcare that I've met up with recently, there's one of the guys who is over at Greenock; and he took me to have a tour around an alcohol recovery unit which he's been working through and I met his support worker and one of the nurses who was working with him as well. So there is that connection, and he does have that support of Faith in Throughcare and those organisations as well. And what we hope is that we can invite people back to Camas on Work Weeks, for Garden Weeks, to continue the connection that we have with them, and potentially they can come and be volunteers as well. And it makes for a bit of a different type of experience in Garden Weeks. It's very inclusive: we have families there, we have friends, we might have relatives of staff, we might have guests that have been during the year and come from difficult circumstances, and then we might have Iona Community members come as well, or just people connected to the Iona Community. And that's really important because actually most of the people that come to Camas come through existing connections. Advertising? You can't really describe what Camas is like. If you describe what it's like: no electricity and vegetarian food and cold water and basic bunkroom accommodation, that puts most people off (*laughs*). So in order to get people to come they have to talk to someone else who's been who can actually describe that it's about hospitality and community. And that's not something that you can very easily communicate on a bit of paper or on a website …

Neil: You work really closely with the Iona Community Youth Workers based in Glasgow.

Jon: Yeah, they do a lot of work with youth groups that come up to Camas. So they'll be in the youth groups, week in, week out. And if we see someone who we think needs particular support or needs an advocate in some particular way, then they're in Glasgow to pick that up …

Neil: Jon, I've noticed you use the word *privilege* a lot when you talk about Camas: a privilege to be in such an amazing place and to listen to people's stories and get to know them over the years.

Jon: Yeah … and I think what we've focused on is the place and the guests but also equally important is the staff and the volunteers. For me personally one of the greatest joys that I have is actually sitting down one-to-one with a member of staff or a volunteer. I think Peter Macdonald described the purpose of the 'monastic life' or living in community is actually to strip away the layers. And you do strip away the veneer of attitude, you know, the presentation that people want to put to the world. And sometimes that's really painful for people, and sometimes it's a real joy, and generally the light of people actually escapes and shines through. Everybody goes through difficult patches when they're at Camas, and I've gone through very difficult patches. But being able to sit down and work through some of that stuff is fantastic. And when I listen to volunteers talk and say how much they value the experience of being there, that fills me with a great sense of pride and joy really.

D [volunteer] is a fantastic advocate for what we've done. He was talking at the end of the season, saying his goodbyes, about actually it being one of the most important periods in his life, where he felt included within a community; he felt really supported by all the people who were around and able to do the work: actually engage with young people, get on with things, and with a clarity. I think that's probably one of the fortunate, lucky things about being at Camas, that it's very easy to have clarity about what you're trying to do. It really is about hospitality. And at the beginning of each year we've sat down with volunteers and residents and said: 'Look, actually what is it that we're about, if we distil that down into a couple of sentences?' And this year was very much about welcoming people to the Centre, so giving them unmitigated hospitality. It's about allowing people to be heard, creating that space. And when things don't go right, or people are defensive, then just hitting them with, I think the phrase this year was, 'the love bomb' (*laughs*). So whatever they throw at you, meeting it with compassion, with love. And you know, people find it very difficult to actually resist in the long term.

It's a short space of time, a very enclosed environment. So it is actually possible to try and deliver those things in a really consistent way, which wouldn't be possible if you were outside in the city or in a different environment where you have different influences coming in or people's attention is diffused to different things. So it's incredibly intense, but it is six months. And quite often people say: 'Is it sustainable?' No, it's not. It's not sustainable. But for six months it's possible. And then you have a rest in the winter if you're a member of staff, or if you're a volunteer you can do something different. Then you come back with renewed energy and do it again …[4]

Jon Lloyd and Neil Paynter

Home from home

I remember when I arrived for my interview for the Camas Gardener job, I remarked to Jon, the Coordinator, that I felt like I was in a dream. He replied with 'I've been here for two years and I *still* feel like I'm in a dream.' I was captivated as soon as I arrived, like so many before me.

I didn't really know what to expect when groups started arriving at the beginning of my first year, but by the end of that season I remember being struck by a real sense that something worthwhile happens at Camas. I enjoy, so much, witnessing young folk from Glasgow and beyond – who I've now seen grow over the last three years – stepping out of their character from the city and feeling free to run on the rocks catching winkles and crabs, gutting fish and jumping in bogs, running into the sea with their socks on (because they 'don't like the feel of sand'), or announcing a meal they have cooked for their peers. This doesn't always happen in one week, but often, over the years, people take ownership of Camas and for the week they are here it is a home from home, which is remarkable and very humbling to be part of.

I feel very lucky to have a deep love for this work, the land and the people who come and share it with us, and for belonging to a long legacy of people who have felt the same for this very special bay.

Abbi Mason

The fear had ebbed away …

Gaining self-worth and a sense of belonging are at the heart of what we are trying to achieve at Camas. So often the granite quarry where we abseil provides opportunities for individuals to challenge the constraints of hardened self-doubt. Triumphs include the lad with impaired sight who struggled across the rough terrain to successfully reach the foot of the quarry. 'Nah, not putting a harness on, not going climbing.' Eventually he agreed to put on a harness and helmet, 'but not going climbing'. After half a dozen colleagues had been up, he announced that he might give it a go – and did. And for the rest of the week casually remarked to new people he met, 'Yup, I'm a rock-climber.'

And from the top of the cliff, abseiling down, friendships are cemented. A young woman from central Glasgow, extremely scared, muttered a mantra: 'Do it for Shonna. Do it for Shonna': Shonna was intensely terrified of heights, and had used all her resources just to *get* to the quarry. She could hear her friend though; and, later in the week, on an exposed rocky scramble on Erraid, Shonna, with the help of her friend, coped confidently: the fear had ebbed away …[5]

Jon Lloyd

Coming home

Camas is an amazing place to live and work. For somewhere so remote and wild, a lot happens down the track. This year we've welcomed almost 500 people, all making their way from different starting points and from a diverse range of backgrounds. At the end of the season, it can be fun to think about the numbers and what makes Camas tick. Here are some of my favourite estimates:

2,500 scones freshly baked;
a quarter ton of porridge served;
over 10,000 volunteer hours contributed;
nearly 2,000 native trees planted in the new woodland;
at least 800 wheelbarrow runs up and down the track;

and 9,000 kilowatt-hours generated by our wind turbine, keeping our fridge cold and our showers (reasonably) warm!

And yet that's only touching the surface. What about all the stuff you can't quantify very easily? There's people saying they feel at home here and returning year after year, and feeling proud for having faced the challenges of being at Camas – eating vegetarian food, abseiling off the quarry wall, jumping into cold seas, and coming through it all; people becoming inspired to follow the spirit of adventure and continuing to roam and explore in the outdoors after Camas; the chance to talk to and get to know people they wouldn't otherwise have met; the unique opportunity to be switched off from smartphones and social media for a while; feeling safe enough to venture beyond one's comfort zone and sing in front of others or speak up in a group – and then there's playing games like 'Whoosh!' where you might end up crying with laughter!

What is it that makes a week at Camas such a special experience, and what inspires people to care so deeply and give so much to the place? Everyone who knows Camas will have their own answers I'm sure, but here are three things that are important to me:

First, Camas is a place of change. We all know how quickly the weather changes, but the seasons, the tides, the resident team, also all come and go. No day is ever the same or fixed. Yet there's an easy rhythm and ritual to the day – meals together, activities, washing dishes, playing music, gathering for reflection – that keeps us rooted, knowing what to expect next, and softens the bare edges of a place that can often be tough.

Secondly, Camas does not belong to any one person or group. It is open to anyone who feels at home and connected here. This is something that people often express: the sense of belonging they find at Camas, as though they were coming home. Camas is supported and nourished by this wide network of people who have a deep love for the place.

And lastly, the Camas team itself goes through many of the same challenges and emotions as the groups and individuals who come here for a week, such as making do with the simple lifestyle, limited electricity and fewer material comforts; living together, having differences, and needing to get along; being able to go through the ups and downs and having to look out for each other; doing things that take us outside of our comfort zones. I think that makes it a more real and authentic place to be. The people living here and hosting groups know the challenges, and so are able to genuinely relate to others.

I'll finish with my favourite memory of this season. We had a group from a football team called United Glasgow. Many of them were refugees from places like Sudan, Syria and Eritrea. They were due to go and play in a tournament on Iona on the Saturday, so a few days before, we went to the beach at Knockvologan for a warm-up game. This was during an incredible spell of weather in June where it was just sunny and still day after day. When we got there, they couldn't believe somewhere like this existed in Scotland – a huge white sandy beach surrounded by turquoise sea and clear skies overhead. Someone said it was like being in their home country. Playing football on the sand was a lot of fun; there was music and dancing – and I even managed to score a goal![6]

Darragh Keenaghan

A conversation with Mark

Mark Jardine is an Isle of Iona resident, a former Camas staff member, and a former member of the Camas Committee. He is interviewed here by Mary Duncanson, a former Camas volunteer and a member of the Iona Community.

Mary: When did you first visit Camas and what were your first impressions?

Mark: It was on a day trip during one of our many family holidays on Iona when I was a boy. As my father (John Jardine) had worked for the Iona Community as the Youth Secretary, he was familiar with the work of the place as both an activity Centre and a fishing station. At the time of my first visit I had no inkling that later it would have so much significance for me.

During my student days, I was working as a volunteer at the Abbey as 'Van Driver' and I went one day to Camas to help load and unload a boatload of building materials. Never one to miss a boat trip, I was quick to step forward to help! Deryck Collingwood, then Leader at Camas, asked whether I could stay overnight there to assist with moving the materials indoors at low water. Maybe this put me more on the map at the time, and he subsequently asked if I would like to come as 'Artist in Residence/volunteer' the following summer for a couple of weeks. Somehow the couple of weeks got extended and I continued with the volunteer work long after the mural was completed. I left college, and left home in Glasgow, and in 1979 I went to work in what was a bit of an experiment at Camas at the time.

Mary: Why is Camas still so special for you?

Mark: There are a few reasons, but probably a key one is that it was my first experience of actually living year-round on the west coast, something I had determined I wanted to do once I finished college in Glasgow. I learnt so much on all fronts – and I had plenty to learn! The truly basic existence there suited me fine. I had been going on camping and bothying trips for several years, and liked the outdoor life, the practical tasks and the micro-community. In the winter it was just the four adults and one toddler. Each evening we would be in the Chapel of the Nets with the wind howling out of the bay and the slates rattling, then down in the living room by the fire and a hot chocolate before we went to bed. Living without electricity moulded me for life; many of the old ways seemed good and the connection with the past was very close. The longer I lived there, the more I came to see the value of the work the Iona Community was doing. Coming from Glasgow I even understood the banter that many of the groups used!

Mary: You'll have many memories of Camas, but can you pick out a couple – good or challenging?

Mark: My Camas memories are a mix of the enduring and the one-off. There are the big events. One of which that lingers in my mind was Ross Morton and Karen Church's [former Camas Coordinators] wedding in 1998 – with a brilliant gathering of folk, some hilarious comic moments and the heartfelt love and emotion of the day.

The edgy thrill of the unexplained has been used to advantage by many at Camas to add a bit of spice to an evening round the fire.

One day we planned ahead, foreseeing a few spooky fireside tales. So, I rowed across to the quarry side of the bay during daylight, unbeknownst to any of the group, and placed a lit Tilley lamp in the ruined smiddy, whose gables stood visible from the opposite side of the bay. After dinner, as the evening wore on, more and more fantastic tales were spun – and soon nobody would venture outside to the loo without a pal. Eventually, of course, the glow was noticed where none should be, in a long-deserted, roofless building. Excitement reached fever pitch as more of the group ventured out to verify the haunting evidence, and various explanations were proffered by willing resident local historians!

Animals have featured on and off during different eras at Camas. While I was there, we had goats for a while. The first one was of very strong will. Jenny provided us with milk, which in those pre-fridge days was a welcome change from the powdered non-perishable stuff, but it came at a price. One evening I arrived home after a very long journey from Aberdeen. That night I was the only person at Camas, so it fell to me to milk the goat, by now in hours of darkness. Jenny was clearly annoyed at my late arrival and overdue to be relieved of her milk. In the feeble glow of a hurriedly lit hurricane lamp she took delight in treading in the milk pail as my inexperienced hands went to work. Not content with thoroughly contaminating the milk, she administered her final revenge, just as I completed the task, by kicking over the pail. By the end of the session it was clear that neither of us was very pleased – but I think she was the more satisfied!

Mary: Your love of boats and the sea must've been deepened at Camas; and were you also involved in the salmon fishing work?

Mark: I was intrigued by the salmon fishing and Camas enabled me to explore my fascination with the coast and the sea. At the end of the 1970s the buildings at Camas were still very much shared with the salmon fishing, which had quite an influence on the atmosphere and balance of the bay.

Bertie MacRae, the fisherman, was a stocky, larger-than-life character with great experience at sea and huge ability to run, fix or make anything practical needed for life on the coast of Mull. He had also a great sense of fun and a non-judgemental attitude which enabled him to win the respect of not just local folk and Camas staff but also the groups of young people coming then, as they do now, from challenging backgrounds and often used to inner-city life rather than the basics of survival at Camas. I admired Bertie just as much as the visiting groups did and expressed an interest in working with him if the opportunity arose.

For two summers I worked as the third hand on the salmon fishing; this meant I was less directly involved in working with the groups using Camas during the day, although sometimes Bertie might take one or two folk out to the nets if it wouldn't interfere with the fishing too much. I loved the work, the camaraderie with Bertie and Willie Wood, his assistant. Willie had a very strong accent and was hard to follow but he had a heart of gold and also liked a practical joke. I learnt a lot about ropes and boats and I couldn't have too much of it. The salmon in those days were still quite plentiful and some of these lithe silvery specimens were so big you struggled to keep their tail off the ground if you carried it by the gills, as was the tradition. The nets were set off the headlands, one to the east and several to the west of the bay. They were anchored to the shore and to an anchor some distance out and stretched by poles to keep their shape. To fish the nets, done on the ebb at Camas, we would go out in the boat, untie the poles to collapse the net up to the surface then empty the inner chamber, 'the bag', by unlacing a door and lifting the fish carefully into the dinghy.

The fish were gutted quickly and transported by Bertie in his 'Haflinger', a small four-wheel-drive pick-up, back up to the main road, then they were either sold locally or, if there was plenty, they went to Glasgow on ice in fishboxes. We had to change the nets every ten days or so, and when we brought them ashore they would be washed, then hung up to dry with the help of the poles on the green and a block and tackle. Any holes would be mended, and then we would carefully fold and stow the nets on a handbarrow so they would run out smoothly when we put them back out.

Many years later, I had a second spell as a salmon fisherman, this time with Jane Griffiths, who had taken over from Bertie when he retired. Jane had worked with Bertie for many years so continued the tradition of able womenfolk fishing and we enjoyed working together. Sadly, the wild salmon stock was in major decline and we found we could not make a living as had been possible in the days when fish were plentiful and there was no competition from farmed fish. Despite our best efforts, by 1996 all the Scottish west coast salmon stations were closing down. Though the fishing at Camas came to an end, its part in the life of Camas remains.

Mary: Why is Camas so important for the Iona Community?

Mark: Well, in my opinion it's about several things. What the Iona Community does at Camas is something very practical. I'm referring chiefly to the work with young people from disadvantaged backgrounds, but not exclusively, as clearly what takes place during other weeks is also valid, whether it be with university students, tree-planting work parties, families or adults with other challenging, or unchallenging, lives. It's often still transformative and beneficial. Camas continues its positive contribution, the value of its work modestly uniting with other signs of hope. In a world where the battles for monetary gain, political power or domination threaten people, families and entire countries, not to mention the very planet we inhabit, Camas works very locally, but its example still applies. The successful mixed species tree-planting scheme is a good illustration of one direction that land custodianship can go in. The growing movement in Scotland for more accountability over land use, and the move towards more local community-owned land and businesses, is something that holds some improved hope for the viability of the Highlands and Islands. 'Sustainable' is surely one of the most key words in the world today.

Mary: Camas has developed very good links with the local community on Mull and you were the local representative on the Camas Committee for a number of years. Do you have any ideas on how the links can be developed further?

Mark: Over time there have been varying levels of integration and involvement with the resident population on Mull and Iona. It is no accident that many former staff have chosen to settle in the area. When folk are consciously or unconsciously thinking about staying in the area their default attitude is inevitably more likely to be one of getting involved with local life, and that means Camas stays on the map. Attendance at local events is the beginning. Camas inviting and hosting things is logical and ongoing involvement with schools, local initiatives and supporting local lobbying where there are key areas of concern (for instance healthcare provision) are all good directions to continue. Camas is also arguably in position on occasion to lead by example; it shares lots of the demands of and challenges to island life, with a few of its own layered over that, but many of the global challenges have to be tackled at a grassroots level, and Camas is arguably that kind of place.[7]

Mark Jardine and Mary Duncanson

The Camas Boys

This light-hearted song was created in 1964 when Iona Community member Leith Fisher worked at Camas. It was sent to him nearly forty years later in a letter from Andy Findlay. Andy wrote:

'I'm Andy from the Glesca Toon … I remember lumpy mattresses, open fires, carving my name in one of the seats … I also remember being told that we had to hike what seemed like miles to Camas through these famous bogs and ditches. I remember who helped me carry my suitcase, thank you again. I remember the discussions we had round the table or at the fireside, never realising at the time how it could shape your future simply by being part of your past. Those early days were so formative for me.'

The Camas Boys

Hello, hello, we are the Camas Boys.
Hello, hello, we are the Camas Boys.

We're up to our knees in candle grease;
If we stay much longer, we're bound to freeze.
We are the poor old Camas Boys.

At least we got tae Camas after miles and miles and miles,
Through bogs and o'er ditches, through gateposts and o'er stiles,
Then Jeanie made a cup of tea and then we were all smiles.
We are the poor old Camas Boys.

Oh, my name is Andy and I come from Glesca Toon.
How I wish that I had gone for a week doon tae Dunoon,
Even with Polaris which might blow us tae the moon.
We are the poor old Camas Boys.

My name is Davy and I am very tall,
Everybody else looks very very small;
Please excuse my voice, I cannae sing at all.
We are the poor old Camas Boys.

She is Jean and she is the cook,
But these old potatoes, they make you want tae puke.
We are the poor old Camas Boys.

Andy Findlay and friends

The common room

All the years of laughter
surround me tonight,
as I sit alone
in a common room.

A common room …
fragile floorboards and ragged rugs
spotted by stains of season after season.
Wooden benches and chairs carved with generations claiming:
'WE WERE HERE!'

Through a worn and draughty door
'welcome' whistles gently in the wind.
A peat fire glows, sizzles and spits
reminders of songs sung,
stories shared and
friendships formed.

Thick whitewashed walls,
patched with clouds of grey,
whisper the voices of years gone by …

voices of excitement and fear at new experiences,
voices of wonder and worry at a week without 'luxuries',
voices of anticipation and trepidation at the challenge of change,
voices of tangled emotions, frustrated feelings held safe in this place,
voices of pleasure and pride, adventures and awakenings.

As I sit alone, and this room remains the same,
I sense the jump of joy in Love's heart,
as her children play once again.[8]

Rachel McCann

Notes:

1. From the *Times Educational Supplement*, 21.09.84
2. From *Coracle*, the magazine of the Iona Community, 1990, Kathy Galloway (Ed.)
3. 'A Priority Area is a community where deprivation rates fall within the bottom 5% across all of the social and economic indicators. The Church of Scotland currently designates 64 congregations as Priority Areas.' (From the Church of Scotland website: www.churchofscotland.org.uk)
4. Adapted from *Coracle*, the magazine of the Iona Community, 2016, Neil Paynter (Ed.)
5. From *Coracle*, the magazine of the Iona Community, 2015, Neil Paynter (Ed.)
6. From *Coracle*, the magazine of the Iona Community, 2012, Neil Paynter (Ed.)
7. From *Coracle*, the magazine of the Iona Community, 2019, Neil Paynter (Ed.)
8. From *Coracle*, the magazine of the Iona Community, 1997, Kathy Galloway (Ed.)

FAITH AND PHILOSOPHY

The Iona Community seeks 'new ways to touch the hearts of all', and Camas embodies an inclusive, creative spirituality that permeates the whole of life there. Of particular significance is a commitment to care for creation, as former Leader of the Iona Community Norman Shanks explains: 'Camas fulfils a distinctive role within the life of the Iona Community … and adds an important dimension to the community's approach to spirituality, with its emphasis on the outdoors, the adventurous and its awareness of the significance of the environment.'[1]

The values and ideas that underpin and inform the work at Camas are explored here by writers from a variety of backgrounds and spiritual paths.

An inclusive community

I am not really religious at all, but you do get a sense of the environmental side of spirituality here, living and working so close to nature. The groups that come to Camas are not particularly religious and don't usually go to church, so what we do here is give them a sense of a spiritual way of life, and that's what appealed to me in being at Camas. You can be who you want to be here and there are no prescribed ways of thinking. It's an all-inclusive kind of community. All people from all faiths and backgrounds are accepted and welcomed and there is freedom for all of us in that.[2]

Sarah Chapman

Camas – a faith reflection

For many years, Camas was a summer offshoot of the Iona programme, and worship in the Chapel of the Nets reflected the kind of worship held in the Abbey. For its time, it was considered innovative, with an unusual degree of participation for the Church of Scotland (in which tradition the Abbey worship originated), but it was thoroughly conventional Christian worship, using the theological language of the church (sin, redemption, salvation, etc.) and of course, almost exclusively masculine in its formulation, as the Abbey worship was till well into the 1980s.

In the 1970s and 1980s, during the Intermediate Treatment years, Camas became much more autonomous, with its own small, year-round

Resident Group, who maintained a pattern of Christian worship based primarily on the experience and preferences of those living there. So for a while, there was a 'Camas Liturgy', and Camas Morning and Evening Prayers appeared in the 1984 version of the *Iona Community Worship Book*. Other patterns were based on Franciscan forms of prayer. Again this was traditional, orthodox and really quite formal.

The 1980s was a period of intense creativity and innovation in the worship of the Iona Community. Many gifted liturgists and songwriters, and in particular, the work of John Bell, Graham Maule and the Wild Goose Worship Group, revitalised the worship in the Abbey. Added to this, the explosion of words and music of the world church into the Iona Community, and a new awareness of liberation and feminist theology, meant that the Community's worship underwent a transformation unequalled since its earliest days that is still continuing.

The Camas challenges

But this transformation largely passed Camas by. Its emphasis, use and impact was on Iona and on the mainland. By the 1990s (by which time Camas had gone back to being a summer camp, without a Resident Group) Camas was beginning to ask its own questions about worship. These were sparked by a number of challenges Camas was facing:

1. While the groups who came to stay on Iona were increasingly church-based and liturgically literate, the groups who came to stay at Camas were increasingly ones which had little or nothing to do with the church, and were completely unfamiliar with worship of any description. Indeed, many of the people coming were 'unchurched' for several generations, and had never been in a church, opened a Bible or gained any accurate knowledge of Christianity (though some had 'orange' or 'green' versions of it).

2. To people who knew nothing about Christianity, the forms and language of Christian worship, even the more open forms followed on Iona, were not so much objectionable as boring, incomprehensible or devoid of meaning, and the idea of 'going to worship', such an integral part of Iona life, was alienating, even threatening for many.

3. Additionally, a significant number of the Camas staff and volunteers, people who brought considerable gifts and skills in outdoor activities, group-work, arts and crafts, etc., were also not people who described themselves as practising Christians. Some were people from a Christian background who could no longer comfortably stay within the church, some were from other faith backgrounds; some described themselves as spiritual rather than religious, and quite a few had a spirituality that could most accurately be described as 'ecological'.

4. As well as the feminist and liberation perspectives that were already being assimilated into the Iona Community, the importance of ecological and interfaith perspectives was becoming increasingly evident. This was particularly so at Camas.

5. In a small community like Camas, and with the particular needs of people who experienced themselves as excluded and powerless elsewhere in their lives, the importance of safety in every area of the life, of acceptance of people where they are, and of real ownership by the groups of their week together, became paramount.

Responding to the challenges

One possible way of responding to these challenges would have been to emphasise Camas as a Christian Centre, to continue to have morning and evening worship, and to concentrate on finding a language and tools for Christian evangelisation. There are quite a number of Centres in Scotland which use outdoor adventure as the basis for evangelisation, and it's possible that this works to some degree.

Successive Camas staff did not choose to go down this road (correctly, in my view). Instead, another direction developed, which, for want of a better term, I would like to call '**theological hospitality**' (rather as we offer Eucharistic hospitality on Iona). This evolved, rather than being decided on as a fully developed policy, and there were markers along the way.

• The re-designation of the Chapel of the Nets as an **open space**. This happened in about 1993 or thereabouts, when Tassy Thompson, an

artist and long-standing member of the Worship Group, was a Programme Worker at Camas for the summer. She transformed the Chapel
of the Nets (which by then was a dark, cluttered and dusty space which
imposed certain expectations and constraints on what could be done in
it) by clearing it out and cleaning it, emptying the space, and putting
into it instead a variety of artefacts from the daily life of Camas. From
this time dates the weekly practice of a group organising the space
together as they want it to be, and taking ownership of it as theirs from
the beginning. This changing of the space was, looking back, enor-
mously significant. Not only did it give the possibility of dynamic use
of a space that had been static for decades, it also posed the question –
what is appropriate in this free and open space?

- The renaming of worship times as **reflection**. This took from liberation
  theology the notion of *praxis* (practice) as the fundamental starting-
  point in the life of a community committed to transformation. Praxis is
  the integration of action and reflection; so we act, and then we reflect
  on our action, and that reflection in its turn shapes our subsequent
  action. So, we learn from experience, we discover what it is that we need
  to nourish and sustain our acting, and we identify and name that nour-
  ishment, whether it is song, prayer, silence, creativity, laughter and tears,
  the stories of a place, a people, a religious faith, or whatever. For groups,
  the things of daily life together (meals, chores, outdoor activities, games,
  conversations, arguments) are all part of the action. In the reflection
  times, groups can name their experience of nature, of community, of
  work, of relationships, reflect on it, and take that into the next day.

'Theological hospitality'

Having used this term, I'd like to explain it a bit more. I would suggest that
at Camas, we make a hospitable space in which people together can reflect
on what are the features of real significance in their life in the community
of the week; and that the ordering also, rather than being laid down in a
particular (in this case, Christian) way by the Iona Community, is given
over to that community, with the process guided and safeguarded by the
Camas staff.

I think there is a clear rationale for Camas being a good place to do this. Because I am a Christian, I choose to describe it in a form which is meaningful to me, that is, a Trinitarian form. One classical Christian formulation for the Trinity is, God as Creator, Redeemer, Sustainer (or, as the patriarchal version has it, Father, Son and Holy Spirit). But this formulation also reveals the nature of life, and that life is very evident at Camas:

Creation

The Celts spoke of reading God in the 'little book' (the Bible) and the 'great book' (the creation). People who would resist reading the Bible readily read the creation at Camas. I think we are offering them a space to do that, and to give them freedom to draw their own conclusions, and not impose our conclusions on them. Remarkably often, people draw the conclusion that the creation is something to be grateful for, to be respectful of, and to cherish.

Interestingly, Camas is a place where the Bible can actually come alive, as **story**. Much of it, particularly the gospels, draws on metaphors from nature and subsistence. In our urban, comfortable life, these are mediated to us, we are told about them. At Camas, they are immediate, we depend on them, participate in them – light, water, wind, bread, boats on stormy seas …

Incarnation

Among the characteristics of Camas are that it is a place where people are required to live in the 'here' (this place) and 'now' (this moment). We don't have to be defined by either our damaged past or our possible dismal futures. We are accepted in the here and now. It's also a place where bodies matter, and we cannot be disembodied intellects or spirits. Together at Camas, we have to feed our bodies, heat our bodies and deal with our bodies' waste. We have a direct involvement in this at Camas like few other places. Camas is a very embodied place, and it communicates the message that bodies matter, that they are holy, whether it is the human body, the bodies of other creatures or the earth body itself. This life in the present and this holiness are incarnational.

Transformation

Camas is a place of significant change and new possibility for many people. The experience of creation and incarnation in new forms, forms that cut across what they know, is a liberating one. Christian orthodoxy might call this 'resurrection'. It is this unusual combination of empowered action and reflection that has led funders to recognise the value of Camas for young people. What it does is give people a new way of looking at what really matters, what is most important, and challenge the hegemony of possessions, status, celebrity, appearance, luxury, power, violence, sectarianism, racism and all the other idols of our society.

These three aspects are in a dynamic relationship which is expressed in and through community, interrelatedness. I have named them in a way that is implicitly Christian (though of course this is by no means the only way these same three things could be named). They reflect for me the interrelatedness of the Trinity, the community of God. But I don't name them thus, and believe that this is the way life is because I'm a Christian. I'm a Christian because I believe this is the way life is. Because I have faith in this 'pattern of reality' (as George MacLeod called it), I feel quite confident that we can offer this theological hospitality as the Iona Community, and allow God, or the Spirit, or however we wish to name the deep thing that happens to people at Camas, to move and inform people as it will. If the pattern is true, it will reveal itself. If it's not, then all of us need to face that challenge, however many services we go to in the Abbey.

What does this mean in practice?

Of course all of this is not really theoretical, more a description of the way things have developed and actually are at Camas. But perhaps it's helpful to try to name some guidelines.

1. **Everyone – guests, staff, visiting Iona Community members and new members – has to be free to be, and be accepted, for who they are, and what they believe.** This does not mean that we have to like or agree with that, but that we recognise the right of people to be different, and to remain different.

2. **We reserve the right to differentiate between beliefs and practice.** Some of the beliefs and attitudes expressed by people at Camas may be deeply abhorrent to us. They may be racist, sexist, sectarian, homophobic, violent, etc., or they may just be in contradiction to our own religious views. Denying people the space to express their opinions will not make them change these opinions; it will simply push them into a dangerously unexamined place. But while we accept people's freedom to express opinions, we do not accept their right to practise them without limitation at Camas, in contradiction to the Iona Community's Peace and Justice commitment. So we will not accept racist, sexist, sectarian, homophobic, violent, practices. *We are committed to a practice of respect for everyone*, practices that infringe that commitment are not acceptable. The freedom of expression we offer to all will only work if it is a mutual freedom.

3. **Creating a safe space for acceptance and dialogue means paying sensitive attention to power dynamics.** If people – guests, staff, Iona Community members, etc. – are to feel comfortable and safe in expressing their opinions, we need to pay attention to some of the factors which inhibit them. This is especially important with people whose habitual experience is of being silenced, ignored or marginalised, or who experience themselves as disempowered in a variety of ways. Power tends to tilt in favour of those in the majority, those with structural authority, those with greater, or insider, knowledge, those who are most articulate. In any given week at Camas, these balances will shift somewhat, according to the group in residence, but there is, I think, an onus particularly

- on Christians to be sensitive to the fact that non-Christians may feel inhibited if they are in the minority

- on those in leadership roles at Camas to be sensitive to the need to reassure staff that they can express beliefs and opinions freely without worrying about 'getting into trouble' or being thought disloyal

- on staff to be sensitive to the advantage that being the 'insiders', those who belong, gives them over people who have just arrived, or who may be in a cultural context that is unfamiliar and threatening to them

- on those who are fluent with words and confident in expressing themselves to be sensitive to those who are more hesitant

All of these are basic principles of dialogue – equal voice. Furthermore, I would suggest that since Camas has a particular commitment to those who are marginalised, there should be a bias to giving way to those who have been silenced in either the Christian or the secular context. This is not an easy thing to do (I speak from experience) and requires a considerable degree of self-discipline, but also the use of methodologies which are designed to maximise participation, and which operate on the basis of asking questions rather than giving answers.

4. **The daily reflection times should be recognised as the standard Camas practice.** Because the community life at Camas is praxis-based (the integration of action and reflection), it should always grow out of the experience *of* Camas. This should apply whoever is staying, including the times when there are no guests. This is not just something we 'put on' for the guests, a part of the programme. It is a basic dynamic of the common life. To replace this reflective dynamic with imported worship is not, I think, appropriate.

5. **Any group should be free also to additionally hold their own religious practice, whether that is the Iona Community daily office, a communion service, Muslim prayers or a pagan ritual, and invite everyone to share in it, if they so desire.** But this should be additional to reflections, not instead of them.

What happens at Camas is, in part at least, a recognition of the fact that, perhaps unlike Iona, the majority of people who come as guests, and a significant minority of staff, are not Christians. It also represents a considerable voluntary dispossession, a giving up of power, by the Iona Community, who could quite validly insist that Camas maintains daily Christian worship. In that, perhaps, it reflects the actions of Jesus who voluntarily embraced powerlessness so that the weak and vulnerable could be empowered. It also reflects the kind of living within limits, of voluntary self-restraint, that we embrace as an ecological value, and sees it as a spiritual value. It requires considerable commitment, and perhaps sacrifice, on the part of staff, who forego the certainties and nurturing of Iona worship. So it also requires the Iona Community to support them, and to see this, not as a compromise or 'second best' but as a genuine engagement with a non-Christian culture, and an honest effort to create the conditions for interfaith (including secular faith) dialogue. It is a spiritual process, putting staff in somewhat the same context as many living with serious constraints on the practice of their faith (although no one's life is at risk here).

Above all, it takes as its basis two fundamental principles:

- An emphasis on our common humanity, and all that nurtures and sustains that, including the environment

- An emphasis, not on getting people to agree, but on helping people to love one another, though we are different and will remain different.[3]

Kathy Galloway

In the morning and evening we got to think and talk about things, and everyone sat in a circle and listened to each other.

Young person

We did 'sit spots' where we each found a quiet spot in the bay. We went back to the same spot each time and listened to nature all around us. I loved the smell of seaweed and variety in my spot. It felt so peaceful and calm.

Young person

Tom Forsyth – the Camas land reformer

Back in the 1980s, I used to be the Business Advisor to the Iona Community. Sheila Russell (now Bates) was the Camas Team Leader, and from time to time I'd walk down the winding track to talk through management and fundraising issues.

In those days there were still the salmon fishers operating from the bay. I remember that one of them was a woman, and this seemed strange and rather revolutionary to me, having been raised on the Isle of Lewis, where we were told that two things didn't mix with boats: women, and church ministers!

I loved the Chapel of the Nets at Camas. It invoked the power of that scene at the foot of Salvador Dali's painting of *Christ of Saint John of the Cross*. There, a shadowed sense of Jesus, almost invisible in the background, wanders towards the fishers, calling them to 'Follow me' and to become fishers of men. No wonder minister types didn't mix with boats. Too readily distracted from the job!

I recall, also from those days, the horror stories that Sheila had about kids from hard-pressed parts of our cities who'd never before experienced nature so much in the raw. Sometimes they'd have run away by the Monday morning. The police might have to be alerted. Come the Wednesday, however, they'd almost all be loving it. By the Saturday, some would have to be literally dragged in tears back on the bus. I've seen it for myself. Once, after running a week at the MacLeod Centre on Iona jointly with the late Margaret Legum and her husband, Colin, I too had to cajole a severely autistic young man back onto the bus. It shows how deeply these places can speak to qualities for which the soul yearns, but which are often lacking in the nature-deficit of city lives lived out in poverty.

The story about Camas that I want most to share here, might be an unexpected one. A near-forgotten and untold one. It's about those strange chains of events that just so happen. In the spring of 1991, I had finished working as the Community's Business Advisor, except in an honorary capacity that continued for a few years. I had moved to teaching human ecology at Edinburgh University – the relationships between the social environment and the natural environment. One day a call came through to my office. It was from John Harvey, then the Leader of the Iona Community. He explained that he was sending through to see me a sixty-year-old man called Tom Forsyth. Appointed by George MacLeod, he had been the Iona Community's Youth Secretary in the 1950s. Based at Camas, he had helped to run some of the camps for young offenders, the so-called Borstal boys.

'He's an original, is Tom,' said John, or words to that effect. 'He's a lynchpin of the crofting community at Scoraig, near Ullapool, and he has an idea for community land ownership on the Isle of Eigg. I told him I'd put a few quid in if he ever gets it off the ground. And I told him to go through to Edinburgh and talk to you.'

Tom's story was that God, for him, resided more in nature than in doctrines. He wasn't very successful at getting either the Borstal boys, or himself, along to church on Sundays. He wasn't even a member of any church. Eventually, this led to a starchy ultimatum.

'Either you join the Church,' said George, 'or that's it.'

'That's it,' replied Tom.

But the wily old founder of the Iona Community was already one move ahead. He knew that on the pilgrimage of life, God likes to send folks on the Hebridean scenic route. So it was that he shoehorned Tom into a new position with Jane Blaffer Owen at New Harmony, Indiana, in the United States. Here was where the industrialist Robert Owen, who was born in 1771 and who had created New Lanark on the banks of the River Clyde, had gone with his vision to build a utopian *community of equality*. Jane was related to Owen by marriage. She was an enthusiastic advocate of his ideas.

When George later visited New Harmony, he was impressed by what he saw of Tom's work there. One day they shared a long car journey. 'How about you, with your Quaker tendencies,' George proposed, kind of madly, from out of the blue, 'as Warden of Iona Abbey?'

An astonished Tom responded by drawing up a twenty-four page 'manifesto' for how he'd lead things. It was for a 'whole community'. Vegetable gardens, baking bread and fishing would interlace with the teachings of Thoreau, Merton and the Desert Fathers.

Probably, more consideration was given to getting bums off pews than onto them. Whatever, it was all too much for some of the dog-collared clergy of the time. Tom's future was not to be with the Iona Community. At least, not except in spirit. Instead, he adopted ten abandoned crofts at Ruigh'riabhach on the Scoraig Peninsula. He had met his first wife, Ray Soper, at the north end summer youth camp on Iona. Together they went on to raise their children Fergus, Morag, Fiona, Aaron and David. The Scoraig Peninsula had no road or mains electricity. Their 'back to the land' approach to rich but simple living helped to open up a fresh vision for crofting, and its diversification into areas like renewable energy.

This was not to forget the big world outside. Rather, as Tom later wrote, it was *'to become more fully human'*. Here he was, now, in my office at Edinburgh University. With encouragement from a few key islanders and a couple of accomplices, the artist Liz Lyon and a Lochwinnoch sheep farmer, Bob Harris, he had been working on a manifesto for the Isle of Eigg Trust. Together, we launched it a few months later. Here was a true human ecology, where the human and the ecological grew together. In Tom's own words in the document:

'When a shoot is grafted on to an established root, the green of the root must meet the green of the stalk. The green, or cambium, is the only living and dynamic part of the plant. In the cultivation of human beings the same natural law must apply.'

Tom passed away in 2018 after living in sheltered housing in Ullapool. His experience at Camas as a young man, of sharing a green vision for the Abbey with George MacLeod and of his crofts at the Ruigh'riabhach end of Scoraig are now the cambium of memory.

And Eigg? That's history. June 12th, 2022 will be the 25th anniversary of the community buyout. The process was complex. It involved many key actors. Tom's intervention played a catalytic role in the early days. Every time I now go to Eigg, I think of that early 1990s manifesto. I look at the local production of food. The islanders' own electricity grid that runs off renewables and attracts visitors from around the world. The affordable housing for the young and old. The plethora of small businesses. The restored little gem of a Catholic church that gives ecumenical service. The immense artistic creativity of both permanent and temporary residents, and the wonted work that it creates. I look at all these things, and I smile, for Tom's early manifesto has been far exceeded.

I think how, partly and in hidden ways, that had roots in Camas, on Iona, and with old George MacLeod. The mustard seed has blossomed to a mighty tree, scattering more seed across the world.

Tom knew about the cambium, because he had trained in horticulture at the Royal Botanic Garden in Edinburgh. Trees helped to give him patience in setting out and following a vision, a vision grafted to the deepest taproot.

We are talking here of faith that's sown in prayer. We are talking here of scenic routes that lead to being fishers of men. We are talking of a tree of life, the leaves of which are for the healing of the nations.

'That's it,' said Tom to George. Aye, that's it.

Or, to use a Hebrew word that means much the same thing. Amen.

Alastair McIntosh

A 'reflection'

'The Compass' at Camas is a cleared area in the woodland, a place for people to come and sit. But it also has four standing stones, marking the points of the compass, and in the middle a cairn, which is formed of big boulders and wee tiny stones, a variety of shapes and sizes. They have all been brought up from the beach by groups as they come up for reflections. Each of them represents a hope, a fear, a burden, a relationship … One stone has 'new beginning' written on it alongside two figures: the first figure is behind bars, and the second is outside in the sunshine. The stone was painted by one of the boys from Polmont YOI. We asked them to write a hope or a plan for the future on their stone and then put it on the cairn. It was very, very touching to see that. The young man who took part explained: 'We had a stone each and we had to write something on it that reminded us of an experience we had during our time at Camas. All the stones were placed together, and I wrote on mine "a new beginning" cos once I get out of the jail it would be good for me to start something good, in college or university, and start totally different to how my life was before.'[4]

Lizz Spence

I liked the 'reflection' when we went off and found something that represented our week at Camas and then brought it back to the circle of people. I brought a football cos I enjoyed playing football there, and because all week we worked well as a team doing jobs and having fun and everyone in the team matters and we all helped each other.

Young person

I will think about spirituality as part of everything I do.

Young person

Aristotle and Pooh would have understood

Since the Iona Community began running Camas, thousands of people have passed through either as guests or staff. I think it would be fair to say that for the majority of these people it was a powerful experience. Some, including myself, would go as far as to say that it was an experience which strongly influenced the direction of their life. Many, however, find difficulty in attempting to explain exactly what it is about the Camas experience which stirred up such deeply felt emotions. What happens to people at Camas, how does it happen, and how can the learning gained be understood and transferred back to everyday life? Not easy questions. However, I have a feeling that Aristotle would have understood; I think Pooh Bear would have understood as well. Neither Pooh nor Aristotle are available for comment so, with the help of their writings, I've decided to have a humble stab at understanding the Camas experience myself.

Before looking at what people take away from Camas, we have to identify what it is that Camas intends to give to people. What is the Camas 'mission'?

When George MacLeod set up Camas, he surely recognised that it is a place which has very special physical qualities. It is a peaceful place, a nurturing place, a place which cradles you but at the same time exposes you to the raw beauty of the natural elements of the world. It is the perfect place to make use of external adventure activities in order to facilitate the ultimate adventure: the inward adventure.

I was joint Leader at Camas during 1993 with Craig Ross, and early in the season we recognised the importance of having a clear mission. We'd both recently read Colin Mortlock's *The Adventure Alternative* and resonated with his work. Inspired by his writing, we adopted the following as the Camas mission statement:

'To provide an experience in a wilderness environment which will lead to an individual's development of:

> *love, respect and awareness of self, in balance with*
> *love, respect and awareness of others, in balance with*
> *love, respect and awareness of the environment.'*

Camas makes use of adventure activities in order to facilitate this mission. The activities themselves are only a small part of the overall Camas experience. They are the tool, the medium employed for teaching and learning. This seems to suit the physical surroundings and the client groups at Camas. On the whole Camas' groups are young people from urban environments such as inner cities. Such groups benefit from a setting which is devoid of distractions, totally clear of the day-to-day normalities – no shops, no cars, no pubs, no electricity, never mind no TV. Camas is raw; there is no escape from dealing with relationships.

So how do these activities tie into the overall aims of Camas? What is their purpose and what do participants gain from them?

Activities such as kayaking, raft-building, hillwalking, camping and problem-solving all provide obvious learning opportunities, such as teamwork, listening skills, leadership and communication. It is my opinion, however, that such experience-based activities also provide something much bigger. They are the tools which can be used to provide a specific type of learning, a type which is instinctual and which enhances knowledge of self, others and the environment. Aristotle and Pooh Bear have words of wisdom on this type of learning:

'All people by nature desire to know. An indication of this is the delight we take in our senses; for even apart from their usefulness they are loved for themselves … With a view to action experience seems in no respect inferior to art, and those of experience succeed even better than those who have theory without experience.'[5]

Aristotle, 384–322 BC

'You can't help respecting anybody who can spell TUESDAY, even if he doesn't spell it right; but spelling isn't everything. There are days when spelling Tuesday simply doesn't count.'[6]

Pooh Bear, 1928

Both Aristotle and Pooh recognised that there are two basic types of knowledge. Left-brain or rational knowledge deals with information and facts and is ultimately for problem-solving. Right brain or instinctual knowledge is a more creative and holistic type of knowledge. It is concerned with knowledge of self, others and the environment together with morals and values. It cannot be taught but can only be drawn out and built upon. Western education systems tend to concentrate overly on the left-brain knowledge and from an early age we are taught to separate and divide rather than approach life from a more holistic angle. We need to seek new ways in which to redress this imbalance. The type of experience-based learning which Camas offers is one way of doing this.

I was made aware of the full potential which is offered by experiential learning during a week's kayaking. Our group came across a large section of rapids on the River Findhorn. These rapids were bigger than anything I had ever paddled before and I was very tempted to get out of my boat and walk down the bank. After much deliberation, I talked myself into shooting the rapids. After having successfully negotiated the section, my instructor invited me to paddle back upstream and to play on the larger stoppers (standing waves). Once in the stoppers, I found that my body was relaxed and acting without thought. The same thing happened when I capsized. It was as if I was in the roll position before my mind had time to tell my body to get into it. It was a completely instinctual action without thought process. What did I learn from that experience? That my abilities are far greater than I had expected. That I felt very comfortable and supported within the group. That I could relate to the river in a whole new way. For a few seconds I was flowing with it and was part of it. I had not conquered it: it had allowed me to play with it. A direct experience had provided insight into myself, my companions and my environment.

The outdoor activities at Camas call mainly on the right-brain thought processes. Participants are asked to re-employ the type of in-built learning skills with which they taught themselves to walk and talk. If participants are judged in any way, it is by their effort and not upon their success. We live in a society which is forever judging and forever putting down. Throughout our schooling we are endlessly tested, and for the majority of Camas guests this testing can be equated with failing. At Camas, however, there is no such thing as failure. Spelling Tuesday never counts at Camas!

Within the safety guidelines at Camas, there are a number of activities that can be offered and tailored in such a way as to provide participants with the type of breakthrough adventure which I previously described. Something as straightforward as getting into a kayak can be a breakthrough for some visitors. Climbing a steep hill will be a breakthrough for others. Of course, the adventure need not involve physical duress. Watching a sunset or feeling a peat bog between your toes can provide equally powerful breakthrough experiences.[7]

Neil Harvey

Circle-making

Over the years I went backwards and forwards to Camas, first as a volunteer and then as a facilitator, I shared many 'circle-making' or 'mandala' workshops with schools, youth groups, adult groups and as part of staff training sessions.

Why do this in circles/mandalas?

The circle is a potent symbol.

With no beginning and no end, a circle radiating light from its centre has been reproduced again and again across time and cultures as a deeply felt representation of the nature and mystery of the universe and creation.

Circles and spirals are found everywhere in nature, appearing in the minutiae of shells, flowers, cells, nuclei, atoms – and in the vastness of swirling galaxies.

The purpose and value of mandala-making

In many societies and spiritual paths, circle-/mandala-making is a form of prayer or meditation. As a shape the circle has unique power to satisfy our longing for an image and experience of wholeness.

By placing their individual experiences within the context of circular wholeness, circle-/mandala-making was a useful reflection tool to enable groups to take stock and have an overview of their time at Camas; to feedback to themselves highlights, challenges and lessons learnt. They were also often used to help people think about broader questions and what they might take forward with them from Camas when they crossed the threshold back to 'life as usual'. Questions such as: 'What do I really want for myself and my life?' 'What makes a happy, valuable and purposeful life, and what matters to me most?' For both those who came to Camas with very specific beliefs and those who came with none at all, circle-making allowed an open space in which to share core values and ideas.

There are many things that can't be said in words and many self-discoveries to be made beneath language. Circle-making allowed for a depth of self-expression that lies in a place deeper than talking. It was an immediately accessible way for individuals to develop confidence in their own creativity, often when they felt they hadn't got any. They could be engaged with it at whatever level felt comfortable as a way of sharing a window into each other's lives and perspectives.

Making a mandala

We always began our circle-making with a settling activity, such as a guided relaxation to create focus and stillness. This was followed by a blindfolding activity in pairs, with one person blindfolded and the other leading in companionable silence. This supported participants to be more deeply connected with their senses in the moment – to stop, look, feel, smell, touch and listen with full awareness.

The next step was always to find the 'right' place – a spot which individuals felt naturally drawn to in the Camas landscape. The circles could be large or small, abstract or pictorial, some were highly intricate, some very simple, some an exploration of pattern, texture and the joy of colour. It was always emphasised that the process of making a circle was more important than the finished product. Because they were almost always made outside and from natural materials lying around (nothing growing was ever picked) – stones, feathers, seaweed – the circles felt like a continuation of Camas itself and the direct contact participants had throughout their week with the elements, when daily immersed in nature. They were a treat for the part of us all that still loves to beachcomb and forage, finding treasures for making everywhere.

We took time, when all the circles had been made, to look at and appreciate one another's creations but without imposing analysis or judgement. I was always surprised with, and often moved by, what people came up with. The range and depth of their creativity was huge, sometimes profound, often funny. One young man had his girlfriend sitting in the middle of his.

There were countless patterns made with sheep poo, with comments like 'life can be shit', 'shit is spiritual too', 'we do it, we need it'.

We very rarely, if ever, photographed them. As they were often built along the tideline, hour by hour the wind and the waves dismantled them, leaving no trace: a truly ecological activity echoing the impermanence of all things.

Debra Hall

Circles

… and there was not enough time (for this is life)
and there was all time, for the circle goes beyond time
and in the time beyond time we dreamt a dream together
of the circle and the seasons
of the power of the waters
and the generations of humankind
of giving and receiving and suffering and learning
and the Great Spirit whispered our names in dreams
the name of all who love the mystery

and we saw with amazement
that everything we needed
was contained within the circle
all healing
all justice
all hope
all courage
all knowledge …[8]

Kathy Galloway

We came to Camas with another church group; we didn't know each other before. At first there were tensions as theological differences came to the fore … and then a reflection about 'loving your neighbour' reminded us of what really matters. That's when the friendship started to grow and everyone started to relax.

Group Leader

I was inspired to see our group sitting listening intently to each other in the Chapel of the Nets. We are going to try to introduce reflection times back home.

Group Leader

Encounter and exchange

There is a challenge in putting down words about Camas on a page, as it is so rooted in the power of experience: the experience of sharing the common life, the experience of outdoor activities, the experience of living simply with nature, and the experience of each individual and group. These experiences take place through the encounter and exchange that happens daily at Camas – with self, others, the sacred and the environment. Former Abbey Warden Brian Woodcock once talked about '*accepting the Mystery*' and this resonates at Camas, where this heart-opening, somewhat indefinable experience is often affectionately called the 'Camas magic' – for me this is Love weaving Her way through people and place in the ordinary, everyday, down-to-earth things of planting trees, baking bread, singing songs, swimming in the sea and washing up.

The Iona Community is known for its words – liturgy, poetry, prose, protest and justice and peace statements are all a powerful part of its theological and creative expression. In 2001 the Camas team was asked to write a liturgy for a book. A typical Camas week involves walking down a boggy track for a mile and a half, possibly in pouring rain, with a group of young people – half-filled with excitement, half-filled with anxiety – singing, complaining, asking questions, laughing and shouting: this may not be the typical context for liturgy that comes to mind! Yet, having walked the track many times, this experience is grounded in justice and peace and has a rhythm and ritual that feels like an embodiment of liturgy. Camas epitomises the engaged theology and the concerns and values of the Iona Community – in working with vulnerable young people and adults, in caring for the earth, in creating community and in welcoming people of all faiths and none.

Rhythm and ritual are present in the daily, weekly, seasonal and yearly experience of Camas. These are cornerstones that support a safe and sacred space within which there is freedom and flow. In a place where physical safety is paramount, spiritual and emotional safety are essential. Camas is a place where the spiritual – that which is rooted in the core of all – can be explored and expressed freely; where respect, understanding, difference and diversity are honoured and encouraged.

It is a place where young people and adults who are often silenced or oppressed can be heard, seen and welcomed, a place where they can engage with what matters to them in their own words and ways. A place where those who are often classed as 'different' or even 'less' by society can find a voice and glimpse something of their own potential. At a time when young people face so many pressures – homelessness and poverty; debt and drugs; questions about identity, belonging and worth – safe places to relax and rest, to explore and grow, are invaluable.

There are many creative ways to enable young people to explore a sense of the sacred in their own way. At Camas the emphasis is on being alongside people, on listening with loving kindness, on creating conversations and learning and sharing with young people with openness and acceptance. Because of their life experiences, many of the young people are vulnerable, yet often worldly-wise beyond their years. Tough shells often hide deep hurt and painful stories. Many come from places where the church is a class and culture apart. Strikingly, one young person who came to Camas had spent time sleeping rough in the porch of his local church but had never been inside.

Reflections take place at Camas each morning and evening and are short, focused times when people can slow down and connect. For me, they mirror the way in which Jesus used the environment around him to tell stories and encourage dialogue rather than imposing meaningless rituals on his followers. Taking their themes from the experiences of the day, and using ideas from liberation theology and experiential learning, reflections offer a creative way of 'growing in love, awareness and respect' (from the Camas mission statement). For example, a reflection on trust uses the experiences of the day's abseiling; a reflection on friendship uses the feelings generated by pitching a tent together. For young people, who may have a sense of spirituality, but who may not verbalise this in traditional religious terms, these reflections offer an honest and meaningful way to engage. There are none of the usual visual symbols of church services – no sermons, books or collection plates – but there is the naming of hurts and of hopes, there is laughter and love, there is the sharing of doubts and dreams. One young person who came with an LGBTQ+ youth project, and who had been badly beaten and made homeless by his family because of his sexuality, said: 'Camas has taught me I am a valuable person who can care for others and enjoy my life.' Another young person from the same group commented, 'Camas is our spiritual home, where we can be who we are without fear and without prejudice.'

Camas cannot provide answers for the complex issues young people face today, but it can offer a place which complements the ongoing work of the many dedicated project workers who bring young people to Camas. In the terminology of youth work, Camas is about personal development, group dynamics, team-building and issue-based work. In the language of spirituality, it is about healing and hope, affirmation and acceptance, freedom and friendship; it is about justice and peace in loving relationship. If young people take even a fraction of these experiences away with them, then their visit is worthwhile.

Although structured liturgies don't often come out of Camas, the pattern of time there feels like a living liturgy. It is the power of experience and the presence of Love dancing where She will in each encounter and exchange that inspires, challenges, changes and brings life.[9]

Rachel McCann

Struggles and dreams

If Iona, Corrymeela and L'Arche bring worship and issues of social justice and peace ever closer together, Camas removes the divide altogether. The two become one. Set worship disappears; life takes over. To many Camas guests, the words, symbols and formality of the church are alien. Shared reflection must and does arise from the guests themselves, when they are ready, with their words and symbols. They literally share themselves – their struggles and dreams.[10]

Brian Woodcock

We were worried it might be a bit 'churchy', as none of us go to church. But it wasn't: the reflections in the morning and evening started and ended the day really well; they made us think about things that matter. People were interested in what we thought; no one tried to tell us what to think.

Young person

On the last night when our group led the reflection, we got everyone to write down something positive about everyone who had been there that week, including the Camas team. There were tears and laughter as each person read their messages; everyone felt encouraged and affirmed. It was a special evening I won't forget.

Group Leader

This has been one of the most wonderful and meaningful experiences of my life and I just want to thank everyone.

Young person

Ropes of connection

As I write, Dragon-class megatankers of fracked ethylene gas arrive from the U.S. to be refined in Grangemouth. Indigenous groupings from all across North America gather over the proposed Dakota oil pipeline to protect clean water; but why is it that our own nations don't gather en masse to protect our own streams, rivers and seas?

I am one with the idea that it is because of ancestral trauma that there is no awareness, respect or love for the environment, and because of this there is no visceral connection to it. This cycle of disconnection is reinforcing; for three generations now, our youth have been denied a basis tenet of human health, denied the basis of creativity: access to free play in nature.

In *Last Child in the Woods*, Richard Louv notes: '*Our society is teaching young people to avoid direct experience in nature. That lesson is delivered in schools, families, even organisations devoted to the outdoors, and codified into the legal and regulatory structures of our many communities. Our institutions, urban/suburban design, and cultural attitudes unconsciously associate nature with doom – while disassociating the outdoors from joy and solitude.*'[11]

Atrophy of environment, then, is as much a cultural catastrophe as it is an ecological one. If we are to survive as a culture, then we have to cultivate an attitude of co-creation rather than a degenerative one. Research is telling us that time in nature is not leisure – it is an essential component for human growth.

After a nine-year study of wilderness programmes, James Kaplan conceived his idea of the '*restorative environment*'; he outlines that in unstructured, spontaneous experience in the outdoors lies the optimal way to train coordination and concentration. He went on to prove that: '*Directed attention fatigue (is) marked by impulsive behaviour, agitation, irritation, and inability to concentrate … If you can find an environment where attention is automatic, you allow directed attention to rest. And that means an environment that's strong on fascination.*'[12]

In his summary of Kaplan's research, Richard Louv goes as far as to say that: '*the fascination factor … is restorative, and it helps relieve people from direction-attention fatigue*'.[13]

Strings become ropes …

This has held true for my experience at Camas. The best ideas have been sourced from the resultant 'quiet mind' found in unstructured time outside, against the impossible odds and hours, through non-directed attention, practising the core routines of nature connection. These ideas have directly informed my practice, and our volunteers have consistently heard the call: '*Support curiosity over and over and you will find passion in that individual. If you find passion in that individual, and support that passion over and over, you will get vision.*'[14]

A visceral interaction with one species becomes a tangible string to that aspect of creation, *if* the experience is reflected upon with mentors or peers who possess good questions and a listening ear. As neuroscience tells us: '*As we fire we wire*', i.e. if a young person develops a relationship with that same species or place over time, strings become strong ropes of connection. We tend to care for things that we have strong relationships with. This is why we emphasise reviewing direct experiences during our daily reflections at Camas.

8 chapters of the Book of Nature

I offer, then, these '8 chapters of the Book of Nature' as a multi-sensorial relationship of meaning and memory to a culture that has forgotten how to play. It is an integrated coding of a central idea: 'honour the integrity of creation'. Its author, mentor Jon Young, in his conception of the 8 chapters, plotted them sun-wise on a wheel, starting in the east. One imagines it is not unlike the regenerative wheeled cross that our Celtic ancestors would serve. Young advises full immersion into all the chapters, '*balancing knowledge and experience of all aspects of nature by cycling through these eight chapters, seizing opportunities as they arise in the moment*':[15]

1. *Hazards: a call to be alert and to use common sense*

2. *Motivating species: things to catch, eat and climb, and tend*

3. *Mammals, and other hard to see, yet totally trackable, critters*

4. *Plants: nature's grocery store and medicine cabinet*

5. *Ecological indicator species: how it all works together*

6. *Heritage species: wisdom of the ancestors*

7. *Trees: tools of human survival*

8. *Birds: the messengers of the wilderness.*[16]

This flexible and open-eyed approach not only honours nature's way of organic unfolding, but also honours the varying interests of your participants and co-mentors.

It is this emergent curriculum that arises out of direct experience, in a spirited, cooperative enquiry with participants and volunteers, that gives rise to collective and individual meaning. These relationships are so real, they cannot be taken or explained away from an individual. When awe and reverence arise, unfettered and unblinkered from any pedagogy, out of direct relationship with nature, spirituality is revealed in its naked form. As the Camas mission statement reads: '*We seek to enable growth in love, respect and awareness of ourselves, each other, God and the environment.*'

Hazel tree boy: A Camas story

During Work Week in October of last year, eight young boys from Muir-house joined us on a group forage of the Atlantic rainforest remnants around Pennyghael, collecting hazelnuts from the treetops in buckets for growing on at a tree nursery in the Camas garden. The week's graft had been supplemented by the fun of fishing, along with reflective tales of the relationship between salmon and the hazelnut. The boys set to the task with glee, shaking the boughs and clambering over each other to collect the nuts. Adults, being slightly more sedentary, stayed at ground level and shouted words of encouragement and direction. One boy, eyes ablaze with excitement, shook his bough with hands and feet – and suddenly there was a loud 'crack' as a branch gave way. I lunged forward as he rolled gently downwards through the canopy, suspended by layers of branches, before wriggling and falling to the next; another 'crack' issued and he fell the last few feet and I caught him in my arms as a silence descended. We got eye contact and I could feel the energy coursing through him. He was *fully* alive. 'Again! Again!' he shrieked with excitement.[17]

Rhyddian Knight

I loved being outside for the reflections, especially in the woodland when we listened to the birds and touched the trees. We were joking and calling each other 'treehuggers', but we all enjoyed it really.

Young person

Simplicity and generosity

'Garden Week' was a full-on 'eucharistic' experience shared with twenty-five or so other people. 'Eucharistic' because we shared what we had with each other, and above all shared ourselves. This community is off-grid and broadly self-sufficient, and it opened my eyes to how little we humans really need! But what we did genuinely need for our physical well-being in terms of food, clothing, friendship, dignity, compassion was given in abundance, and was really powered by the loving intention of the group as a whole.

It made it real for me that 'All you need is love'. It really is as simple as that, because from love/connection flows all else in life. I virtually lost all sense of 'needing' though, due to the generosity of the environment. I also had a deep feeling of safety, knowing that if I did need something, the community would enable it.

There's something really wonderful about simplifying our lives like this. Without the usual excess, you can see what you have with so much clarity and from that flows gratitude, and from that flows joy and trust. And from those things flows even more love.[18]

Angela Kurton

It's a soul-searching place that made me feel good about myself.

Young person

Slowing down and stepping away from phones and computers to reflect on life and be in nature was something us leaders valued as much as the kids did.

Group Leader

I have felt more at peace and have thought more about others' feelings.

Young person

The Chapel of the Nets

At the beginning of each week when guests arrived, we would all gather upstairs, sit round in a circle on the nets and hear the story of Camas: quarrying, lighthouses, fishing, borstal boys, adventures … We'd think about all the people who have spent time at Camas and been part of its story, and then each week the people who were there would re-create the space in the middle of our circle anew. Each season, each week, the people that are at Camas are the people who belong to Camas for that time.

Dot Stewart

A new community

When we welcome a group each week to the first group reflection, we start with talks about the history of Camas and the different communities who have lived here over the years. We then, using artefacts, or 'junk' left at Camas over the years, mark out the new community which has been formed, making a sculpture together. We might notice how different we all may be – our backgrounds, culture, experience and beliefs – but we then highlight the one thing that joins us – the experience of being at Camas: living here, living simply, living together – sharing the experience of the week. The sculpture is a symbol of the group – and no two sculptures will ever be the same.[19]

Mary Ireson

Something there

The Chapel of the Nets changes with different groups and individuals adding and subtracting artefacts over the years. In this way they own it. With its flickering candles, rattling slates and dimly lit faces, it is an evocative and special place: 'If the walls could speak …' Many young people, despite their scepticism, have found something there and I don't feel I need to define what it was; these people include staff as well as guests, and although the place of reflection has evolved it still is one of several key things that sets Camas apart from being 'just another outdoor Centre'.

Mark Jardine

What it means to be human and connected

Camas is a place which is constantly trying to create a space within which people can explore the very truth of what it means to be human and to be connected. A space that is as much about the outside as the in. In this space, 'the church' is the Chapel of the Nets, a beautiful space full of random discoveries which speak of the faith – in all facets of God, Christian or otherwise – of all of the people who have sat and shared stories in it. Previous young people who have found themselves here have left their mark. It is a space that the visitor owns, but also holds responsibility for.

Alex Clare-Young

Chapel of the Nets

Remembered – left
at the back of my mind
like an old, closed book –
a loft full of dusk,
nets, a gathered sense
of reverence and tradition.

But now we enter
a big echoing room –
a bare space
like a blank sheet of paper
waiting to be written –
open to become, in our hands,
a place of worship again.[20]

Jan Sutch Pickard

Despite the dark

Sometimes it is not strange to think that God
is out behind the darkness of the night;
that there is hope, however small and odd
the thought might be. Sometimes it is all right
believing that the good will yet win out
against the weight of hate, and that the light
will shine again when all the voices doubt,
and you have fought the dark with all your might.
Lift up your hand and see its grace anew,
and open up the window to the dawn
to hear the birds that sing the morning in.
For this is still a thousand times more true
than fear and lies and giving in to wrong.
So keep your faith – believe, begin again.[21]

Kenneth Steven

I carry hope

I carry hope
like the kite in the boot of my car,
waiting
for the moment to let it fly … high.
Sometimes it goes days without coming out
but I know it's there
and given the opportunity I'll launch it.

I've launched it on beaches with friends
and outside hospitals
when hope needs to be seen
to be tugging at life
and showing the way.

I launched it on the track this week;
at first tangled and unable to fly
when there was no wind,
the kite battered along on the ground at risk of being torn,
of not being able to fly again.

But the track cleared
and the wind came
and up she went
like a beacon in the sky.

Launching hope makes you late for dinner …
It makes you walk more slowly,
looking up
instead of head-on.
You see things never seen before,
the pattern of the unseen
is what holds hope up there;
it is proof that there is more than we know.

So I tucked the kite in my bed,
worried that hope might get stolen and broken,
and it was there when I climbed in with my pyjamas.

The next day, as the sun shone and the wind blew,
I knew that the time had come –
and boy did hope fly!
She danced and dived,
tugged and dropped,
and hands young and old universally understood.

For a time I lay sleeping on the beach,
hope held in someone else's hands …
and then I went to find her.

Freedom released
into the wildness of the air
whilst on the ground I danced,
twisting and turning,
rising and falling,
the St Bernard's Waltz on the ground
with my partner in the sky.
From a distance hope could be seen
like a smoke signal declaring my love
in colours bold and bright.

The kite didn't fly on Wednesday,
a feeling
moving inside me,
sending me
spiralling
down,
like when
the wind
drops.

But hope visited me in cups of tea
and in eyes that really looked with love
and soon it was time to move –
and the only way was up!
I climbed and climbed, up and up,
with the kite first in my hand and then in my backpack.
I scrambled and feared I would never go up or down,
but be stuck
in this halfway point
that made me tired and dizzy and
wishing I'd never brought others to this place.

Then the sky was calling to me,
the sea too,
and the adventure of travelling a path I had long
avoided.

Hope waited at the top
resting,
but watching,
ready to move,
but giving enough string for me to
come into my own flight.
And through the movement I was born for,
not the stationary paralysis built by fear,
but the climbing through past memories that haunt me,
I reached paradise.

The water was turquoise and sparkling
like an Aladdin's cave dropped in the ocean;
and as far from all the things in our lives that
steal hope like a thief in the night,
we were all free and living out hope.

There was swimming and climbing,
and snoozing and chatting.

There was feasting on loaves baked with love and
loaded with bananas and chocolate
and not one of us there was anywhere
but
in
that
moment.

Hope lived there.
As the kite flew at her highest,
she had other places to take us.
For as we filled with our own hope
and this true joy,
she went higher still –
calling to somewhere new.

The kite tail flapped behind me
as I climbed onwards from paradise,
striding out to discover butterwort and sand martins' places of residence.

Over crags and through bogs we travelled a new way,
with invitations to beaches undiscovered
and pointers to a life lived long ago,
with cows and sheep and places to shelter.

For hope lived then too,
in the same sand and hills and sea
and I know she will dwell there for all time,
such is her way.

The return brought us rest and refreshment;
a return of life and another beach
and another feast.

We gathered to be well-fed;
to laugh and tell stories and wonder at our lives and

how a Lorne sausage could be the gateway to this life.
The fire was stoked and
hope found a new home
as it burned and warmed and gathered us in.

Hope was keeping our beds warm too,
a snug hot-water bottle,
making the cold of the night
seem warm and inviting.

Hope was still there in the morning;
with her bags packed
and the load shared she set foot
on a familiar path.

Hope made a circle and with gratitude said goodbye
and got on the bus.
But she got in the car with us too,
and she went back down the track
wrapped around wrists in wool.

Sarah Brown

For the Camas staff

We give thanks for the Camas staff,
for their creativity and commitment,
love and laughter,
passion and patience,
and for their work and wisdom.

With open hearts and skilful hands,
they offer welcome and care to young people;
may they *'grow in love, awareness and respect of self, others,
the Creator and the earth'*.

May all of us, wherever we are,
welcome the stranger,
hear your whisper in the trees,
see your beauty as the heron soars
and honour all of creation.[22]

Rachel McCann

Notes:

1. From *Iona: God's Energy: The Vision and Spirituality of the Iona Community*, Norman Shanks, Hodder and Stoughton, 1999, second edition, Wild Goose Publications, 2009
2. From *The Sacred Garden*, BBC Radio Scotland, 2004
3. From *Living by the Rule: The Rule of the Iona Community*, Kathy Galloway, Wild Goose Publications, 2010
4. From *The Sacred Garden*, BBC Radio Scotland, 2004
5. From *The Basic Works of Aristotle*, edited by Richard McKeon, Penguin Random House Press, 1948
6. From *The Tao of Pooh*, by Benjamin Hoff and E.H. Shepard, Mandarin, 1991
7. From *Coracle*, the magazine of the Iona Community, 1995, Kathy Galloway (Ed.)
8. From *The Dream of Learning Our True Name*, Kathy Galloway Wild Goose Publications, 2004
9. Adapted from *Coracle*, the magazine of the Iona Community, 2000, Kathy Galloway (Ed.) and *Holy Ground: Liturgies & Worship Resources for an Engaged Spirituality*, Helen Boothroyd and Neil Paynter (Eds.), Wild Goose Publications, 2005
10. From *Holy Ground: Liturgies & Worship Resources for an Engaged Spirituality*, Helen Boothroyd and Neil Paynter (Eds.), Wild Goose Publications, 2005
11. From *Last Child in the Woods: Saving Our Children from Nature Deficit Disorder*, Richard Louv, Algonquin Books, 2019
12. From *Last Child in the Woods: Saving Our Children from Nature Deficit Disorder*, Richard Louv, Algonquin Books, 2019
13. From *Last Child in the Woods: Saving Our Children from Nature Deficit Disorder*, Richard Louv, Algonquin Books, 2019

14. From *Last Child in the Woods: Saving Our Children from Nature Deficit Disorder*, Richard Louv, Algonquin Books, 2019

15. Jon Young, Village Builders programme, 8 Shields: http://8shields.com

16. From *Coyote's Guide to Connecting with Nature*, Jon Young, Ellen Haas, Evan McGown, Owlink Media

17. From *Coracle*, the magazine of the Iona Community, Neil Paynter (Ed.), 2010

18. From *Coracle*, the magazine of the Iona Community, Neil Paynter (Ed.), 2018-2019

19. From *Coracle*, the magazine of the Iona Community, 2010, Neil Paynter (Ed.)

20. From *Pushing the Boat Out*, Wild Goose Publications, Kathy Galloway (Ed.), 1995

21. From *West*, Kenneth Steven, Wild Goose Publications, 2019

22. From *In the Gift of This New Day: Praying with the Iona Community*, Neil Paynter (Ed.), Wild Goose Publications, 2015

A sense of place

The Iona Community is committed to ecological justice and states that, 'handled with integrity, creation can provide for the needs of all, but not for the greed which leads to injustice and inequality'.[1] At Camas this is evident in a sustainable lifestyle that is educational in theory and practice. Being in tune with the cycle of the seasons, the rhythms of the earth and the elements is both a way of life and a necessity at Camas.

For many guests who come from an urban environment, being in a wild place can be a powerful experience. As Kathy Galloway says: 'The work at Camas is so important – it offers an alternative vision of community, ecology and sustainability to young people whose experience of those things is often entirely absent or destructive'.[2]

Groups and staff engage with the environment through the programme of activities – kayaking, coasteering, swimming, abseiling, nature connection, gardening, foraging, cooking, tree-planting, beach and hill walks, wild camping, conservation, peat-cutting, creative arts, reflections … and through all aspects of the daily life and work of the centre.

The following pieces reflect the ecological ethos of Camas and focus on key places in its landscape – the garden, the woodlands, the buildings, the sea and the track.

We've had a fantastic, challenging, enlightening week in a beautiful, wild place.

Group Leader

The best thing about being here was how peaceful it was. The scenery is nothing like you would expect. The thing that surprised me most was how I had lived in Scotland for twenty years and I had never experienced how nice it was.

Young person

I think the particular magic of Camas is that there are so many things you can get individually in other places, all in the same place – the isolation, the sea, hills, air, the wildness, the activities, rocks, caves.

Group Leader

The pushback

The commitment to a subsistence lifestyle is one of the handshakes of the regenerative design movement. It's part of a responsible 'pushback' against the mainstream; meeting our needs creatively in right relationship with our non-human neighbours.

Shared tasks at Camas are, for the large part, rhythmical, cyclical and seasonal: Bread is baked; food is harvested or foraged from garden and shore; eggs are fresh from the coop not the Co-op; kelp and human waste becomes friable humus for our fruit crops to complete the circle. All items we can't provide for under our own steam are linear – to be specific: wheel-barrowed from the tarmac down the track.

Rhyddian Knight

A simple lifestyle

Living simply and with respect for the environment around us is a given here at Camas. We rely on the wind and sun for power to heat the water and operate the fridge and washing machine. The weather impacts on what activities we can do and the way our week gets shaped. The elements are so much more fundamental to what happens in our day, as most of our days are spent outside in nature's great playground. One of my favourite comments from the evaluation forms is this from a young person:

'Camas is better than Xbox 360. I would give up TV for this lifestyle.'[3]

Mary Ireson

The thing that I love about Camas is that it is a place where almost nobody has what they want, but everybody has what they need. There's no electricity, you can't bring your electronic gadgets, but everybody has enough to eat, good companionship, a nice peat fire to sit round and we are surrounded by beauty. It does remind you about what really matters.[4]

Kathy Galloway

I will go outside more and enjoy life.

Young person

I will treat our planet with more respect.

Young person

1. The Garden

Myriad dedicated people have tended the Camas garden and woodlands over many years. It's notable that by the middle of the 1800s, the quarry-workers at Camas were known across Mull as having productive vegetable gardens.[5] Here some of those involved in more recent times tell their stories ...

Reflections of a one-time Camas Gardener

At my interview for the Camas Gardener job, I declared with confidence that I could double the area of garden ground under cultivation. I took up the post on the first day of spring 1983 – and wore wellies most days for the following eighteen months.

I chose to make my home in a modestly insulated shed previously occupied by my horticultural predecessor, Ingrid. I liked the proverb she left pinned up on the wall: *'If you have two loaves, give one to the poor. Sell the other and buy hyacinths to feed your soul.'* I liked the affirmation we uttered daily in the Camas liturgy too: *'Neither length of time nor distance of space can separate us from those whom we love.'*

I had been personally inspired by the then Iona Community Leader Ron Ferguson's new year pep talk to young volunteers, saying to the effect that Columba, like Jesus before him, had been just one person, who had effectively achieved positive lasting change in the world by putting vision and commitment into action, and living out personal beliefs with uncompromising integrity. Accordingly, it follows that nobody should underestimate the difference their life and actions may potentially make, when they know they are being true to a greater good, even (and perhaps especially) in adverse circumstances.

I also came to appreciate the wise advice of salmon fisherman Bertie MacRae. Early on he declared to me: 'You can keep a garden, or you can keep goats, but in the end, you can't do both.' Right enough – my efforts to upgrade garden fences with select scraps of firewood imported from the Pennyghael sawmill were endless, and all too often futile. All new arrivals at Camas were strictly instructed concerning the importance of keeping garden gates closed, but I could only be philosophical about the ingeniously determined and sometimes astoundingly athletic break-ins of our inscrutable milk providers, Nancy, Bessie and especially Zimba. Besides free-range sheep, we also had to contend with occasional visits from straying cows too, so I was glad of Bertie's guidance when it came to putting up a proper fence from scratch, fit for purpose.

A version of the Benedictine motto *'Laborare est orare'* ('To work is to pray') was freshly repainted on the door of the Chapel of the Nets in those days. If it be true, then I spent most of my waking hours in prayer of one kind or another. I took proud satisfaction in the blending of soiled goat and chicken bedding with collected sheep droppings, seaweed, green bracken and weeds to create steaming heaps of vital compost. This essential alchemy generally failed to win much appreciation or engagement from Camas colleagues or visitors alas, alongside competing attractions of kayaking and orienteering adventures, and such daily obligations as mustering firewood for the evening. Some seemed not to share my enthusiasm for developing a more holistic ecosystem, even suggesting that trees did not belong at Camas! In this light, it is all the more heartening, a generation later, to behold the wee forest thriving there, affording shelter for more effective crop production and biodiversity.

A visiting chum more than earned his spartan keep and shed-floor space by mentoring and supporting me in breaking ground in the newly fenced 'park', where the land had been out of cultivation for perhaps a century or more. The two of us used spades to cut and flip a long straight line of hinged turves, before slicing another set of parallel grass flaps and folding them back to within a spade spit of the first row. The grassy gap remaining between the upturned sods was filled with manure, compost and seaweed before planting seed potatoes, which were progressively earthed up with gravelly soil scraped from flat-bottomed furrows two spits wide, between each mini raised bed.

It has been suggested that practitioners of this expedient method of planting a potato crop in new ground be termed *'lazy bastards'*, since it is based on a hybrid combination of traditional *'lazy bed'* cultivation and a bastardised form of *'bastard trenching'*. It is actually quite hard work to begin with, but in the second season, the ready-made dip between ridges made in the first year is filled with more organic material and used for cropping. Potatoes were more easily earthed up using the long lines of decomposed turves remaining after the initial harvest. By the end of the third harvest, the whole area should have been enriched with organic matter to some depth, by repeating this technique.

I remember, too, an expedition to Pigeons' Cave to recover guano in potato sacks for toting back to Camas, and also the incredulity of some lads from Possil at my enthusiasm for importing more organic material to improve our growing prospects. I bribed them with the promise of a pint in the Argyll Arms if they helped me fill sacks with years of accumulated cow manure from Ronnie Campbell's byre in Bunessan. 'Och, no wi yer bare hands!' they baulked, as I grovelled in the dung they had loosened with clumsy hayforks. We transferred a trailer-load of filled sacks by tractor to Bunessan pier and loaded them into a friendly fisherman's boat for delivery by sea to Camas.

Another memory is of harvesting honey from a Camas beehive but being called away for lunch before completing the job of slicing the honeycomb into jars. By the time I had eaten my soup and crackers, thousands of bees were swarming in and out of gaps in the shed door, to claim back every last drop of their precious food supply. I was helpless to intervene because I had left my overalls and bee veil in the shed. Sadly, despite reclaiming virtually all their bounty, and subsequent feeding with sugar syrup, the bees did not survive the following winter in their windblown situation, with little but seasonal heather flowers to sustain them.

We mostly accommodated groups of teenagers 'at risk', because the Scottish Office had been persuaded to support Camas as a centre especially well-suited to welcoming 'Intermediate Treatment' groups for residential programmes, led by qualified professionals.

Our young guests couldn't do much damage to the place, though there was once a (rapidly resolved) theft from a local shop; and another incident of graffiti sprayed on the north wall. In general, Camas groups caused no real affront to anyone. Indeed, on one notable occasion, members of an Easterhouse gang were readily motivated by their leaders to helpfully tidy and scrub graffiti off walls of the Nuns' Cave at Carsaig, by the offer of a lift back to Camas after a night of camping.

I once sent two goats into a particular volunteer's shed because he was still in bed at morning coffee time. Nobody had told me he was a recovering heroin user sent to Camas by his enlightened social worker. He got through it, but explained that the first hit would be free as soon as he went back to Glasgow, so he knew staying clean would be a challenge. Happily, we became lasting friends, and recently shared some laughs over memories when he visited Mull again for the first time in twenty-five years or so, having long since straightened himself out.

Once I had contributed what I said I would in terms of enhancing potential for food production at Camas, it felt more important for me to invest energy in trying to do some kind of helpful good closer to the front-line in Thatcher's savagely uncaring Britain. I called quits on the last day of summer 1984 and took up residence as a benefits claimant in the home neighbourhood of my pal in the shed next door – the second worst area of multiple urban deprivation in Scotland at that time.

That winter, I was astounded to realise how very many teenagers in the housing scheme were drug users, but also profoundly touched that those who had shared the adventure of Camas evidently harboured such positive memories of the wider horizons and good times we had enjoyed together on Mull.

So: This many years later, what do I make of my wee stint at Camas?

I feel privileged to have played a fleeting humble part in the ongoing story of the uniquely remarkable off-grid microcosm of island life that is Camas. I feel enriched by enduring memories of all kinds of people with whom I shared all kinds of experiences, and a special affinity with everyone else who has ever known and loved the place.

More than that, insights gained at Camas were integral to deciding to establish my home and raise my family just a couple of miles west along the coast, so I continue to share the same elemental wonders and wonderful wider community I first discovered as a twenty something, over 30 years ago.

Terry Hegarty

Camas Gardener

'*Camas Gardener*'. The words jumped out of the job ad in the *Big Issue* and mugged me with a feeling of rightness. With not a doubt in my mind, I persuaded my husband, David – a dyed-in-the-wool townie too – that he would love it, and clinched the deal by suggesting it'd be a great place for the dog he wanted to get.

Hearing that my interview had been a success, I was delighted to be getting a proper garden to look after: my training had been in amenity horticulture and I'd been working as a landscape trainer – too much grass-cutting, too many slabs. Ahead of me lay this Hebridean paradise preserved in my memory of happy New Members Weeks as a sun-drenched, wave-lapped horticultural nirvana.

Upon arrival at the foot of the track I ran along the front of the buildings, and such was my excitement to be back that I completely missed the fact that I'd run over a substantial pile of Ballachulish slate which a double-figure gale-force had thoughtfully deposited there. 'Er, look at the roof,' said David – always the one with an eye for detail – 'that's quite a big hole.' He always had a talent for understatement. We went on to see a twenty-foot gaping hole in the roof above the Chapel of Nets. The contents of the rest of the building were like items in the worst charity shop in the world: elderly blankets, the national collection of plastic boxes, dodgy curtains and a three-piece suite which I knew for a fact had been purchased third-hand and carried down the track by my pal Helen Gray when she'd been Coordinator some fourteen years previously.

The garden was a weedy wreckage of overgrown beds and home to two elderly sheds, which had been serving as much loved and coveted staff accommodation. Most gardens, particularly production ones, look hellish after winter, so this is no judgement on my gardening predecessor. Leave any cultivated land alone for long enough and it'll turn into a forest eventually. Camas hadn't had an all-year-round paid gardener for about 20 years, so any progress made by seasonal volunteer gardeners was usually reclaimed by the unstoppable moorland herbage and the ravages of the winter winds. The idea to reappoint a Resident Gardener had come from the previous Camas staff team and the Camas Committee, and the Rank Foundation provided the funding.

So here before David and me was a challenge and an opportunity.

The hole in the roof was quickly repaired by a lovely builder from Fionnphort, who also taught us the local names for the fish in the bay as well as how to catch and cook them. We were joined by David Berger, who had been appointed as Coordinator, having worked previously as a volunteer – his knowledge of how to find things and make them work was invaluable in those early days. Together the three of us set about the task of mucking out the building to make it habitable for the other resident and voluntary staff, who came along in April.

We spent much of the first year reclaiming ground in the walled part of the garden and reinstating the 'lazy' beds, an archaic term for this traditional method of cultivating difficult land – there's nowt lazy about the process of digging out sodden peat for drainage, removing obelisk-sized boulders and hauling endless wheelbarrows of kelp up the hill from the shore to feed the soil. A shape began to emerge from what had been established many years previously. A stand of Sitka spruce provided good shelter in the upper garden; in addition, many native species had been planted in more recent years and the woodland was starting to achieve good coverage. For all the problems presented to us – the rank-grasses, rusty fencing incapable of repelling a herd of determined cows and hungry sheep – the sheer beauty of the place, the fertile peat soil and the goodwill of guests and staff alike kept us from wearying.

There is, however, only so much that determination and spadework can achieve: it was clear that the garden needed a decent budget and a few more key resources. The first came via Community member John Polhill, who helped raise funds to equip us properly; and the second came via Brik Halcrow, the Bursar on Iona, who persuaded her neighbour Anne Tolleson, an associate member, to donate a disused polytunnel from the grounds of her house. I have enough memories of my years at Camas to fill several volumes but the standout one was the day we set out with the entire staff team to dismantle the polytunnel – bolt by rusty bolt – and carry it back on foot a mile over the moorland hill from Ardfenaig: a glorious team effort and a 'demanding common task' worthy of George MacLeod and those early rebuilders.

We sited the polytunnel in the most sheltered part of the garden, behind the dry-stone dyke (a dyking style which I think is unique to Mull, being single-faced, achieved by rolling huge stones up an earthen ramp, and having been constructed with great skill by islanders during a famine). Concreting in foundation tubes was essential to securing the tunnel against those winter gales and we managed to dig nine out of the ten holes quite successfully. Hole number ten, however, contained a granite boulder which would've challenged Obelix the Gaul – there were tears that day. The problem was solved by Gordie Rutherford from Historic Scotland; having worked for many years on the restoration of the Abbey, Gordie knew more about dealing with granite than anyone else I knew. 'Cut your tube short and concrete it onto the boulder – it'll take.' Sure enough. By the end of year two we had a fully constructed and newly skinned polytunnel with space to extend the growing season, and a damn good venue for a sneaky staff party/New Members Week late-night session.

The funding also secured the purchase of a strimmer to keep down the rank-grasses, and this enabled us to plant around 2000 trees and hedging plants to provide shelter and habitat. Controlling the grass and bracken saw the re-emergence of the native herb layer that had been choked out over the years. An over-winter visit from some deer, the repeat visits from the open-grazed sheep and one memorable invasion of a herd of cows made it necessary to re-fence the garden and to extend it. We built two sheds: a proper potting shed inside the garden, and a hermitage for Kathy Galloway while she was Leader of the Iona Community.

Many hands (and sore backs) – residents, volunteers, work-weekers, colleagues from the Iona Centres – were added to our own to create the basis of the all-year-round Camas garden. New Members Weeks were always a welcome source of labour and we sure as hell put them through their paces – cutting bracken, mixing concrete, raking up sheep shit. Calvinist boot camp, but always marked by good humour and lots of singing!

The garden introduced lots of young people to nature – quite a few had never been outside of a town before. Seeing the astonishment on a kid's face when they realise that tomatoes actually grow on a plant is quite something. Seeing the boiling flush on a kid's face after he's decided to scoff a whole red chilli that you warned him against is quite something too. Sarah Neale, then Camas Coordinator, often described cooking dinner at Camas as 'the art of disguising vegetables from suspicious children'. Indeed, one pudding made with garden produce proved extremely popular, with third helpings being demanded, until the unwitting teenagers discovered that the secret ingredient was courgettes; it was as if we had betrayed some sacred trust.

In our final year David and I stayed on while Extropy Construction, Bill Watson and colleagues, worked with their skilled team to produce a sympathetic and appropriate reconstruction of the old buildings. We continued with the development of the garden, while the builders cleverly made new window spaces by reusing old hearth stones, knocked down walls to create brighter rooms and installed solar-powered showers to make living at Camas less hard work. The installation of a clever low-tech compost toilet system was, I suppose, one of the most satisfying aspects of the transformation. Part of the gardener's job was to manage the old bucket system of the toilets in order to produce compost for the tree plantings – good fertiliser indeed and immortalised in a custom-made Latin motto courtesy of a visiting Classics teacher: *'Per merdam crescimus'* ('Through shit we grow'). For staff and guests alike, emptying the buckets had been – hands-down – the least popular chore, and emptying the septic tank (a winter job which fell to David and me) quite eye-wateringly disgusting.

I've yet to meet a gardener who'd tell you that they think their garden is finished. It is the nature of seasonality that each year we dig over the mistakes of the last and sow optimistically in the hope that this will be the year of the great, golden harvest: some years it is, some it ain't. David and I never 'finished' that garden but succeeding gardeners, staff teams and visiting kids continue to work and develop it – and that thought always makes me very happy.

Lizz Spence

The best part of the week was when we dug up potatoes from the garden. I didn't like the worms, but we all worked together as a team.

Young person

I liked collecting things from the polytunnels for everyone to eat. I didn't know what some of them were but people explain it all to you, so you don't feel nervous.

Young person

We have a community garden at our school. I didn't think I would be into it, but helping out in the Camas garden and trying food from there meant I enjoyed it when I got back home.

Young person

The chicken whisperer

The real value of the environment for me is how it impacts on the individuals who spend time at Camas. Early in the season (before mink had destroyed several of our chickens), it was a nightly ritual to entice the ladies back to their run in the garden with a rattle of corn in a plastic tub. Herding chickens is seldom an easy task and we often invited a couple of the visiting group members to help. By far the best was a lad with ADHD who had caused mayhem by rushing headlong into bogs, bracken, tables – you name it; however, it turned out he was the chicken whisperer. Gently coaxing, slipping behind trees, working around the sides, 'shooing' in subdued tones, he was a completely different character – and highly prized. The chickens are a wonderful asset to the Camas staff team; their patience at being constantly lifted up, chased or spoken to about being turned into nuggets is admirable.[6]

Jon Lloyd

Courgette pizzas

When I was a volunteer cook one of the challenges was to make use of all the courgettes that Terry would bring from the garden. I found a limit to the number of courgette pizzas the Camas guests would eat! This reflects the balance and integration of all of life at Camas, with food from the garden on the table each day – and yet the staff have to adapt always to the needs of the groups who arrive – making concessions, while also holding out the possibility of another way, a new 'taste', or unfamiliar experience, with which to experiment and to expand comfort zones.

Ruth Harvey

'Pure helfy, man!'

The home-cooked, home-grown food here proved unappealing (boggin' was the more polite term used) for some but turns out that's not a problem if you've packed your bodyweight in chocolate, Pot Noodle, juice and sweets in your rucksack. One group showed us what *real* food is when they served us up chips 'n' curry the final evening. 'Pure helfy, man!' Thankfully they spared our Camas chickens from the pot.

From the Camas blog

The pivotal potato

Whilst fairly common on day one, by day two the sea air and activity usually overcame guests' suspicions of the vegetarian meals. However, after three days of watching a guest eat nothing but the sweets he had brought with him, the subject was finally broached …

Ross   (*Camas Coordinator*): Why are you not eating the food, K?

Guest: Don't want to. Not hungry.

Ross: But you must be hungry …

Guest: No.

Ross: Go on, try something, you might be surprised …

Guest: NO!

Ross: OK, but why not?

Guest: I DON'T eat vegetables!

Ross: OK, then what do you eat at home?

Guest: CHIPS!

Ross: Errr, but chips are made from vegetables …

Guest: No, they are not!

Ross: What are they made from then?

Guest: They're made from fat!

Ross: Err, OK. Umm, David, could you help K make some chips please?

Me: Sure, come on K let's go out to the garden …

And so, some of the first potatoes from the newly created gardens were dug up and taken to the kitchen. There K scrubbed, peeled, chopped and fried them, and once the alchemical transformation had occurred, proudly and reverently carried them through to the dining room. They were eaten in an awed and epiphanal silence … followed throughout the rest of the week by several helpings of everything else that was put in front of him …

David Langton

Watching the garden grow

The leaves of the aspen are in full power, the bed of self-seeded delights have turned into a jungle of greens to eat, the grapes in their infancy fascinate me and how tall the sweetcorn grows! The asparagus, too, I could watch it stretch. The potatoes, raspberries, salad crops, apple blossom and rhubarb. The kale and the chard, turnips and beets, the strawberries are ready to eat!

Fresh herbs from the herb canoe and a sea of sunflowers – I could sit for hours and watch the garden grow, the birds bouncing from branch to branch, the adders curl in the sun, the tidal ebb and flow and the chickens' mischievous charm.

The bees come for the borage, as do I. Infinite pickings of nettles and 'weeds' from the sea and ground, sorrel is my favourite zesty treat to find on a forage. A gift freely given, food for food's sake. Beauty for beauty's sake.

I could sit for hours and watch the garden grow.

Watch how the light moves across the rocks at the roundhouse, how the rowan leaves turn with the moving sun, how the infant trees are made quickly small by the increasingly tall bracken; one day it will be reversed.

The willow dome is complete now, a secret to retreat to and look out from within the leaves. The baby apple trees are flowering too and that pine we cut has its use. We sit on the logs around the fire, telling stories, united by our mandala.

I could sit for hours …

Abbi Mason

Prayer

Almighty God, Creator:
the morning is Yours, rising into fullness.
The summer is Yours, dipping into autumn.
Eternity is Yours, dipping into time.
The vibrant grasses, the scent of flowers,
the lichen on the rocks, the tang of seaweed,
all are Yours.
Gladly we live in this garden of Your creating.[7]

George MacLeod

Living in Camas

The sheep seek shelter in the woodshed,
while stars remember sleeping in long rows
around the island.

Candles make shadows of our faces,
the soft amber glow adding depth
and life to stories,
groves of trees, ravines, rocky coves, the open sea,
all in our night,
mapped across our faces
in the darkness and soft flicker of
each of us before the fire.

The pumpkin collects water in
dimpled leaves,
mirror of moons,
soft dappled light showing
me where to step in the garden
between the drains,
stepping heavy across neat paths
into the scent of rolling tobacco and cooking apples.

Beyond the garden, after the mesh gate is secure,
along the coast and into the hills,
the bog keeps the past rusty and golden;
remains of the history that hides
beneath the lazy beds, between the bracken.
The peat is a sweet archiver to curiosity.

I go to bed, weary and thinking of
the ruins over the land.

The sheep seek shelter in the woodshed,
while the stars remember sleeping in long rows
around the island.

Eric Wojchik

Notes:

1. From the 'Justice, Peace and Integrity of Creation Commitment of the Iona Community'
2. From *Living by the Rule: The Rule of the Iona Community*, Kathy Galloway, Wild Goose Publications, 2010
3. From *Coracle*, the magazine of the Iona Community, 2010, Neil Paynter (Ed.)
4. From *The Sacred Garden*, BBC Radio Scotland, 2004
5. *A History of the Ross of Mull*, J. Stewart Cameron, Ross of Mull Historical Centre, 2013
6. From *Coracle*, the magazine of the Iona Community, Neil Paynter (Ed.), 2012
7. From *The Whole Earth Shall Cry Glory: Iona Prayers*, George MacLeod, Wild Goose Publications, 1985

2. THE WOODLANDS

The Camas woodlands have been developed over the years and are a crucial part of the overall ecological ethos.

Simple in means: Rich in ends

Through the many areas of concern with which the Iona Community is involved, we can help to shape values, morals and attitudes to enable society to be more sustainable. One such area where the community looks creatively at these concerns is at Camas. We updated the Camas mission statement to reflect this. It reads:

At Camas, the Iona Community seeks to provide the opportunity for small groups and individuals to address concerns of justice, peace, ecological aware-ness and personal development through:

– *sharing a simple lifestyle and building personal relationships;*

– *creative and adventure activities;*

– *reflection, discussion and spiritual exploration;*

– *helping everyone to take responsibility for their own participation and for the functioning of the whole group.*

In response to developing the aims of Camas, we undertook much work to provide a holistic and integrated programme which addresses the main themes of 'interdependence' and 'sustainability'. However, words are just words unless they are given meaning through action. As such, we have striven hard at Camas to ensure that the sustainable ethos permeates to the very fabric of the buildings.

Indeed, this went as far as the toilets at Camas, which were identified from guest feedback in 1997 as being the most negative part of the 'Camas experience'. For those of you unfamiliar with the experience, let me remind you of the chemical toilets: slopping out and dumping the contents over the side of a boat into the sea. Not environmentally friendly, and very unpleasant.

True to the aim of living sustainably, we decided to create a practical and educational experience, and transformed the chemical toilets into compost toilets. Thus we created a method of turning a 'waste' product into a valuable resource. Through this means of waste management we create less pollution and less hassle, whilst using no valuable fresh clean water.

So what do we do with this human resource?

On New Year's Day 1998, we decided to plant a small native woodland at Camas: as a symbol of new growth and regeneration. Scotland's landscape has not always been the treeless desert that we witness today. But rather, it is a legacy of our historical tendency to live short-sighted and unsustainable lifestyles. The great oak, birch and pinewoods of Caledonia are to be found only in isolated pockets of our much-mismanaged land. The Highland Clearances cleared Mull of many of its forests as well as its people.

It may be only a token gesture towards regenerating our woodland society, but the seeds planted in the minds of the young people who come to Camas about our responsibility to the environment is where the real growth will take place. On a practical level, it is even possible, with a little forward thinking, that a coppice management strategy could be developed which would provide Camas with a self-sustaining wood supply.

It is onto these trees that our composted human 'waste' will go. Once it has been broken down over a two-year period the resulting compost is safe to handle and is a very rich source of nutrients. Efficiency at its best; sustainability in action.

We also resurrected the organic garden at Camas, after an absence of eight years. Why import food from afar when perfectly good, inexpensive, environmentally friendly and better-tasting vegetables can be grown in your back garden? Grown without the aid of chemicals; and using natural fertilisers such as seaweed and comfrey is by far a more sustainable means of providing healthy food.

Once again the value of the garden exceeds the practical and is extended into the educational. The groups at Camas do not simply eat the food they encounter there: each group is introduced to the garden at the start of each week and are encouraged to become more involved in the growing and cultivation of produce. The sense of connection with their food is continued into the kitchen where they help in the preparation of the vegetables for lunch or dinner. An everyday occurrence for many of us, but for many youngsters brought up on convenience and fast foods, it is a truly enlightening experience.

A further development of the organic garden was the reintroduction of lazy-bed farming to Camas. Lazy beds, or runrigs, are the traditional means of crop production in the Highlands, dating back hundreds of years. There is an extensive system of lazy beds on the land surrounding the Centre which are a legacy of the people connected to Camas in the past. Although they require a lot of work (if ever a misnomer there was, 'lazy beds' is it), they do provide a sustainable and efficient means of producing food from otherwise poor soil.

There are educational and cultural benefits to be gained from incorporating the lazy beds and their history as an integral part of the Camas programme. Groups have much to gain from learning about, and feeling the reality of, life before our time at Camas.

The environmental ethic followed at Camas is reflected in the amount of waste we are left with at the end of each week. Everything that can be composted is, and is then fed to the garden and lazy beds to provide further food. All glass, tin, cardboard and paper is recycled, and we are usually left with only one or two bin bags of waste each week.

We can all live like this. We have not inherited the earth, we have simply borrowed it from our children, and we have a responsibility to these children and to the earth. Our aim at Camas is to help facilitate and increase in 'love, respect and awareness of self, others and the environment'. God is present in all these things, and thus through our work we help increase 'love, respect and awareness of God'. We have much to learn from this way of life. But perhaps the real value of this environmentally connected and sustainable lifestyle is best summed up in one simple sentence: 'Live simply so that others may simply live.'[1]

Ross Morton

Planting hope – a new woodland

Staff and visitors continued to plant trees at Camas on a small scale from 1998 on. However, in 2017 the Camas staff team launched an exciting and ambitious project to plant 4,200 native trees – largely donated by the Woodland Trust – on 1.4 hectares of land around Camas. A hugely successful and inspiring Crowdfunder appeal raised £18,345 to pay for the deer fence, labour and transportation. About half the trees were planted in March 2018, with a ceremony held beforehand to honour and thank all who helped to make the vision a reality.

The Camas staff said: 'We are inspired to make this happen for future generations and we are putting something back into the landscape to provide a place for young people to explore nature. The woodland will enable them to have night walks, campfires, to tend the wild and to take part in the planting and care of the trees. The trees will also provide nuts and fruit, and young people will be able to experience a direct connection with gathering and eating food, as they do now with our vegetable garden.

'We are very grateful to everyone who has generously supported the project. It's an exciting step forward in the story of Camas, the Ross of Mull and reforesting Scotland.'[2]

Rachel McCann

A big beautiful woodland

I live and work here as the Resident Co-Gardener with my partner and our young daughter – growing her as well as growing vegetables – which I'm particularly grateful to be doing in this community and this stunning landscape – a very nourishing environment.

In our work with young people at Camas, we try to create a safe space, especially for those who don't usually get the chance to be out in nature. We give them opportunities to explore nature and to find out more about themselves through doing so. I have spent a lot of time in the garden with young people and adults and have often observed them finding a sense of satisfaction in doing purposeful work. I have one specific memory of a couple of boys planting potatoes and beaming with the sense of pride in doing something useful. It's always felt a great privilege to work alongside others as they discover the fun and value of gardening!

I was at Camas as a volunteer in 2001 when our original woodland was only about two years old. We did a lot with the groups in the woodland back then, mulching the baby trees with humanure and great piles of seaweed and cardboard, and almost without exception, people would get stuck into the task and find a lot of joy in it – in tending these little tree beings whilst hearing stories about how big they were going to become. Then, a few years ago, I came down the track after a gap of seven or eight years – and was immediately struck by the trees and how big they were and by their beauty. Even now, after living here for a year and a half, they catch my attention almost every time I walk by and stir up a happy state of wonder in me!

So now, with a much bigger tree-planting project, I find it exciting to think that when my daughter is 18, these new wee trees will have formed a big and beautiful woodland.

Laura Gamwell

We sat in a clearing in the woodland around a fire and some people were playing guitars and singing and telling stories and jokes. It was a fun evening.

Young person

We helped out pulling bracken to make room for the trees. My arms and legs were aching but it was brilliant to know we were a tiny part of helping to regenerate this area.

Group Leader

Seeds of change ... Dare to believe!

Hopefully others have written about the track and the eternal repairs; the fake lightswitch gag on the groups' first evening; the sacred nights of song lit by fire or full moon; the groups that came and went leaving indelible impressions; the sense of purpose, comradery and mucking-in-together-ness; and the exhaustion-induced flare-ups and tension ... so I want to share something through a wider lens.

I can still remember the meeting in the old, dingy staffroom (before the buildings were refurbished), when someone said, out of the blue, 'Wouldn't it be amazing to one day be able to say, "Come on, everybody – let's go up to the Camas woods and play"?!'

For when I first met Camas, in the 1990s, it held a desolate, barren and raw beauty. Everything outdoors cropped to nothing by hordes of sheep and everything indoors encrusted in what they left in their midge-laden wake. Due to daily doses of chemicals from the old toilets, the bay was devoid of all life – even seaweed. In the skies flew nothing but a few passing gulls and a pair of resident, offspring-less oystercatchers. In the bogs and on the hills sprouted no plant larger than bracken and marsh grass. The 'garden' was a 2'x3' bed of herbs; and in and around the buildings and sheds there wasn't anything that could be deemed comfortable or that hadn't been salvaged or recycled. To be there was hard … and I loved it!

It was during this time of one of Camas' lowest ebbs – with buildings fairly unsafe to use, finances extremely tight and the Iona Community questioning Camas' continuation – that the aforementioned meeting took place.

Going against the tide and all the evidence and advice, it was decided to behave as if the place was still going to be going – thriving even – in 20 years' time. The tiny garden was extended up the hill, where, incredibly, strips of taller bracken still indicated where the quarrymen's lazy bed system had been; compost toilets were created; the roof, windows and doors were repaired, making everything more snug and weathertight; kitchen equipment was rescued from an Abbey clear-out; peat-cutting was begun as a more suitable and sustainable source of fuel – and even a few pine trees were daringly planted. It all felt a bit foolish and pointless much of the time, but still we sowed the seeds …

20 years on from my last visit, with much trepidation and my two children in tow, I once more strode down the, umm, surprisingly complete boardwalk of the track. The goat willow I had planted in boggy and inaccessible places had taken – and spread right across the hill. Those original pine trees were now huge … and surrounded by so many other trees … and can those possibly be polytunnels?! The buildings were sound and well-presented and – who'd have ever thought it – even boasted hot(ish) showers! The bay turned out to be teeming with diversity, vibrant and alive with seaweed and literally piles and piles of winkles and whelks on the rocks – and birds! The birds had found it all and made it their home too. There was an actual, real, noisy dawn chorus …

Camas had been 'believed in'. I want to take this opportunity to thank and bless all those who, over those twenty years, helped to create such an oasis of biodiversity, such a model of sustainability and positive human development. They have made Camas even more of a special place! Just as it should be!

On our second day, already full up emotionally – and physically, after a wonderfully unchanged-by-time breakfast of rib-sticking porridge and scones – a volunteer stood up and said, 'Hey, everyone, when we're finished, why don't we go up to the Camas woods and play?!'

David Langton

The John Muir Award

At Camas we run the John Muir Award. This is an award that fits very well with the ethos of Camas. It *'encourages people of all backgrounds to connect with, enjoy and care for wild places'* (www.jmt.org). Young people can take back the environmental learning from Camas and apply it to their everyday lives; and hopefully they will be inspired to continue exploring and learning about the environment and the whole wide world! As one group leader commented: 'Young people and adults have a greater understanding of the impact they have on the environment – and they learn to eat vegetables.'[3]

Mary Ireson

Giving something back

The John Muir Award challenges you to discover a wild place, explore it, do something to help conserve it, and to share your experience with others. Having become familiar with this pattern from the first two levels of the award, and moving to Mull to live and work at a small outdoor Centre, I thought that working towards the Conserver level would be a useful way to provide some additional motivation for understanding my new home landscape, and getting out and about on my days off.

Meeting the 'Discover' challenge has been easy – just moving to live at Camas, in its own bay, and a mile and a half off the road down a boggy moorland track, meant I was immediately surrounded by beautiful wild places. I've developed a new awareness of the changing tides and seasons here, never growing tired of the view from my bedroom window: on clear days I can count seven different islands; on foggy days I feel completely isolated from the outside world as a wall of cloud blocks off the mouth of the bay; at sunset the pink granite rocks glow in the evening light; and in winter stormy north winds bring the sea almost to the front door!

So I've spent an enjoyable year exploring all the habitats of Mull, Iona and the nearby Treshnish Islands – white sandy beaches, rocky shores, regenerating native woodland, machair, salt marsh, cliffs, mountains and moorland bogs – walking, camping and sleeping out under the stars for the first time in my life. I've been recording the experience through environmental art, taking photographs and keeping a nature diary.

Our lifestyle here at Camas is designed to conserve the wild places around us. As there is no road access everything must be brought in by boat or the ever-reliable wheelbarrow, organic fruit and vegetables are grown in our garden, and we produce our own renewable electricity from the wind and sun. Attending a 'Leave No Trace' training course has given me additional skills for camping alone, and to lead some of our groups on wild camping trips; we have cleared litter from several beaches, leaving them in better condition than we found them. I've also joined in with drystane dyking on a local National Trust for Scotland conservation work party, and contributed wildlife sightings to a number of national bird, plant and marine surveys.

So is Mull a wild place? The golden eagle certainly nests here, as do white-tailed sea eagles, and I've been privileged to have several sightings of these huge 'flying barn doors' – but this is no untouched wilderness. These are islands whose tourism industry is influenced by the popularity of the children's TV show *Balamory*, Iona as a place of pilgrimage over the centuries, and above all their spectacular wildlife. It's a place where people and wildlife come close together. For example, this year a pair of kestrels chose to nest on our abseiling ledge; last year my best birthday present was watching dolphins jumping clear of the water as they followed the ferry. But this doesn't mean that wildlife is tame or easy to see. I've looked out into our bay every day for a year and a half now, and only once caught sight of basking sharks.

Although the maps show large areas of Mull as empty of human settlement, I've come across many abandoned shielings and crofts, walked well-trodden paths past disused rig-and-furrow now covered in bracken, and followed the tracks of feral goats through lost worlds of ivy-covered boulders between cliffs and sea. As well as the obvious villages, it's easy to stumble across traces of people working this landscape, even in places which at first glance seem to be untouched: disused quarries, rusting farm machinery and the constant presence of small fishing boats tending lobster creels off apparently deserted coastlines.

The Celtic saints – famed for long sea voyages in tiny boats and hermit cells on small remote islands – had a reputation for seeking out wilderness. This gave them a great respect for nature, a legacy left behind in the Celtic tradition upheld by the Iona Community. There's still an element of 'living on the edge' here, in spite of broadband internet access! The weather can certainly be wild, with stormy days cancelling ferries and sending waterfalls upwards in spectacular fountains of spray from the clifftops. However, there have also been surprises – one memorable February day warm enough to spend over an hour lying in the sunshine above a deserted stretch of beach, looking out towards the hills of Jura, or days when the calm flat sea mirrors the mountains in a perfectly still reflection.

Sometimes it has been uncomfortable to challenge myself to learn the skills to lead outdoor activities, or to complete wildlife surveys correctly, or to explore in new ways, in all weathers, and to have to rely on myself rather than on others to show me what to do. It's also tempting to be very lazy on days off from a job which is very satisfying, but which takes so much energy, when you look out the window and see this beautiful bay as a workplace, with the wildest thing out there seeming to be the enthusiastically noisy group of teenagers playing football on the lawn!

Sharing experiences comes naturally when living in community. I've been able to get Camas registered as a John Muir Award provider, and several groups have completed their 'Discovery' awards alongside our staff, learning about the impacts of our lifestyle on wild places, exploring through kayaking, abseiling, walking and camping, watching and recording wildlife, beach art, environmental games, sharing songs, poems and stories around the fire in the evenings or during reflection times.

Of course Camas is a very different place in the winter, away from the busy summer season – especially when a north wind is blowing straight into the bay! But winter has its own beauty: navigating the track purely by starlight with the stars reflected in every puddle along the way … watching a huge full moon rise over the hill and light up the white wave-caps of a choppy sea … sitting on the island on a calm day listening to the swell and watching sunset light transform a grey cloudy day into purples, pinks and blues, as a seal swims past checking out what the humans are up to today – it's still an amazing place to call home.

Overall, I've gained a new appreciation for this island I once dismissed as just a dull, boring expanse of moorland and forestry plantations, not really worth visiting. (That was before I lived here!) I've tried to pass on this inspiration and change in my own attitude, and in turn have been inspired by working and playing with colleagues, guests and visitors with their many different ways of communicating how much the experience of this unique wild place has meant to them.

Completing this award has helped to motivate me to do as I keep encouraging others to do: to get out there and explore and appreciate our surroundings, to notice the small details as well as the big landscapes, and to try to give something back to the places I've grown to love.

Emily Wilkins

Sacred soil

pine crackles
warming salty toes
from cold October mud,
the sea whispers of love
and the hands that feed us.

today is Sunday,
conversation wrapping us in warm embrace,
the birds chase and erase
the face of fakeness
from our days.

can we rewind
to the beginning of time?
this ancient mystery
bringing us together,
roots entangled in time.

grey lady rock
rumbles beneath,
gives life to new trees
as our wind friend
spreads seeds

and tall they'll grow
as time rolls slow,
planted with love
into the future

we go …

Mairead Spangler

Faith

The oystercatchers consummate spring,
a brief awkward fluttering.
Three speckled eggs
in a simple nest of scraped sand.

Living close to the shore, I share
the female's pretence
that she isn't there,
smiling as she fails to blend
with a sandy backdrop:
black-and-white bird,
bright traffic-cone beak.

Neither is the fleet mink fooled.
One grey morning the eggs are gone;
the oystercatchers utter hollow *kleep kleeps*
that blunt my heart.

In early summer, they try again;
a hoodie crow awaits its chance.
Passing sheep disturb the female from her nest;
sleek as death, the hoodie stabs each egg,
scooping yolk to feed its own coarse brood.
Later, broken, I cup the empty shells in my hand,
curse oystercatchers and their stupid, fruitless faith.

That's how you found me.
You walked down the track, met a man
hell-bent on a hard shell.

It's mid-summer, my love.
In the oystercatchers' nest,
a single speckled egg.

Dougie Strang

Notes:

1. From *Coracle*, the magazine of the Iona Community, 1998, Kathy Galloway (Ed.)
2. Church of Scotland
3. From *Coracle*, the magazine of the Iona Community, Neil Paynter (Ed.), 2010

3. THE BUILDINGS

The Camas buildings require constant ongoing work and financial and prac-
tical support. In recent years additions to Camas have included a roundhouse
and a pizza oven. The following stories, however, highlight major events in the
life of Camas' development – and are further reminders of George MacLeod's
well-known phrase 'only a demanding common task builds community'!

The roof went on after a hundred years!

Whilst all Camas staff undertake the ongoing maintenance jobs (especially
after a rough winter), and George MacLeod had had his groups working
hard on the buildings, the first major architectural work at Camas was
undertaken by Deryck Collingwood and his team. Using basic tools, volunteers and local resources, the project was, by necessity, low impact. The
plan was to put a roof on the single-storey smaller building, which had
been left unfinished when the quarry was abandoned in the 1870s. This
was no easy task, with limited resources and a limited budget. Dercyk tells
the story:

'During the summer of 1976 we intended to build the cottages to provide more
indoor space for bad weather, and we obtained the services of the young
offenders groups to put up the rafters of the unroofed building. Despite constant
treks to the village phone and endless promises from the sawmill, the timbers
arrived a week after the lads came! Eventually, as the last rafters were being
nailed into place, the architect arrived to announce an unforeseen delay in plan-
ning permission and requested that the rafters be dismantled! Though the work
on the roof was delayed for six months, the rafters remained in place. The
bigger job was to dig up the healthiest topsoil and grovel our way through fif-
teen inches of mud-packed small stones. Tons and tons of sand were wheelbar-
rowed to the cottages where concrete was mixed for the new floors. It was a
mammoth undertaking without mechanical aids or even horses, and most of
the work was done by parties of young people under social work supervision.
It was so good to be able to tell them that they were doing something which
tradesmen would not take on. Most of them left feeling justly proud.'[1]

Mark Jardine helped to finish off the work:

'When I arrived the single-storey cottages had only fairly recently had their roofs completed. Part of our work at Camas was continuing the building work to make these buildings a usable part of the Centre. We spent a lot of our winters building steps, manholes, plumbing, plaster-boarding, even making doors and windows. Deryck had trained as an architect but our building skills were very basic, though we learnt as we went.'

As a result of the team's hard work new staff accommodation and new downstairs dormitories were created. The team also put a roof on the building that became the kayak shed – no easy feat in itself!

Rachel McCann

Growing Hope

The next major building project was in the mid-2000s. In the late '80s and early '90s, as a result of changes in funding and staffing, the Iona Community went through a time of soul-searching with regard to Camas, at one point even considering closing the Centre. However, during Community Week 1998, the then Camas Advisory Group presented a strong vision and business plan to members of the Iona Community, which led to a renewed understanding of and commitment to Camas. Ruth Harvey was a part of that group and commented: 'As a group we were deeply committed to the long-term development of Camas, and were convinced of the potential that is built into the bricks of the place. We put Camas at the forefront of the Iona Community's reinvention of itself.'

As a result of this work, the Camas Committee was formed in 1999. Initially co-convened by Ruth Harvey and Kathy Galloway, it offered the specialist support and oversight Camas had needed. Ruth said: 'The co-convenership enabled the two of us to join forces and to share the responsibility of the task in hand. It was also a way in which I could be involved in a leadership role as a new mother – so Maeve, born in 2000, came with us to all committee meetings.'

In 2001, the committee started a major piece of research and consultation on the way forward for Camas. Staff, groups, local people and Iona Community members gave their views and, although one or two of the initial ideas (asphalting the track!) had to be honed down, the process gave a clear direction as to what was needed at Camas.

In 2004, the 'Growing Hope Appeal', led by committee convener Margaret Stewart, was launched. This had the aim of raising funds to develop Camas into a more comfortable, sustainable and professional centre for staff and groups to enjoy. Prior to the redevelopment, there were serious problems – including rotting floorboards, a kitchen that was prone to flooding, damp dark dormitories and poor staff accommodation. Driven by health and safety regulations and a need to bring Camas up-to-date as a modern facility, the challenges of the financial and practical aspects of the project were considerable and many people worked hard behind the scenes, including, and especially, then Support Services Manager, Graham Boyle. However, the Iona Community is never short of vision, courage and faith. As Kathy Galloway commented: '*I very much appreciate that the Iona Community is open to learning, open to new things, open to risk, to being adventurous. In one sense raising lots of money to run an outdoor centre on a sandy strip on the Ross of Mull is not the immediate thing you would think of doing.*'[2]

Core to the project was environmental integrity, and Howard Liddell from the Gaia Group was appointed as architect. He brought great experience and expertise in ecological architecture and sustainable development, and he instinctively grasped the ethos of Camas: '*Camas is a stunning place, a place with a sense of arrival. A "genius loci". I see our job as having as light a touch as possible to retain the atmosphere of Camas. It would be nice if it could be left alone – but the modern world includes health and safety legislation – and it's not unreasonable.*' Howard recognised that the challenge was to introduce essential improvements, without losing the simplicity of the Camas experience. As he explained, '*The work involved finding imaginative new uses for existing materials, as a general ecological principle, but also retaining the character that these materials contribute to the history and sense of place.*'[3]

The redevelopment also sought to find the balance between comfort and challenge. For young people coming from backgrounds where secure housing and material comforts may not be readily accessible, additions like warm showers and a drying room were important. Camas offers a wilderness experience, and basic conditions are a valuable part of that, but it also offers a sense of safety, community and nurturance. As the then Camas Gardener Lizz Spence said: '*This renovation and the work of the Growing Hope Appeal honours the young people who have been coming over the years, and all the ones who will come in the future.*'[4]

Rachel McCann

Work in progress

Camas was closed up, and the building work began in 2006. My husband David and I chose to live on site while the work was being carried out, to act as a liaison between the Iona Community and the contractors, and also to continue the work in the garden.

I could look out of my *new* window (in the games room, a loft-style apparent) and to the left see the tranquility of the bay, and to the right, several pieces of heavy machinery, muddy scars on the lawn, piles of spoil and boulders: the debris of construction. The weather had been wonderful, and my nephew Gavin and I took ourselves off for a constitutional to Trig Point, where we had a bird's-eye view of the whole site. From the old pier we were able to appreciate the astonishing progress that the builders had made on the roof of the south building: stripped of its fragile old tiles, it was resplendent in a bright-green breathable membrane. From our vantage point we could also see that the digger-driver had reached the bottom of the track with the trench for the mains water pipe, after cutting through a mile and a half of very difficult ground. We saw the line of the level-access path in front of the north building that Drystane Dougie [volunteer] had been constructing so beautifully.

What the contractors, Extropy Construction, had achieved in twelve weeks was astonishing. Whole new floors had been fitted; modern plumbing installed: the aquatron (an environmentally friendly septic tank); old rotten materials replaced with new, fit-for-purpose stuff. All of the work was carried out to a high standard – a robust building for robust purpose.

Lizz Spence

At Camas

Alone at Camas
on a blue May afternoon
a brisk wind blowing in from the north
whisking up white froth in the bay
and the rare Camas collection of antiquated artefacts
casting sharp strange shadows on the grass.

You'd think it would be quiet, but
my street in the middle of Glasgow is quieter!
Things rattling and creaking
doors banging
tattered bits of cloth flapping in unexpected places
birch trees shivering and rustling
waves breaking on the shore
slapping the stones, ebbing and shlishing
little rivulets lapping their way into narrow grooves,
rippling over the causeway
the rumble of a weight of water moving
the deep bass bumping and thumping of sea on rock
in the kitchen, a kettle whistling
high overhead a plane beginning the long descent from Canada
lambs bleating woefully, their mothers panicking dolefully
gulls squawking, oystercatchers wailing,
the ravens in the quarry cawing
a lark calling

the noise is cacophonous

this morning there were other sounds
the generator humming
the digger grinding across the rocks
the thud of heavy bags dropping onto soft earth
voices shouting. It's no quieter now they've stopped.

Good sounds, all of them.

Kathy Galloway

Open for business

After a year of being closed for the building work, Camas reopened in 2007, with Dot Stewart at the helm as Camas Coordinator.

We are delighted that the renovation work to secure and insulate the buildings has been completed, on budget and on time (no easy feat in a remote island location two miles from the nearest road). The redevelopment has been done to a high standard of environmental sustainability.[5]

Kathy Galloway

Camas has reopened its doors for guests. Following a hectic early season of endless Work Weeks and a stream of willing volunteers who painted, cleaned and cooked, we are now ready![6]

Maggie Birley

When I first sat down to write this piece, I was going to write about how we are entering a new stage in Camas' history. About how exciting it is to have our very own electricity from the wind turbine and to shower in water heated by solar panels. About how fabulous the buildings are looking and how grateful we are to everyone who has given their time, money, expertise, energy, skills, etc. just to help get us to where we are today. All of this is true.

But this morning I came across some papers dating back to the 1980s and I was struck by how much of what has been said in the past still resonates today, both in terms of the practicalities of running the centre, and in terms of the plans that were proposed for the future. Recommendations included 'the installation of a small wind- or solar-powered electricity generator'. Well, we have done it! Most of the paperwork was about what actually happens at Camas: comments about the different groups, activities and experiences that people have shared, which reminded me, once again, that these buildings are only important because of what happens in and around them.[7]

Dot Stewart

Sharing and celebration

Camas welcomed its first group of young people to the redeveloped buildings on 2nd June, 2007, and on 11th July a day of sharing and celebration took place. It was a joy to celebrate the Camas renovations with an outdoor liturgy in the glorious July sunshine. Those of us who gathered with our packed lunches were members and associates of the Iona Community, families, staff, locals, young people, representatives of Extropy (the builders) and Gaia (the architects).

The style of the day reflected the vision of Camas: inclusive, informal, thoughtful and fun. Many of us shared Camas experiences and the air was full of stories as we explored the buildings, discovered flushing toilets, showers and stoves. We commented on the amount of 'new' space upstairs and the great living area created by removing the wall between the dining area and the community room – and all of this whilst nothing had been spoiled and it all felt the same!

In the middle of the day we joined in a short 'Blessing Ceremony for Camas Tuath' with the intention of expressing and consolidating the heart of Camas as a safe place, with all that means to guests, visitors and staff. We began at the top of the garden and made a *caim* with young people, staff and leaders, placing stones to form a protective circle as Camas was encompassed with prayer. We then moved down to the grassy area in front of the buildings where the internal space was blessed, with bundles of scented herbs from the garden placed in each room.

As the final action in the ceremony, everybody who was able to joined in the new circle ceilidh dance called 'Camas', which included steps representing the twice-daily movement of the tides, the arms of the wind turbine and the making of new friendships.

We have succeeded in our vision for Camas! We renovated Camas at a cost of about £675,000, most of which came from and through our own supporters, from fundraising events, personal generosity and sacrificial donations. At Camas we saw and celebrated the result of this.[8]

Margaret Stewart

From 'A Blessing Ceremony for Camas Tuath'

There is an old Highland tradition of praying for protection and assurance that God, the saints and angels surround us and accompany us in times of distress, crises or decision. This ritual of encompassment, or *caim*, drew an imaginary circle of prayer which enclosed and accompanied a person as they walked or travelled, safeguarding and upholding them.

Together we make a *caim* of protection and remember the saints and angels of Camas past and present:

We lay a stone for the crofting families of the Ross of Mull, who for countless generations have worked the land and sea …

We lay a stone for all those who were forced by poverty, hardship and brutal clearance to leave the Ross in the 19th century, and took ship for an unknown future in Canada and elsewhere …

We lay a stone for the quarrymen and their families, from the Ross, from Aberdeenshire, from Donegal, who built these houses and whose labour provided red granite for the Skerryvore lighthouse and many other constructions …

We lay a stone for those who built the Galloway dry-stone wall that leads to Camas, as a poor-relief project …

We lay a stone for all who fished for salmon at Camas …

We lay a stone for George MacLeod, whose vision first brought the Iona Community to Camas …

We lay a stone for all the young people who have visited Camas from young offenders institutions, especially Polmont …

We lay a stone for the thousands of young people from difficult backgrounds who have found in Camas a welcome home …

We lay a stone for all the builders who have made the vision of a renewed Camas into a reality …

We lay a stone for all new members of the Iona Community who have dug ditches, laid track, painted rooms and shifted endless piles of stones …

We lay a stone for all Community Kids who have found freedom and adventure here …

We lay a stone for all Camas Committee members, past and present …

We lay a stone for all Camas gardeners and tree-planters, past and present …

We lay a stone for all Camas outdoor instructors, past and present, whose skills have made Camas a safe place for adventure …

We lay a stone for all Camas staff and volunteers, past and present, whose care has made Camas a safe place for the Spirit …

We lay a stone for people across the world who love Camas …

Creator Spirit,
today let us be grateful for changing things:
for cloud patterns and seasonal landscapes,
for the restless sea and multi-coloured earth,
for branch and leaf and fruit and flower,
for rocks, weather-carved like an old face which could tell stories,
for wind and water and all that was never meant to stand still,
for the lilies in the field.
This is your economy: teach us its value.[9]

You have given us a vision of a new heaven and a new earth,
resources conserved, earth tended,
atmosphere cleansed, trees planted,
injustice ended, oceans teeming, nations at peace.[10]

Bless all people and organisations working to care for the earth:
all who seek to live more simply and walk more lightly on the earth,
all who are committed to change,
and may we be included among them.

Kathy Galloway and the staff at Camas

The wilderness rejoices

'Mike, will you look in each direction and say what is the same, and what has changed?' asked Becky, the Camas Gardener. I was with four of the Camas staff for the morning reflection. It was during the balmy days of April 2011, and we were in sunshine, gazing at a calm blue sea, standing a stone's throw from the Camas buildings, on the little island – the one that gets cut off as you daydream and the tide comes in. I was returning to Camas after a break of about 10 years, having first been there through the summer of 1990.

To the north, the outlines of Gometra, Ulva and Little Colonsay were familiar friends. Favourite rocks on the island in the bay still invited me to sit. It was people who had been the agents of change. A few yards to the east there was a lovely simple stone labyrinth, and to the south strong new huts. To the west were the buildings, which I recalled as impractical, damp and cramped. Restoration has made the walls, windows and roofs weather-tight. An attic added to the lower building includes a drying room – another major difficulty solved. Solar panels heat water; a wind turbine charges a huge battery, mainly for a fridge and a washing machine – joy of joys: we used to boil the tea towels, and take the other washing to Iona.

Installing mains water has solved many problems. Showers – and flushing loos – have ended night-time stumbles on uneven stone paths. The rough paths have also been made smooth, both beside the buildings, and on the track to Camas, with slip-proofed wooden walkways over the mud. I had heard nothing but praise for the renovations at Camas, and I shared that enthusiasm.

Camas remains a challenging place to live and work in though, and remains a place where only torches, candles, fireplaces and lanterns shine – and stars can still be seen. I had no doubt that the current staff would provide the energy and skills to use the place with the visiting groups – as has been done consistently for as long as I have known Camas. The people living and working there had of course changed, but the spirit, energy and humour with which they were preparing for the new season were familiar.

The previous afternoon we had been talking about how visiting groups could be encouraged to use all their senses at Camas, to build relationship with their surroundings: from that comes the impulse to care and conserve, and to share enthusiasm – expressed so well in the John Muir Trust Award scheme now an integral part of the Camas programme. So, on the island that morning we paused and listened … and I heard something that was different. There was new birdsong carried on the air of Camas. To the south, woodland planted around ten years ago was already mature enough to give shelter to the birds, and protection from wind to a garden now vastly bigger and more verdant than the one that was struggling in the early 1990s. Helping Becky (or perhaps hindering) for an hour or two the previous afternoon had made me realise the huge effort over the decades in turning that rough ground into garden.

Looking from our island that morning, the wind turbine seemed a suitable symbol of Camas, responding to the possibilities and challenges of this age. At our feet were other symbols of Camas. The very rock of the bay, pink granite, is a coming together of three minerals. Upon the rock the algae, then mosses and grasses grow, and an ecology, a natural community, develops. That same coming together of diversity, to build something beautiful and new, continues each week as new visitors are welcomed into community.

In 1990 there were concerns about localised issues of acid rain, pollution, the hole in the ozone layer. These were known to be reversible with rational policies. Yet these were the signs that unfettered commerce, industry and acquisition were unsustainable and damaged the planet. Today we know that we are generating global change – to the climate, in loss of biodiversity, in ocean acidification.

Reversing these is not so straightforward. In many circles in 1990, talk was edging forward from being about domination of the earth towards the need for stewardship. We now know that the connection to the planet that needs to be recognised and re-created is not merely one of stewardship – but of us as an intimately linked part of the planet. At Camas I imagined air, water, land, life interweaving like the lines of a Celtic cross, an interweaving that included humankind.

It is a radical hospitality that the Camas staff offer – an offer of community with them, certainly, but also with the place, the land, the history of Camas, and with the earth and stars, without the masks and distractions of city life. Camas embodies the attitudes and relationships needed to heal the planet. If a prophet hadn't started Camas in the 1940s then the Iona Community would have to start it now.[11]

Mike Mineter

My favourite room at Camas is the common room – we had lots of fun in there, playing games by the fire.

Young person

We came to Camas with a group before and after the redevelopment, and the changes mean it is much more 'liveable'. The new dorms are much better and we play 'spot the wind turbine' as we get closer to Camas on our way in!

Group Leader

The changes make Camas a much healthier and more comfortable place for staff to live and work – it is even cosy in the winter!

Camas staff member

Comfort

Ask me about comfort
and I'll tell you of a room,

of an old, slatted door
holding its own against a healthy wind,
by the rusting strength
in its metal rattling latch,

of a shuddering, salt-cornered window
reflecting leaflets on times of tides
and the occasional bus to the ferry,

of damp, whitewashed walls
that leave their mark
on your top layer of woolly warmth,

of newspaper-stuffed boots
snuggling up to a peat fire

that glows your face to a flaming red
but leaves your back cold-shouldered,

of steaming socks and dripping trousers
hung over fishing-net twine
slung from a soot-blackened ceiling,

of a room filled
with the comfort of acceptance.[12]

Nancy Somerville

Notes:

1.   From *Coracle*, the magazine of the Iona Community, 1979
2.   *From The Sacred Garden*, BBC Scotland, 2004
3.   Quotes by Howard Liddell from *Coracle*, the magazine of the Iona Community, 2007, Ruth Harvey (Ed.)
4.   From *The Sacred Garden*, BBC Scotland, 2004
5.   From *Living by the Rule: The Rule of the Iona Community*, Kathy Galloway, Wild Goose Publications, 2010
6.   From *Coracle*, the magazine of the Iona Community, 2007, Ruth Harvey (Ed.)
7.   From *Coracle*, the magazine of the Iona Community, 2007, Ruth Harvey (Ed.)
8.   From *Coracle*, the magazine of the Iona Community, 2007, Ruth Harvey (Ed.)
9.   John Bell © Wild Goose Resource Group
10. John Harrison, from *Holy Ground: Liturgies & Worship Resources for an Engaged Spirituality*, Helen Boothroyd and Neil Paynter (Eds), Wild Goose Publications, 2005
11. From *Living Letters of the Word: Readings and Meditations from the Iona Community*, Neil Paynter (Ed.), Wild Goose Publications, 2012
12. From *Pushing the Boat Out,* Kathy Galloway (Ed.), Wild Goose Publications, 1995

4. The Sea

As well as its past role in Camas' salmon-fishing history, the sea plays an important role in current Camas activities: bringing in equipment by boat, kayaking, coasteering, swimming and sailing-boat trips. It provides beautiful views and a habitat for wildlife, with sightings of otters, seals, seabirds, dolphins, minke whales and even basking sharks. Trips to beaches, including Market Bay, are always popular with guests, and for some young people it is the first time they've seen the sea – more than one Camas guest has charged straight in on arrival! Camas is nestled in a beautiful bay, and people often comment on how it feels 'held' between the hills and the sea.

Camas Bay

On the final evening we paddled out on the calm, clear and ever-so-magical water. We were not the only creatures out to play in Camas Bay that night. Four dolphins came to dance and dance around our kayaks! Breathtaking really. Here's to Camas Bay and all that dwell here.

From the Camas blog

The Chapel of the (Cotton) Nets

I remember George MacLeod coming to preach to the 'Borstal boys' in the Chapel of the (Cotton) Nets. The world has changed a great deal since then.

The difference in the world from then to now is particularly interesting from the fishing perspective. At that time most of the materials in use were of natural origin; there was next to no plastic. The move to artificial fibres around the end of the '50s and early '60s was significant. Ropes made of courlene, polypropylene and nylon were introduced. The new ropes were much stronger but it took some time for the fishermen to trust that a much thinner and lighter rope could do the job just as well as the traditional materials. Nets made from artificial fibres were also much lighter than before, which meant easier handling. They were also much more resistant to damage. When basking sharks collided with cotton nets on their summer migration, they tended to break right through, leaving a large and annoying hole in their wake. The new materials often caught the sharks instead; and it is quite likely that the resurgence of basking shark numbers in recent years is a result of the end of the bag-net fishery.

The decline of wild salmon stocks was accelerated at this time. All this was part of a change of culture. Traditional fishing included an unspoken awareness of the need for conservation. The greatly increased fishing effort, the introduction of fish farms, pollution and acidification mean that wild salmon, which were plentiful in the early days, are now close to being classed as an endangered species.

In the little pools of water outside the Camas buildings you used to often find elvers. Eels were also plentiful then. Eel numbers are down 90% since those days. You need look no further than this ecological history at Camas to see evidence of why talk of environmental disaster is more than just rumour.

The great news of course is that growing awareness of environmental damage is provoking another change of culture. Camas is a great example of environmental awareness: with the use of renewable energy, composting, cutting back severely on the use of plastics and increasing recycling. It also plays a role in educating today's young people to a more enlightened understanding of the natural world. Let's hope that the work of Camas over the next seventy years helps to bring a renewal and regeneration of the natural world which sustains us all.

Douglas Canning

This line of golden light

One of the most amazing experiences I've ever had was going out to Lunga with Mark Jardine and the group in his boat the *Birthe Marie*. We sailed out from the south coast and went round to the little island at the north of Iona and we were fishing there. Then we went right out to Lunga and camped on Lunga. We got up early in the morning and saw all the puffins coming in: those classic ones, with the sand eel in the mouth. We walked up round the corner – and there was a sea stack with thousands and thousands of birds all over it, cormorants on the shore and puffins and razorbills

– it was like something off a David Attenborough show!

Another memorable experience was camping at Market Bay and watching the sun go down with a group and a couple of staff, and there was a golden ball going down into the sea and this line of golden light coming across the sea – and then these dolphins came across the sun, jumping up and down – it was just the most incredible experience.[1]

Jon Lloyd

Cre8 enjoy the sea

Beach and dolphins!

Yesterday afternoon was a walk to Market Bay. We played non-violent games, including beach wrestling, sea football, 'grab onto the giant floating log in the sea', 'bury Matt in the sand and everyone jump on Tom'. We've seen porpoises here before, but never dolphins – they were HUGE. We saw them twice, once from the Camas boat and also later when Jon and Rob were out sailing. There was a pod of eight to ten, a mixture of what looked like adults and younger animals swimming alongside. We were following the pod; they would turn towards the boat, come close and then turn away again. Dolphins!

We are sailing

Camas is surrounded by beautiful clear-blue sea. We swim in it, kayak in it, jump into it and on occasions we also get to sail on it. Mark Jardine has this wonderful traditional sailing boat called *Birthe Marie* which he brings round to Camas, and picks us up to go sailing. Today the conditions were perfect: light winds, sunshine and a calm sea. So we went fishing. Mark lives on Iona but used to work here at Camas and he always makes room to do young people's trips during his busy summer. It's one of the ways we really benefit from the Iona Community and its commitment to disadvantaged young people. We're thankful.

From the Cre8 website

Basking sharks

This week we had an incredible group from Glasgow come and stay with us. The week was full of tons of activities – and basking sharks! We went out sea-fishing and on the way we had basking sharks come right up to the boat with their huge fins and humongous mouths; we all watched in awe, as we could literally almost reach out and touch these whale-sized sharks! We even had basking sharks in our bay, and they even came pretty close in towards the buildings!

From the Camas blog

A magical experience

Coasteering was on our rota for this week. It includes getting into wet-suits, buoyancy aids and helmets and then heading out, not completely fearless, to the islands in front of the Camas buildings to climb around them on the rocks and in the water. To finish the whole thing off, you simply jump off a big rock at the end and go for a swim. After you've done that, you come into the common room for a nice evening in front of the fire.

On Sunday night everyone was on a night walk down by the bay, and we discovered there was phosphorescence in the water of the bay. Sadly, no pictures could capture the beauty we saw, but those of you reading this who have ever been lucky enough to have experienced this wonder of nature in person will know what a magical experience it was. With a simple brush of a finger or raindrop on the smooth black surface of the water you could release a trail or pinprick of green light, and the splash of a rock turned into a natural firework explosion out in the bay. Some folks even ditched their wellies for wetsuits and went swimming, despite the cold, just to see the trails of light their strokes left in their wake.

From the Camas blog

Portrait of Camas

Ravens sliding down the blue sky,
helter-skeltering over the hills
and bouncing off ridges.
Sheep arguing across the valley,
breezes dipping in and out
of gently moving waters,
flicking, in passing, the wagtails' feathers.
Buzzards calling in the souls
of long-dead salmon-fishers –
and otters before breakfast.

Is time suspended here, locked
in the pink and white crystals of the granite;
stranded like the seaweed on
the strand between the tides?

No, time is not suspended, but we are;
our lives are far too short to register
the long, slow, pulsing rhythms,
the birth of rock in fire and heat,
the cooling, shattering, splitting uplifts,
the long, slow grinding down:
persistent, gentle seas, the ice, the frost,
the breathing of the earth;
the long, slow flowering of plants.
No, time moves on:
the builders, quarriers, fishers came and went,
as we will too.

And, in God's own good time,
these rocks, these hills, these seas
will move and change again,
responding to His rhythm.

But somewhere still, I dare to hope,
there will be
otters before breakfast.[2]

Alix Brown

Camas lullaby
(For H.M.B.)

Bracken and rock and rose-pink heather
will carpet the land for you.
Oystercatchers will dip and a heron
skim over the bay for you.
Bog-myrtle and wild mountain thyme
will scent the air sweetly for you.
Daisies and celandines and tormentil
will dance in white and gold dresses for you.
And the sea and the seals and the gulls
will sing an island lullaby for you.[3]

Kathy Galloway

Notes:

1. From *Coracle*, the magazine of the Iona Community, 2015, Neil Paynter (Ed.)
2. From *Coracle*, the magazine of the Iona Community, Kathy Galloway (Ed.)
3. From *Pushing the Boat Out*, Kathy Galloway (Ed.), Wild Goose Publications, 1995

5. The Track

The Camas track is a mile and a half walk across boggy moorland, which is part of a wonderfully rich and diverse ecosystem. The track is a place of connection and conversation, of silence and stories, and of mud and magic. It is a liminal place of beginnings and endings, of welcomes and farewells. Anyone who has worked with youth groups at Camas will also know it as a place of humour and complaints from young people beginning to step out of their comfort zones: 'When do we get there?' 'This is boggin'!' 'How far is it now?!' It has also been a place of grit and graft for many staff and guests, who have dug ditches, built bridges, laid wood and patched up paths. As former Camas Coordinator Jon Lloyd once said: 'Journeys (and track work) never end.'

It was boggy and wet and went on forever! But we got talking to new people and arrived eventually. I was glad there was tea and biscuits when we got there!

Young person

The one and a half mile track, that scares some people, don't let it scare you … that's my favourite part of Camas, cos you are always magnetised to one of the leaders at the start, and they'll be your best pal for your whole week at Camas.

Young person

Camas as a place is pretty beautiful. But emotionally it's been harder than I thought it would be. It's worth it, as it builds up your confidence a lot: you have to trust yourself. Even coming down that wee track, you have to trust where your feet are going, you have to trust where you are walking is safe, so it builds up your confidence to trust in yourself.

Young person

Walking the track

In May 2009 at Camas a group of adult guests on Kathy Galloway's 'Reading the Big Book' week were considering the theme of 'landscape'. At the morning reflection session we told of our journeys to reach Camas – then we visualised the walk we had all taken down the track …

You begin where the track leaves the main road, among cars, mailbox, dustbin, firewood pile and wheelbarrows. Far away you can see a wind turbine, and the people who meet you tell you 'beyond that turbine is where you are going'.

A farm gate, usually with a large puddle just inside it, leads to a stony farm track, with fenced fields on each side. After a short, steep slope it is straight and level for a while, though sometimes with deep muddy puddles. You can walk beside your companions and get to know them. When the track gets rougher a walkway of wooden planks appears on the left-hand side. Using this makes it easier to push the heavy wheelbarrow, if you are the one bringing supplies, especially when the track dips sharply down again.

Another gate leads to a wide, flat wooden bridge over a burn, and then to a smooth, wide, grassy track, open to the moor on either side. But the track turns sharply to go up and round a rocky knoll, and we've completely lost sight of our destination. After the sharp bends the slope is gentler, but the ground is so boggy that more planks have been laid. Walking on these should keep your feet dry, but sometimes an unwary step produces a fountain of black muddy water.

Another gentle rise leads to a wider view. The track stretches away, apparently smooth and level, and there is a clear view of the small hills with the wind turbine on top. It looks a long way still, but all very simple.

It's only as you travel along that you discover the pitfalls – steep drops, muddy holes, places where you really need the planks, which are sometimes smooth and new, sometimes rough and worn, with flat stones filling gaps.

Halfway along is another bridge over a deep burn. Now the track begins to rise again. Reaching the far side of the level moor, the track bends again, becoming a stony stream-bed, and finds its way up between small rocky hills. A pair of gateposts on the right-hand side leads nowhere. Now there is a high stone wall on the right-hand side, and steep hills on the left. You climb steeply and can no longer see where you are going – while the turbine still whirs steadily on top of the hill.

As the track levels again, becomes smooth and grassy and bends to the left, a new view appears – a valley below you, leading to the sea. Soon you have your first sight of the rooftops of Camas – but now, suddenly, the track becomes a steep, stony downward slope. You need to walk slowly, trying not to stumble, but the heavy wheelbarrow, bouncing and clattering, is trying to run away with you. You are focused so much on this that you hardly notice the back of the buildings. But you pass the blue name-post and suddenly you land on a wide, smooth lawn – the sea is right in front of you, doors open and friendly faces and voices welcome you to Camas.[1]

Joan Jones

'New Street'

Everybody who stays at Camas becomes familiar with 'the track'. Locally it used to be referred to as 'New Street', because previously access to Camas had generally been through Ardfenaig. When Bertie was using a vehicle to bring fish out, a lot of drainage was done and the track was just passable, but there was always a chance of getting bogged! Living at Camas I became so acquainted with the track that I could traverse it in the dark with no torch on even the darkest of nights, and often did so to get the post, or a gas cylinder or whatever was needed for life to continue. Indelibly imprinted in my mind was the exact route I could get a wheelbarrow down without mishap. And then there is just the experience of trudging up and down the track, in summer and winter, be it in 'pissing rain', or on lark-symphonied spring mornings, or in the pitch dark with the treacherously slippy mud waiting for your stumble, or lightfooted on a day off – away for a summer bike ride with not a care in the world. People arriving for the first time at Camas were sometimes misbelieving that they were actually going to arrive at the coast!

I remember one night Deryck Collingwood was filling in at Bunessan Parish Church for the minister; he had to change some of his clothes at the car at the road end to be respectable for the job – only to discover that he had left his keys back at Camas. I got a mention at the service, as it seemed more appropriate that I be the one to go back down and up the track in the dark to still have the minister there on time. Needless to say I was somewhat less presentable-looking by the time I reached the car for the second time!

Mark Jardine

Track space

The track played an important part in the groups' experience – for both them and us. It intensified their arrival, and the anticipation of turning the corner and seeing the bay open up in front of you. It also gave us time to suss out some of the young people a little. On their departure, the track was a great safety valve as well. It gave us space, and by the time we had returned to base to deal with chores, I had pretty much put aside the events of the week just done and was able to focus on the one about to start.

Sheila Bates (Russell)

Beauty beyond words

Camas lies at the end of a mile and a half of track which traverses drainage ditches, peat bog, low-growing heather, ubiquitous bracken and bog-myrtle forest. Old stone dykes flank much of the track, before it rises to unveil the wonder of Camas Bay, with its distinct tidal island. The old fishing cottages seem as if they are sliding into the sea; and from the rise in the track, one can see the severity of the Ardmeanach cliffs. It was from here that a young guest from a residential school, a young man very nervous about arriving in a place so different from his native Glasgow, proclaimed: 'It's so beautiful!'

The land itself seemed to provoke wonder in young people visiting the Centre on week-long breaks. After this young man affirmed nature's 'beauty beyond words', I always paused at the rise in the track while leading groups to the Centre. Often, I perceived the hard shells of these young people crack under a beauty which transcends class, history, even understanding.[2]

Eric Wojchik

Journeys

The track to Camas is rough, long (if you are as unfit as I am!) and hard work. There are moments of uncertainty – am I going the right way? Are we nearly there yet? Can I carry this pack all of the way? It was a wonderful opportunity to reflect and to pray as a new journey, a new pilgrimage began. During the week, I had the opportunity to help rebuild the track where it had been worn down by a long season. Walking back down it at the end of the week, I noticed how well it reflected the journeys of each New Member that I had met. Journeys of toil and uncertainty. Journeys through oppression and pain. Journeys that are shaped by each moment of life.

Alex Clare-Young

Through sheer effort and a few songs

Work on the track made steady progress throughout the week. The satisfaction of being up to your knees in bog was not lost on our team of volunteers, who managed to get the drains flowing through sheer effort and a few songs. The work on the drains means that over the winter they won't flood and the track should remain relatively dry!

From the Camas blog

The track

Wild geese fly overhead,
burnt umber, the landscape,
hunting ground for the Spirit of God.
She is the huntress;
relentlessly she pursues her prey,
wrestling with us, daring us
       to live, to fight
       to freedom, to passion

    to love, to pain
    to mud and to fire.

She is the Priestess
leading us through the liturgy of the track
each time we walk its length.
We are called deeper into the mystery,
the mystery of what?

The mystery of solitude
the mystery of friendship
the mystery of struggle
the mystery of shared burdens.

The mystery of pilgrimage
the mystery of sunset and moonlight
the mystery of the way
the mystery of God.

Amy Chakif

Both, and …
(*For R.*)

Look! Can you see the daisies
on the drying ground, dancing ground,
at the sea's edge – or is it snow?
Otters at play
in the waves beyond the island, or stray weed
tugged to and fro?

What is meeting you as you walk the track –
is it sun or squall?
It is both, becoming a rainbow.

Is it a wide winter sky
amazed by blue breaking through?

A landscape where fragments of colour
are distinct over great distances –
or is it the broken plates and cups
of households a hundred years ago?

Sea-worn, faded yet living blue,
reminders that human life goes on
and is beautiful, even when broken.

What is meeting you as you walk the track –
is it sun or squall?
It is both, becoming a rainbow.

Is it a bare and barren pole planted on the hill,
like a standing stone
or a signpost to nowhere –
or is it the makings of a cross,

meeting point, place where God is at work?
Is it the voices of children
far from the city, finding a different space,
or the call of the oystercatcher and curlew
at home in this place?

What is meeting you as you walk the track –
is it sun or squall?
It is both, becoming a rainbow.
Is it soft Hebridean rain on your face,
or tears at parting and returning?
It is both, becoming a rainbow.

Jan Sutch Pickard

The way to Camas

There's a stormy road
that can lead to a track
where the heavy mud clogs the pores of your boots
dragging you down,
gluing you to ground level.

But that dark track
can lead to a dawning
where light exposes and banishes
the shaded corners of despondency,
and cool rain brings stagnant pools to life.

There's a road to Camas from Craignure,
a road to Camas from Glasgow, Penang, Toronto
and the rest.
There's a road to Camas from Camas –
whether clear and open,
or hidden by the mist of confusion –

always there,
ready to lead
to the Camas inside.

Nancy Somerville

Returning in winter

Stumbling down a once familiar track,
wondering what will be the same or changed.
Thick ice, night sky, cold feet,
directions confused and knees all bruised …
As so many times before, an angel stranger grabs my hand,
shares his light;
we journey together.

Awakening to January's canvas,
red blaze and grey.
Sea calls at our door,
wind rages her welcome
as slow summer days dance and sing in the smile of my memory …

Oystercatchers screech excitement at the first family flight,
city kids leap (all banter and Irn Bru)
into unknown waters of something new,
blessing us with laughter and teaching us of truth.
Unsure adults, bringing gifts of joy and tears
in the challenge of simplicity, celebrate community,
as the place between stranger and friend disappears …

Winter waves crash and roar around me,
unnerving urban sensibilities,
making me feel so small,
and yet –

I am, we are, this is
created, cherished, entrusted
by the eternal hands of Love.[3]

Rachel McCann

Notes:

1. From *Living Letters of the Word: Readings and Meditations from the Iona Community*, Neil Paynter (Ed.), Wild Goose Publications, 2012
2. From *This Is the Day: Readings and Meditations from the Iona Community*, Neil Paynter (Ed.), Wild Goose Publications, 2007
3. From *Coracle*, the magazine of the Iona Community, Kathy Galloway (Ed.), 1998

Moving on

When the time comes to move on from Camas, mixed emotions can be a challenge for both staff and guests. The ebb and flow of people is a part of the natural rhythm of the place; as George MacLeod said, 'The fact that things change and move and flow is their life.'[1]

Reflecting on the Camas experience and integrating this into the next steps of life are important parts of the process of learning and leaving.

Camas times

My first visits to Camas were when I was a small child; lots of happy times visiting the Collingwood family both at Camas itself and in their caravan at the road end. (Pat and Deryck were really pioneers of the 'staycation' before we even knew 'staycationing' was a thing!)

I returned to Camas for a week when I was about 11 – and that time I pretty much hated it. The track was too long, my bag was too heavy, the sea was too cold, the abseil cliff was FAR too high …

When I was a little older, and wanted to become a member of the Iona Community, I knew I would have to spend time at Camas again as part of the New Members Programme. I remember very clearly giving myself a pep talk: 'Come on, Dot – you can do this. It's only going to be two weeks out of your entire life …'

I am happy that, of course, it didn't end up being only two weeks out of my entire life, as I quickly discovered that Camas was a very special place, where I felt at home, and where I felt I could be more myself than anywhere else. I later went on to be a volunteer, Programme Worker and then Coordinator at Camas.

I learned many things during my time working at Camas:

I learnt about the tides.

I learnt that moon shadows are an actual thing, and not just something Cat Stevens made up for a song.

I learnt that the longer you wear your jeans without washing them, the comfier they get.

I learnt that the pee bucket is actually much more unpleasant than the poo bucket, but if you offer to empty the poo bucket everyone will think you're doing them a favour.

I learnt to drive in wellies and – most importantly – to dance in walking boots!

I learnt that I could do things I didn't know I was capable of, and I had the privilege of watching others realise the same thing about themselves.

I learnt that sometimes, when something feels impossible, other people will come along and help make it happen.

I learnt that Camas doesn't really belong to anyone, but that many, many people can all belong to Camas.

And I learnt that Camas is a place of both constancy and change.

I was fortunate enough to work at Camas both immediately before and after it was renovated back in 2006. Before the renovations happened, some were concerned that to 'improve' Camas might be to 'spoil' it. That somehow if life at Camas were less basic, it might also be less special. Of course, happily, that didn't turn out to be the case. There may now be a little bit of electricity (sometimes), hot water for showers, and even flushing toilets and a washing machine, but the things that make Camas what it is are still there:

Friendships
Challenges
Acceptance
Adventures
Community
Freedom
Singing
Activity
Reflection
Hard Work
The Quarry
The Bay
The Island
The Garden
And of course, the Track

I feel very grateful to have been one of the people who has belonged to Camas over the last 70 years. I am sure that anyone who has spent time there will have names, faces, memories etched into their minds – and hearts (and in the case of names, sometimes they're etched into the rafters too!).

Dot Stewart

At Camas, I learned to face my fears whilst having fun.

Young person

You learn a lot about yourself as well as others. You realise you don't need certain things that you usually think you need; like the internet, you don't need it, it's not a life priority. Camas showed me that there are other things that are important.

Young person

At home we remind each other how we worked together at Camas – building rafts, putting up tents, cooking – and we try to make sure everyone is included and respected, like at Camas.

Young person

Camas is central to the Iona Community's youth work. It also provides a great opportunity for young adults who volunteer there. They have the chance to learn new skills, to have unique experiences and to reflect on their direction in life. Working there can often influence vocational choices and values; this is something that often goes under the radar in how we evaluate the work of the Iona Community.

Peter Macdonald, a former Leader of the Iona Community

Good news

I owe a lot to Camas and I think we need to extend the lifestyle way beyond the track and the island. I'm glad to still be attached to the grid and live much closer to the main road but experiencing Camas over the years shows both what is possible and how difficult it can be. It's not about replicating Camas; it's about soaking up the experience and taking home the ethos, seriously applying it to life elsewhere.

That's good news, that's the Spirit at work.

It could make a big difference.

Thank God for Camas.

Liz Gibson

We are sad to be leaving Camas. The welcome and support of the Camas staff and the beauty of the place has given us a week we will never forget.

Group Leader

The journey continues

The Jubilee year 2000 was a pilgrimage year for me. It was not just that I visited the four Porte Sante of Rome; it was a long and enriching journey, a journey on foot and in both faith and philosophy. The centre of this journey was the five months I spent as a Camas volunteer.

I was captured by the idea of living simply. Perhaps some would think we took things to extremes, living without so much. But stripping things back, we found what is truly essential: namely, that the greatest joys came from living together in community, in work and in play, during meals and in reflection. And I never once minded emptying those compost toilets.

During this time, I realised what it means to be a 'consumer' and how little we actually need to consume. I began to incorporate a love for humanity into my faith, bringing awareness of social issues, of intolerance, poverty, human rights and violence.

Leaving Camas was quite difficult, and sorting through all I had learned, where it had brought me, and where I wanted it to take me, was a challenging task. How is the experience of Camas to be transported from that beautiful bay?

I was fortunate to have the chance to work on that process in Italy. During my visit there, I journeyed to the city of Assisi, and found great peace walking the paths and exploring the grottoes surrounding the Mountains of St Francis.

Here are some of my thoughts from that time:

'How can one describe the peaceful stillness, the quiet whisper of God's voice? I cannot say in words, but the wind speaks of it, the twirling leaf on a spider's web proclaims God's presence. The first real peace since Camas; the stillness enfolds me, and I return to Camas, not in place but in wholeness of spirit. I find a grotto, a circle of stones, small handmade crosses of twigs, sit at the centre. I place tiny stones in a circle, and at the centre, a cross. I see myself

touching the holy in my sculpture, sensing the poetry of nature. I see art and nature become one in expressing God's silent words. Here my Camas spirituality makes sense – it is incorporated into theatre and story, ecology and simplicity. I feel the warmth of God.'

And so, the journey continued and held me close to the gifts and insights of Camas, whilst I gained new awareness of new spiritual homes and kindred hearts.

Natalie Gould

I just want to be back in Camas, playing games, mucking about on the beach and having amazing banter with my mates.

Young person

The Camas week was one of the best I have had. I miss the sea and the people. I learned a lot of new things and one day I would like to go back as a volunteer.

Young person

We always value Camas because it gives our young people the chance to be young – to laugh and play. Some of the stresses and responsibilities they face at home are very difficult. Camas gives them not just a holiday, but a chance to think about things in a new way. We try and remind them of good moments at Camas when they are struggling – how they met a challenge or how they helped in the group. This always brings a smile to their faces!

Group Leader

Starting point for other life adventures

Young people have benefitted from Camas in a variety of ways, ranging from learning from others, participating in activities, gaining new skills and having positive experiences which increase their self-confidence.

For the staff, too, it has been a starting point for other life adventures, influenced future life choices and focused priorities. Being part of the team has benefited some who may have had difficult personal experiences before coming to work at Camas.

Tor Justad

Just back home from a week away at Camas with no electricity, limited hot water … Came home to all the technology I could ask for, yet I want to be back on Mull already. People and friends are all I need to get by; without that, life is just full of pointless technology to keep us on the edge of boredom and insanity.

Young person

Camas taught me about nature, growing my own food, trees and birds. I am much more mindful of the environment now.

Adult guest

Goodbye to Camas

Four years ago I walked down the track with excitement and trepidation about what was to come. Tomorrow I will walk back up with a bag full of the happiest and most life-changing memories.

Thank you Camas for all the songs, the dancing and for unveiling rapper M.C. AbMcFab into the world; for the daily breathtaking beauty of the land and the people and for making all the hard work so incredibly worth it.

Thank you to everyone I have met along the way: for your stories and warmth, your challenges and support and friendship.

Thank you to the chickens – the best youth workers on Mull!
With wholehearted gratitude, cheers Camas!

Abbi Mason

I miss …

I miss being at Camas in so many ways. I miss communing in the common room. I miss eating lunch and dinner together. I miss being at the quarry and seeing people work together to overcome insecurities. I miss being a part of hosting people in community. I miss making food with others. I miss exploring with others and getting to see the different things that different people see. I miss the garden. I miss the bathroom and the many great conversations that happen in there. I even miss the sheep a bit, or maybe it's that I miss making fun of the sheep. I miss the fun.

Kelsey Lavoie

Camas increased my confidence; the support of my youth group leaders and the Camas staff made me feel good about myself, and I will try to help others increase their confidence from now on.

Young person

Manna from heaven

the circle of stones in the sand
will keep its shape only until
the tide washes over it
and tumbles the stones to a new beauty

desire too, white as the midsummer moon
or dark as pools on the shadowed side of the island,
has its ebb and flow

the eye that fills and the hand that trembles
are dry and still before the candles have guttered
and the ashes are cold in the grate

and intimacy is precious and fleeting as the scent of oil
on air and skin

we are going where it is not safe to dance with abandon and ecstasy
where we cannot laugh with trusting hearts
where prayer is not as uncomplicated as breathing in the silence

but we will remember
that we ate manna from heaven
because we were hungry
and lived the truth of ourselves

of our need
and our sufficiency[2]

Kathy Galloway

Friday morning

We three stand there on the rocks,
saluting a glorious morning;
on the edge of the sea,
dazzling under a pink sky,
one group are just leaving,
with tears and lighter rucksacks
to a new beginning …

Ruth Thomas

End of season

Craig depresses the mini-bus clutch
for Ally to slam it into first
and then a cooperative three-point turn.

He drives too fast
on the single-track road
and then thrown together we hug the corner
then rattle downhill, scattering sheep
as others, chewing, look on
with vapid stares.

> Our speed must overtake this time
> and carry us back
> to when there was no rush,
> no sweat,
> when things we felt could be left unsaid
> until later.

Past the pier, clear now
of weekly supplies
to moan or cheer over –
own-brand beans and Jaffa cakes.
We coast the S-bend of the village
to bump and judder left
across the stone bridge.

I stare past the old crack
in the shuddering glass
and for once in my life
ignore the caution signs
just glad for this last day.

Nancy Somerville

Caveat for the Camas alchemists

I thought I had made it,
escaped with my sadness intact,
but at the top of the track
(my crusty shell just within my reach)
Eric brought me down with
a dagger of light through my heart.

Softly wounded, falling in slow motion
onto a bed of green moss,
suspended in sunlight,
scented with bog-myrtle and mountain orchids
and then tears

   'oh, no, not the tears … please'.

They poured down the insides of my cheeks,
balm passing through my aching throat
into the wound created by the dagger,
hot salt shot through with golden starbursts,
melting another piece of lead ingot,
replacing it with daffodils and dandelions.

I have little defence against daggers of light.
I have little defence against golden starbursts.
I have no defence against loving intention.

Stuart Barrie

Camas farewell

So long Camas,
and thanks for all the scones.

You were my sun and stars,
my night, my day,
my seasons,
summer, winter, my sweet spring, my autumn song,
the church in which I pray,
my land and ocean,
all that the earth can bring.

Thank you to the people at Camas,
who were gracious enough to share their time with me.
Playing ping-pong, dancing at washing-up,
on the lawn, in the common room,
conversations serious and silly,
swimming in the bay and off the beach,
adventures here, there and everywhere.

Thank you to the people of the Ross of Mull,
who stopped to chat, chewed the fat
and allowed me to make this my home.
Cosmic ceilidhs, magic music nights, Calmac conversations,
ferry-shop convergences and just being able to say hello.

Thank you to the hills, mountains, white sands, blue sky and bluer sea,
birds and bees, golden light and pink granite
that nurtured my spirit, my body, my soul
and kept me mindful of the beauty and energy of the universe.

Thank you Camas and all who sail in her,
for the love that has touched me so deeply
and given me the trust to look inwardly as well as outwardly.

Thank you to the track that shows journeys
(and track work)
never end …

Jon Lloyd

Goodbyes

'goodbyes are never
the end, true
friends will always
meet again …'

'but I'll miss you and
her and him' she
said

skimming the
water, eyes miles
away on the
journey of miles she'd
to do the next day.

miss waking up to
the ever changing
beauty of the
bay
sound of the
water, cocks crowing
Wendy wheezing

the feeling of
walking on wild
barren prairies
as we'd trudge up
the track

sludge through
mud and puddles to
the pub.

in the early
hours of the
morning, we'll
steal away
by boat, by train

in the early
hours of the
morning, I'll steal a piece
of this place

keep it locked in
my memory to
help keep me sane

eyes brimmed with water
eyes miles away,
on the journey
of miles she'd
to do the next day

Jenny Smith

One day on the Ross

One day you wake
and the sky is a thin icy blue
and you hear the call of the wild geese,
with strong wingbeats disturbing the air
as they land on the shore – but you
know they are only passing through.

One morning you glimpse
a green tide flowing –
transforming the hills, which winter
left pale and tired: the sap of spring rising;
but you know that seasons
keep turning, like waters coming and going.

One day you step
off the path, suddenly wading
through bluebells, fragrant and deep
in hue as the sky's zenith, primroses'
fine embroidery, violets like tiny jewels:
you know they're more precious, because fading.

One day you notice
the cuckoo has come and gone,
gold dandelions have turned into silver clocks,
seeds scattered, fledglings have flown the nest,
and different otters have reclaimed the shore:
like restless clouds, everything's moving on.

One afternoon, look,
reflecting the high-summer sky,
harebells fragile as joy, brief as a breath;
but you know they hold hope –
like that rainbow over the loch – being signs
(though dying) of love that will never die.

One autumn day –
when the burns are swollen with rain –
you see that the bracken's begun to turn;
rowan trees, glowing with ripe berries,
tell scarlet rosaries,
counting the days till winter comes again.

One day you look out
as gathering swallows, one by one, alight
on the wires like musical notes.
They played in the long movement of summer.
It comes to a close. They know
when it's time to go – and now the time is right.[3]

Jan Sutch Pickard

The Light of the world is shining

A poem inspired by a reflection on finding hope in the world beyond Camas.

We placed candles on a map –
the world spread out on a damp, dusty floor,
held down by sea-gifted stones and shells,
circled by the old and young,
the searchers and seekers,
the dreamers and healers.

We placed candles on a map
because we knew that wars were raging
and hate and shame and fear were rising,
because we knew our brothers were dying
and in their arms their children were crying,
because we knew our sisters were starving
whilst greed and wealth and violence were harming,
because we knew our land was taken
and trees were cut and gifts were stolen,

because we knew of pain and sorrow
and our neighbours' fears of facing tomorrow.

Because we knew,
we placed candles on a map,
chartered the contours of care,
marked lines where love lived,
pinpointed places where
people and projects made peace.

We placed candles on a map,
one in each spot:

for the bridge builders in Belfast
and the soul-healers in Sarajevo,
for the young women of Washington Heights
and the earth-carers of Kerala,
for the mothers of Liverpool
and the ministers in Maputo,
for the sister in San Francisco
and the believers in Beijing,
for the joy-givers in Johannesburg
and the campaigners in Chiapas …
for love, for truth,
for justice, for peace
we placed candles on a map.

We placed candles on a map
and in our humble act of honouring hope
we saw the Light of the world was shining.[4]

Rachel McCann

Coriolis

The sky above me
is also over Camas,
where the rising tide
divides and unites around ever-diminishing rocks,
where seas, hills and sky meet to form angles of elements
reaching out to infinity.

But I'm here
in rush hour traffic
looking up from long shadows
to where the early-evening light
sets ablaze the wings of pigeons
homing in on city rooftops –
a flock of glitter spiralling
in ever-decreasing circles,
surrendering to the Coriolis effect,
drawn to their Earth.[5]

Nancy Somerville

Sea glass

The harsh serrated edges of city
rounded by the elements,
made beautiful and faint and scratched,
visible to others,
uniquely flawed, open.
The edges perfected,
played with,
brought home to nature.

A shell,
a broken bottle, litter
turned by sea waves.

We return to city, etched, softened sea glass,
willing to feel the wind, linger longer in the darkness,
hold silence in the street, note mystery in every city face,
every trespassing oak, and the dramas our eyes avert,
until we ourselves become the bay forging the city,
a rounding roughness that is
always glass but resembles shell.

Eric Wojchik

The flow

It's the way you've survived over and again,
the way you float up through your pain
still smiling under water your soft beluga grin
opening your arms to let the raven fly in.

It's the way you try to show yourself in full
your answer to the deeper pull.

How we walked through the bog cotton
in the evening light last night
our friends in front of us
seemed to vanish in the glow
hand in hand with the flow.

We were all hand in hand with the flow.

Debra Hall

Notes:

1. From *Daily Readings with George MacLeod*, Ron Ferguson (Ed.), Wild Goose Publications, 1991
2. From *The Dream of Learning Our True Name*, Kathy Galloway, Wild Goose Publications, 2004
3. From *Between High and Low Water: Sojourner Songs*, Jan Sutch Pickard, Wild Goose Publications, 2008
4. From *Holy Ground: Liturgies & Worship Resources for an Engaged Spirituality*, Helen Boothroyd and Neil Paynter (Eds), Wild Goose Publications, 2005
5. From *A New Beginning*, Brown and Whittaker Publishing, 1999

AFTERWORD

Leave-taking has rituals. There's a ritual at the Camas track-end that has come and gone over the years. The group leaving Camas gathers before the bus arrives, standing in a circle whatever the weather. As a ball of wool is passed from one to the other, a word of thanks – a prayer of gratitude perhaps – is offered for the time that has gone. Once all have shared a 'gratitude', and are now bound together with the wool, each breaks off a piece of that wool, winding it around their wrist, as a memory of our connectedness for the onward journey.

Bound and loosed – experiences at Camas, where adventure is mixed with deep reflection, simple living, contemplative moments and profound community sharing – guests and staff alike form and reform community each time there is a welcome or a leave-taking at the head of the track. We are both bound together in shared experience and we are loosed – from the patterns of daily living that have become 'normal', to patterns of daily living that are freeing. These experiences of being bound and loosed together are brought vividly to life in this collection of writings.

And the track – always the track. That icon of beginnings and endings, the Camas track is a liminal transition space between the life we are leaving behind and the life we are joining, between the now and the not-yet, no matter which direction we are travelling, either down or up the track! The track is a kind of Holy Saturday space of transitioning from one profound moment to another.

Leave-taking has other rituals. On Iona, for guests and staff of the Iona Community, whether you've been there for a week, a month, a year or longer – there are rituals. Waving farewell at the jetty is maybe the most profound. A 'leaving service' in Iona Abbey where those remaining offer a blessing on those departing is another. Passing a stone around a circle, naming the good in each, offering a word of blessing to all, creating songs for leave-taking are yet more. And in times of physical connecting, hugs are a powerful symbol of being bound and loosed in community.

For most at Camas, having visited for a few days or weeks, the leave-taking begins as we set off back up the track. If we're not deep in our own exhausted/exhilarated reverie, or in conversation with others, rucksack

292   Down the track

packed with soggy socks, then as we walk up the track we may remember the 'delight-fear' of abseiling or coasteering as we pass the hanging washing and drying wetsuits on the lawn. We may relish the harvesting, the cooking, the feeding, the composting as we pass the polytunnel, the pizza oven, the lazy beds, the huts.

Gradually the track transforms from rough peaty bogland scattered with wooden planking, through the gate to a more even track and so gradually turning into the rubble and hardstanding of a track for vehicles. As the track takes on the guise of more typical human interaction, so we Camas-emerged souls begin to reach for coins long lost in our pockets, tickets and chargers buried deep in rucksacks as we lift our eyes to the horizon and see the road, hear traffic.

Since the early 1940s, it is people of the Camas community, nestled in the bay at the end of the track, that have been a crucible of transformation for young and old, offering solace, adventure and life-changing moments to all. The Camas 'community' gathered here in this volume testify to the power of community in the face of so much that is wrong with our world. May the Camas track, and the community that awaits all who venture down it, remain an icon of transformation for generations to come.

Ruth Harvey, Leader of the Iona Community

About The Contributors

Keir Aitken is a Scottish director and theatre maker whose work includes VR performance, movement and live audience engagement. He also hosts *Thoughts*, a philosophy podcast, and enjoys a morning swim.

Esa Aldegheri grew up in a Scottish-Italian family. She first visited Mull as a child and vividly remembers getting drenched on a walk not far from Camas. She has enjoyed nourishing times at Camas during the annual retreat held there for GRAMNet postgraduates.

Lucy Allan visited Camas in 2017. She studied Outdoor Education at the University of Cumbria. She loves giving most activities a go – if it means being outside and having fun.

Norman Alm worked at Finchden Manor, a therapeutic community in Kent for adolescent boys, and then in Dundee devising and running support programmes for young people in trouble. Later he was an academic in computing at Dundee University, developing computer-based communication systems for non-vocal people and for older people with dementia.

Maeve Austin enjoys walking, climbing and canoeing. She has been visiting Camas since the age of 10 and loves its sense of community and all the wonderful people she has met there.

Stuart Barrie is a Glaswegian poet and was an annual visitor to Camas over several decades. He worked for forty years as an engineer, and along with his former colleagues features in the film *Nae Pasaran!*.

Sheila Bates (Russell) was Camas cook (May-August 1985) and Camas Leader (September 1985-December 1988). She runs a croft with her husband and is a textile artist.

Jean Belgrove first visited Camas in 1997. She is member of the Iona Community and lives in Brighton, where she enjoys her garden and allotment.

Doug Birley is from Scotland and has had a strong connection to Camas from a young age – this inspired him to become a youth worker. He currently works with young people at Camas.

Maggie Birley was a Camas Committee Convener and member of the Iona Community, who ran Scottish Wood (www.scottishwood.co.uk) with her husband, Jim. Their three children, Kitty, Jo and Doug, have all been Camas volunteers. Maggie died in 2018.

Hannah Blyth first came to Camas aged 12. She was a volunteer in 2012 and 2014 and Programme Worker from 2015-18. Hannah's main passions are the sea, exploring, cooking and food, and most of all sharing these with young people and community groups. She lives in Glasgow.

Alix Brown is an integrative psychotherapist and a member of the Iona Community. Because of her work with young people, many of whom are in Local Authority care, she recognises the importance of Camas as a place which provides support and challenge and enables real personal growth.

Graeme Brown is a former Leader of the Iona Community (1974-1981), who lives in Edinburgh.

Sarah Brown has been a friend of Camas for over 20 years and has witnessed the joy and transformation of many young people there around the fire, watching the tide turn, seeing stars fly and the bell being rung with stones. She can currently be found flying kites in Aberdeen.

Sandy Brunton was born and raised on Mull. He spent many happy summers at Camas as a youngster, along with various cousins. He still lives on Mull and is very active in local community development projects.

Fiona Caley is an East Yorkshire photographer. For six years she lived in Scotland, with three years spent with the Resident Group on Iona. Her love of the land, sea and her faith brought Fiona to the west coast of Scotland and still influences her life in Withernsea, East Yorkshire, along with her other lifelong love of photographing the landscape. These themes are where she finds her strength and inspiration. Instagram @fionacaley, www.fionacaley.org.uk

Iain Campbell spent three years as a youth worker for the Iona Community. As part of that role, he worked with groups before, during and after their visits to Camas. The biggest highlight of this was helping to re-establish the Iona Community's links with Polmont Young Offenders Institute. Iain now works as an artist, mostly painting portraits: www.idcampbell.com

Douglas Canning is retired and lives in Tiroran, Mull.

Amy Chakif spent a season as a volunteer at Camas in 2000. Her poem 'The Track' was inspired by many walks up and down the track to welcome and bid farewell to guests, to collect supplies in the wheelbarrow and to just walk for walking's sake to reflect and enjoy the beauty of the surroundings. Amy stayed on the Ross of Mull for two years, living and working at the Keel Row, Fionnphort, making life-long friends and immersing herself in the stunning landscape. She calls Aotearoa New Zealand home, where she lives with her husband and three wonderful children.

Sarah Chapman and her brother were born at Camas while their parents were the Coordinators in the 1970s, and it was home until she was four. She was involved with the Iona Community and the Iona Youth Associates throughout her teens and twenties. She returned to Camas in 2004/5 as a volunteer – and loved every minute of it. She now lives in Argyll with her husband, Alan, and their two boys, Finn and Calum, working as Community Project Manager for Carr Gomm.

Alex Clare-Young is a pioneer minister in the United Reformed Church and is passionate about trans theology and intersectional social justice. Alex's book *Transgender, Christian, Human* is published by Wild Goose. Alex spent a week at Camas as part of the New Members Programme, where they learnt about taking risks together in community.

Pat Collingwood was a member of the Resident Group at Camas from 1976-1982. She has visited Mull every year since leaving Camas. Pat studied in Edinburgh and became a social worker, practice teacher, lecturer and trainer, specialising in the psychology of learning. She loves the outdoors, travel, India and the Western Isles.

Abbey Charlotte Connelly visited Camas in 2017 while studying Outdoor Education at the University of Cumbria. She enjoys caving and climbing, as well as tae kwon do.

Rachel Daniels came to Camas as a volunteer from northern California for the 2016 season. She dreams of the day she can return to that little hut she called home between a garden and the sea. Her photography can be found at wanderingcamera.net

Viv Davies is a former nurse and midwife. In the early 2000s she brought two groups of homeless people from 'The Ark Breakfast Café' in Edinburgh to Camas.

She hopes that some of them still remember the peace they found there.

Sally Denton (née Bolton) helped to lead weeks at Camas during the summers of 1976-1978 while training to be a teacher. Lasting friendships were made and the experience of Camas put her on the path towards some of life's bigger questions, expanded her horizons and led to a greater appreciation of the world.

Paul Derbyshire was a Camas volunteer in 1979, and the Camas Team Leader from 1982-85. He met his partner, Ingrid, at Camas and they were on the Resident Group together. She is a retired gardener and he is a retired teacher.

Helen Douglas gardened at Camas the year it reopened, in 2007, and again ten years later in 2017. She is a shepherd in Perthshire. She returns to Mull whenever she can.

Mary Duncanson trained as an Occupational Therapist. In 1993 she worked as a volunteer at Camas from May to October. From 1994-1996 she worked for an NGO in Zimbabwe, before returning to Iona in 1996 as Staff Coordinator for three years. She returned to work as an OT with the NHS, retiring in 2012. She became a member of the Iona Community in 2009, an Ordained Local Minister in 2013, and was the Convener of the Camas Committee from 2014-2018.

Emilie Selby Ebbestad visited Camas in 2017 when she was studying Outdoor Education at the University of Cumbria. She is a jack-of-all-trades when it comes to outdoor activities, but climbing, hillwalking and snow sports hold a special place in her heart.

Bryan Evans has worked at Camas many times as a volunteer and was Team Leader at Camas in 1990. Since then he's been working in Glasgow in the voluntary sector, presently for Children 1st: Scotland's National Children's Charity. Bryan is a Trustee of the Iona Community.

Susan H. Evans is a writer and writing teacher/coach, living in East Tennessee. She worked as a volunteer at Camas in the summer of 2007. She is a traveller of the world, looking for adventure and hoping to lend a helping hand.

Leith Fisher was a parish minister in the Church of Scotland in Glasgow and Falkirk, a member of the Iona Community, a broadcaster, and a Convener of the General Assembly's Panel on Worship. He was a gifted speaker (and also a gifted listener) and his pastoral abilities were legendary. Leith led youth camps at Camas in 1964 and 1965. He died in 2009.

Angela Formby was a Camas volunteer in 2017 and 2018 and Camas Environment Worker from 2019 to 2021. After completing an MSc in Environmental Sustainability, she worked as a residential volunteer at Lothlorien Therapeutic Community and Edinburgh Cyrenians Farm Community, as well as being involved in a housing co-op and a workers' co-op in Edinburgh.

Kathy Galloway has led, facilitated or assisted with many programmes at Camas over the last 30 years. From 1999-2002, she was Co-Convener of the first Camas Committee, and as Leader of the Iona Community from 2002-9, she was much involved with the Camas renovations. More recently she was Co-Leader of the Iona Community for two years. She thinks she is the only person to have spent at least one overnight at Camas every year since 1989. She has found Camas inspirational for both her writing and her gardening.

Laura Gamwell was a Camas volunteer in 1999 and 2001. Some fifteen years later, she went back as Resident Gardener for four years. She is passionate about growing organic vegetables and has worked in a variety of community garden settings. She finds joy in dancing (especially barefoot in the mud), building with cob, swimming outdoors and more recently, and most importantly, in being a mama to a wee one brimming with curiosity.

Rosie Gibbs was at Camas for four seasons: first as a volunteer, then as a Programme Worker for three years.

Liz Gibson is a member of the Iona Community, Church of Scotland minister, social entrepreneur, environmentalist, feminist, pacifist, wife, mum, organic crofter, tea grower, bookseller, theatre technician and craftworker. She lives on Mull with her husband, Martyn.

Natalie Gould was a Camas volunteer in 2000 and 2001. Since Camas, she has worked in education, theatre and artisan breadmaking. She now works from home for a software company, which allows her space to explore community and sustainable agriculture on her small farm in California.

Ellie Green visited Camas in 2017 with Cumbria University. As a student of Outdoor Education, she enjoys combining philosophy and well-being with the outdoors, from wandering in woodlands to dipping in the sea.

Debra Hall was a volunteer at Camas in the 1990s. She subsequently lived on Iona then Mull for ten years and became a regular facilitator of groups and staff trainings at Camas. She now lives in southwest Scotland where she writes and records audio meditation scripts for Insighttimer.com and makes poetry and art. The elements that continue to anchor her life are her relationship with her husband and close friends, an intimate friendship with nature, a fire to tend, nourishing food, her work for the world, creativity, fun, Presence and Love.

John Harvey first volunteered at Camas as cook in 1958, and was a strong supporter of Camas as a member of the Iona Community, Abbey Warden, Islands Committee Convener and Leader of the Iona Community. A retired Church of Scotland minister living in Glasgow, he is involved with family, local church and community issues.

Neil Harvey first visited Camas as part of Community Kids Week in the 1980s. He went on to volunteer and then to be Camas Coordinator (with Craig Ross) in 1993, and on his own in 1996. He's lived all over the place – but Camas remains his favourite place in the whole world! A former member of the Camas Committee, he lives on a croft about five miles from Camas and builds camper vans.

Ruth Harvey first visited Camas in the early 1970s and hasn't stopped. As a volunteer at Camas in the 1980s and 1990s she rediscovered her childlike love of wild places and swimming in the sea. In 1993, turning the corner from the track to the green, she met Nick, cleaning the kayaks … and he later became her husband. Ruth is the Leader of the Iona Community, a Church of Scotland minister, a Quaker and a former Director of Place of Hope. She lives with her family in Cumbria.

Terry Hegarty was gardener at Camas from March 1983 to September 1984. He spent four years on Erraid as a member of the Findhorn Community, and then over ten years commuting to work in the Argyll Hotel garden on Iona while bringing up his family on Mull. Since then he has helped to establish various community initiatives and currently works as Coordinator of the Ross of Mull and Iona Community Transport Scheme, and is also a Director of the Scottish Islands Federation.

Linda Hill lived and worked in a small ecumenical Christian community in Roystonhill in Glasgow during the late '80s and early '90s. During that time she took several groups of children and young people to Camas every year.

Hattie Cooper Hockey has worked at Camas as a volunteer and a group leader. Originally from Manchester, she now lives in Norwich.

Bridget Holtom is a participatory researcher interested in how migrants and activists sustain their work for social justice. She uses creative research methods such as poetry, filmmaking and storytelling to work with people affected by violent borders and to campaign for change. She visited Camas with GRAMNet in May 2015. Bridget now works for Quakers in Britain.

Mary Ireson was a Camas 'Community Kid' from about age eight to thirteen but hadn't been there for over 15 years when she became Coordinator in 2009. She met her partner, Jamie, a local fisherman, whilst working at Camas. She left Camas in January 2012 and moved to the northwest of Mull, where she currently runs a seafood sandwich kiosk in Dervaig called the Piece Box, and looks after her three children. In her free time she loves sewing, baking, crafting and of course seeing Camas folk.

Mark Jardine first worked at Camas as a volunteer, and then as part of the Resident Group for two and a half years (alongside working as a salmon fisherman). He lives on Iona with his family and runs traditional sailing boat trips (www.boattripsiona.com). Mark continues his link with Camas by helping with training and taking Camas guests out on his boat the *Birthe Marie*.

Peter Johnson is a former Manager of Muirhouse Youth Development Group (MYDG) and of Venture Scotland. He currently works for Youth Scotland, focusing on anti-sectarianism. He was a member of the Camas Committee and has brought many groups to Camas. He lives in Edinburgh.

Davie Johnstone first came to Camas when he was sixteen, as a group leader with theGKexperience. He found that and each subsequent visit transformative for both the groups and himself. He has volunteered at Camas and was a resident staff member in 2017, and has gained many of his best friends through Camas. Currently he is working in Glasgow supporting people recovering from mental health problems.

Martin Johnstone works alongside people who live their lives at the edge as well as with organisations and individuals committed to ensuring that the wisdom of the poorest and most marginalised is listened to, and acted upon. Over recent years, Camas has been one of these places where he has learnt from some pretty amazing and inspiring individuals and groups. He has been a group leader and Member in Residence at Camas.

Joan Jones worked as a librarian and has four children and four grandchildren. She discovered Camas in her late fifties. She first went as a guest – and fell in love with the place. She worked as Resident Gardener at Camas in 2009, and in 2013 returned to Iona to be Sacristan of Iona Abbey until the end of 2015. She is now the Chapel Verger at Magdalen College, Oxford.

Tor Justad was Youth Organiser for the Iona Community from 1972-75. Originally from Norway, he moved to Scotland in 1972 after training as a Youth and Community Worker in Leicester. He has worked in adolescent psychiatric care, community work, social enterprise and co-operative development in a variety of places. Tor is married to Pat, who worked on Iona as a volunteer in the 1970s, where they met.

Darragh Keenaghan volunteered at Camas in 2010. Following that, he worked at Cyrenians Farm, Ruskin Mill College and Camphill in Edinburgh, where he ran an environmental group for young adults. He was Camas Coordinator in 2018 and 2019, during which time he and his wife, Lizzie, had a son called River. Darragh and his family now live on a croft on Colonsay.

Rhyddian Knight lived for four years at Camas, two years as Programme Worker then, on the birth of their daughter, spent two years as Co-Gardener/co-parent with Head Gardener/partner Laura. Together with his family, he pursues a woodland crofting lifestyle in Argyllshire and subsists as a writer, facilitator and forager: www.rhyddianknight.net

Poppy Kohner was lucky enough to visit Camas three times with GRAMNet. Each time she had that rare feeling of her soul being awakened. After finishing her Ph.D. in the 'Anthropology of militarism, trauma and resistance in post-9/11 USA', she continued working with GRAMNet on their film series. She went on to work as an anthropologist for Forest Peoples Programme, and was a founding member of the Workers Theatre Co-operative. She currently works in arts community engagement and is training to be a person-centred psychotherapist.

Angela Kurton is a city-dweller who is increasingly longing for more contact and connection with nature, and loves the landscapes of the Western Highlands and Isles. She was drawn to volunteering at Camas because of its beautiful setting and the feeling that it would be good to share the experience of gardening with others.

David Langton was at Camas various times between 1994-98. He restored the old veg garden (where the polytunnels are now), helped with the restoration of the old quarry-workers' lazy beds and regularly guerrilla-planted willows on the hills behind Camas. He now lives within sight of Mull with a family of four, still happily landscaping and gardening and loving the great outdoors.

Kelsey Lavoie came to Camas from Canada following a desire to connect with her ancestral roots and to experience living in close community. She volunteered at Camas from April to July 2018 and during this time was pleased to meet all types of people from many different places. She lives in Canada, on the territories of the Lekungen Nation, where she works as a human rights educator.

Avril Leonard worked as Camas Resident Activities Worker from February 2013-November 2015. As well as meeting all of the amazing people at Camas, she loved looking after the buildings and garden and felt like a 'guardian' of the place. Since leaving Camas she has worked for Outward Bound New Zealand as an outdoor instructor, and currently lives in Glasgow, where she works as a counsellor. Aside from her work, she loves adventuring and building community through shared food and singing.

Susan Lindsay lives in Fife and is an activist.

Jon Lloyd was Camas Coordinator from 2012 to 2016. Previously he worked in Outdoor Education in Norfolk and as an instructor with Outward Bound, New Zealand. He loves Mull and lives on a croft there with his partner, Wendy.

Peter Macdonald was Leader of the Iona Community from 2009-2017. He was an inspirational preacher and a committed advocate for social justice. Peter led New Members Weeks at Camas, and was passionate about the transformational opportunities Camas provides for both young people and adults. Peter died in 2020.

Dr Lorn Macintyre is a Scottish novelist, short-story writer and poet. Having spent his formative years on the Isle of Mull, he has written and lectured extensively on Mull and Iona, including interviews with George MacLeod. He has a particular affection for the beauty and achievement of Camas.

Christian MacLean was the first Warden of the MacLeod Centre and is a former Co-Leader of the Iona Community. She loves Camas, having first come across it in her teens through her brother John, who was a frequent visitor and volunteer; more recently her daughter Hannah Blyth was a member of the Resident team.

George MacLeod was the Founder of the Iona Community and a Camas pioneer.

Vincent Manning was Camas Coordinator in 1999, a challenging but immensely rewarding year. He lives in Stockwell, South London, where he is involved in HIV ministry and community activism. He is a member of 'the Community of the Passion', and recently completed his Ph.D. in theology.

Abbi Mason went to Camas in February 2014 as Resident Gardener. After two seasons in the garden, she put down her trowel and picked up the whirlwind of plate-spinning that is the Camas Coordinator job, finishing in 2018. Previous to life at Camas she studied theatre in Devon and completed a permaculture design course in Bristol, which led her to moving to New Zealand where she ran a community garden. Inspired by Camas, she has since set up Big Meadow CSA in South Wales, where she combines organic veg production with residential programmes for young people.

Rachel McCann was a Camas volunteer in 1997 and 1999, Camas Coordinator in 2000 and 2001 and a member of the Camas Committee from 2014-2020. She is a former youth, community and social worker who retrained in gardening. Amongst other things, she enjoys her allotment, crafting, foraging, pottery and making soap. She is an associate member of the Iona Community and a published poet and writer, whose work has appeared in a number of books and magazines.

Stewart McGregor has been a member of the Iona Community since 1957. He became a Youth Associate in 1952 and served as a volunteer leader at Camas North End and Village Youth Camps for four years from 1953. Ordained in 1957, he worked in Aberdeen and Cumbernauld from 1957 to 1970, as Chaplain to the Royal Infirmary of Edinburgh from 1970 to 1998 and as locum minister in congregations in Edinburgh and Europe in retirement.

Alastair McIntosh was involved with Camas as the Iona Community's business advisor, 1986-1990. He is now a well-known writer and the author of, among other books: *Soil and Soul: People versus Corporate Power* (Birlinn); *Spiritual Activism: Leadership as Service* (Green Books); *Poacher's Pilgrimage: An Island Journey* (Birlinn); *Parables of Northern Seed: Anthology from BBC's Thought for the Day* (Wild Goose). Alastair lives in Glasgow.

Barry McLaughlin is a youth worker from Glasgow and first volunteered at Camas in 2013, and worked on the Resident team in 2017/18. Barry is passionate about people, travel, Glasgow and the outdoors.

David McNeish visited Camas as part of the New Members Programme in 2009 and 2010. 'It was a healing place,' he says. He now lives and works in Orkney.

Donald McPhillimy is a forester who has worked in New Zealand, Argyll and SE Scotland. He is especially interested in community, farm, urban and native woodlands and runs training courses in woodland management and coppicing. He is a founding member of Reforesting Scotland and brought groups to Camas with New Caledonian Woodlands.

Mike Mineter came across Iona and the Iona Community in 1989 whilst on a sea kayaking trip. The next year he was at Camas for the summer. Later he was on both the Camas Advisory Group and the Camas Committee. He is a Roman Catholic, a member of the Iona Community and works in climate science at the University of Edinburgh.

Ross Morton was Camas Coordinator in 1995, 1997 and 1998. He met and worked with his wife to be, Karen, at Camas, and was whisked off to the southern hemisphere after 'tying the knot' at Camas in 1998. He was a manager at the New Zealand Outward Bound School for seven years, before three years as Chief Operations Officer of Outward Bound Australia. He currently works at Whenua Iti Outdoors, Motueka, New Zealand.

Cat Muckart was a Camas guest as a young person and went back as a volunteer in 2016, 2017 and 2018, and then as a programmer worker in 2019 and 2020 – which she says was an amazing experience. Cat likes to seek out green spaces with her bike whenever she can.

Neil Paynter is an editor, writer and late-night piano player. Previously he worked in nursing homes and homeless shelters. He is an associate of the Iona Community.

Ely Percy's first publication was a letter-cum-poem in *Big!* magazine in 1994. Since then, they've released a memoir *Cracked* (JKP, 2002), contributed over fifty short stories to literary journals, and published two novels *Vicky Romeo Plus Joolz* (Knight Errant Press, 2019) and *Duck Feet* (Monstrous Regiment, 2021). elypercy.com

Jan Sutch Pickard first visited Camas in the 1960s. Since then – during Work Weeks when first joining the Iona Community, and later when Warden on Iona, and now as a neighbour on Mull, visiting for occasional storytelling sessions – she has seen Camas at many different stages, all embodying a down-to-earth spirituality and real hospitality. She is an activist, storyteller and writer.

Immy Reeves is currently a 4th year student at Strathclyde University, on the BA Primary Education course. She also works for St Paul's Youth Forum, helping to deliver youth work sessions as part of a Faith through Art group. Immy loves to cook and to be outdoors as much as possible!

Derek Robertson is a former teacher at Abercorn School.

Jim Robertson was youth worker for the Iona Community from 1962-69, and then worked at Polmont YOI and Douglas Inch Clinic, Glasgow. He later worked in a teaching and research role at University of Northumbria (1973-2006). His current activities include project management and mentoring on faith-based community work projects. He is involved in Church Action on Poverty North East and Thrive Project Stockton. He also helps to manage the Crossings Project, a community arts and music resource for asylum seekers and refugees.

Lynsey Semple works with children and young people in Glasgow. She was a volunteer at Camas in 2015, accompanied by her dog Mabel.

Norman Shanks is a member of the Iona Community and a retired Church of Scotland minister. One of the highlights of his term as Leader of the Community (1995-2002) was the week each year with new members at Camas.

Rachel Shepton has long had a love affair with Mull and Iona, and worked at Camas in the mid-1990s. After 10 years living in Australia, she returned to the Highlands and has settled with her partner, two children, dog and ponies near Glencoe. She works as a physiotherapist and Pilates instructor, happily balancing work, parenthood, animals and outdoor life.

Jenny Smith is an artist and writer based in Edinburgh and the Isle of Lewis. Jenny worked at Camas as a volunteer in 1988 and wrote 'Goodbyes' the night before she left. During her summer there, she sprained both ankles and, unable to go out with the groups, she spent her days in the art room and started painting the surrounding landscape. After Camas she applied to study Drawing and Painting at Duncan of Jordanstone College of Art, and graduated with a first-class degree. She has won a number of awards for her work, including the Royal Scottish Academy Award for Painting. www.jennysmith.org.uk, www.drawnto.org.uk

Nancy Somerville became an associate member of the Iona Community in 1991, following her first visit to Camas. She returned as a volunteer in 1992. In 2015 she retired from her job as a Community Education Worker in Edinburgh and moved to Craignure. Her experience at Camas and on Mull continues to inspire her writing.

Mairead Spangler is a travelling musician and songstress from Glasgow, collecting songs and stories from around the world to weave the magic of the land into the hearts of her community. Camas has been a part of her life from a young age, and in recent years she has worked as a volunteer there.

Lizz Spence was Camas Gardener from 2002-2006. After Camas, she was Head Grower at Phantassie Organics in East Lothian for eight years, and is currently Manager at Jock Tamson's Gairden in Duddingston, a community market garden and parkland run by volunteers. She is an associate member of the Iona Community.

Kenneth Steven is a widely published poet, novelist and children's writer. Iona has been his spiritual home from childhood days, and it's been at the heart of his creative work for years. His novel *The Well of the North Wind* imagines the story of the creation of the Book of Kells on Iona. His most recent volume of new and selected poems is *Iona*, published by Paraclete Press in the States and very much available here in the UK. Kenneth and his wife, Kristina, lead annual Celtic Christian retreats on the island. He's a great devotee of the work of Camas – past, present and future! kennethsteven.co.uk

Dot Stewart was a Camas volunteer, Programme Worker and Coordinator from 2003-2009. She lives on Iona and is a member of the Iona Community.

Margaret Stewart became a member of the Iona Community in the same year (1978) that her daughter – later a Camas Coordinator – Dot was born. Margaret was Deputy Leader of the Iona Community from 1985-88, and Convener of the Camas Committee from 2002. One very happy memory of Camas for Margaret was when her family spent a wonderful Christmas there.

Dougie Strang had two stints at Camas, first as a volunteer, and then as gardener in the late 1990s, during which he helped to develop the garden and plant the smaller woodland. He and his wife, Em, met at Camas, and now live with their two children in Dumfriesshire, where Dougie is still a gardener, as well as a storyteller and events curator for the Dark Mountain Project.

Neil Squires is a social worker and was a Camas volunteer in 1987. His poem in this book was written on a New Members Week at Camas. Neil remains a huge admirer of the work being carried out at Camas.

Alison Swinfen enjoys visiting Camas with members of GRAMNet. Perhaps better known to some as Alison Phipps, she is UNESCO Chair in Refugee Integration through Languages and the Arts at the University of Glasgow. Alison is a writer, passionate gardener, knitter and poet.

Bob Thomas became a member of the Iona Community in August 2017. He has been to Camas twice, and to Iona many times. A teacher, now retired, and lay minister, Bob also worked for many years with refugees and asylum seekers in Portsmouth.

Ruth Thomas spent some wonderful months at Camas in 1997, 1999 and also brought a youth group to visit a few years later. Nowadays she loves to walk, talk and think out in the Peak District.

Sheena Walker lives on Mull and is a granddaughter of Alan MacInnes, who had the salmon fishing at Camas.

Rob Wardle was the founding Director and Trustee of Cre8. He has been bringing young people and adults to Camas for over fifteen years. He is now a Church in Wales priest and the Vicar of Holyhead. Rob is a former construction worker, a hobby farmer and a community activist.

Emily Wilkins was a Camas Programme Worker from 2008-2010. She still enjoys life on Mull, where she works as a countryside ranger.

Eric Wojchik worked as a Camas volunteer in 2000 and as a Programme Worker in 2001. He spent many years living in Scotland, on Iona, Mull and the Isle of Lewis. He is from Minnesota and is a town planner, poet, gardener, traveller and former youth worker.

Brian Woodcock is a retired URC minister and former Warden of Iona Abbey and member of the Community. He lives in Bristol and enjoys spending time with his family and being involved in the local community and church, with an ecumenical house of prayer and with a charity that addresses rural poverty in South India.

Rachael Yates lives in Edinburgh and has been involved with Camas since 2002, when she went as a New Member. She has brought groups to Camas, served on the Camas Committee, and been Member in Residence and a group leader for a Community Kids Week. She is an English teacher, has two daughters – who also love Camas – and lives with Andrew near the sea.

Photo credits

Cover – photo © Rachel Daniels

Chapter 1   **The Camas pioneer**s – photo of George MacLeod at Camas Archive photo, photographer unknown

Chapter 2   **Life in community** – photo © Hannah Blyth

Chapter 3   **Camas guests** – photo © Rachel Daniels

Chapter 4   **Over the years** – photo © David Coleman

Chapter 5   **Faith and philosophy** – photo of Camas Cross © David Coleman

Chapter 6   **A sense of place** – photo © Fiona Caley

Chapter 7   **Moving on** – photo © David Coleman

How to contact Camas

For enquiries or to book:
email: camascoord@iona.org.uk
tel: 01681 700367

For current information about Camas:
https://iona.org.uk/island-centres/camas-the-outdoor-centre-with-a-difference/
https://www.facebook.com/camas.centre

Camas Centre
Ardfenaig
Bunessan
Isle of Mull PA67 6DX
Scotland, UK

Wild Goose Publications, the publishing house of the Iona Community established in the Celtic Christian tradition of Saint Columba, produces books, e-books, CDs and digital downloads on:

- holistic spirituality
- social justice
- political and peace issues
- healing
- innovative approaches to worship
- song in worship, including the work of the Wild Goose Resource Group
- material for meditation and reflection

For more information:

Wild Goose Publications
The Iona Community
Suite 9, Fairfield, 1048 Govan Road
Glasgow G51 4XS, Scotland

Tel. +44 (0)141 429 7281
e-mail: admin@ionabooks.com

or visit our website at
www.ionabooks.com
for details of all our products and online sales